LUCIFER'S COURT

A Heretic's Journey in Search of the Light Bringers

Otto Rahn

Translated by Christopher Jones

Inner Traditions
Rochester, Vermont

Inner Traditions
One Park Street
Rochester, Vermont 05767
www.InnerTraditions.com

Originally published in German under the title *Luzifers Hofgesind* by
    Schwarzhäupterverlag
First U.S. edition published in 2008 by Inner Traditions

Library of Congress Cataloging-in-Publication Data
Rahn, Otto, 1904–1939.
  [Luzifers Hofgesind. English]
  Lucifer's court : a heretic's journey in search of the light bringers / Otto Rahn ;
translated by Christopher Jones.
     p. cm.
  Includes bibliographical references.
  ISBN-13: 978-1-59477-197-2 (pbk.)
  ISBN-10: 1-59477-197-9
  1. Folklore. 2. Mythology. I. Title.
  BL313.R2513 2008
  201'.3094—dc22
                                                              2007046262

Printed and bound in the United States by Lake Book Manufacturing

10 9 8 7 6 5 4 3 2 1

Text design and layout by Carol Ruzicka
This book was typeset in Sabon, with Charlemagne used as a display typeface.

CONTENTS

PART THREE

Do you know why I have so patiently translated Poe?
Because he resembled me. The first time I opened
one of his books, I saw with terror and
rapture subjects dreamed by me and
described by him, twenty years earlier.

CHARLES BAUDELAIRE

Translator's Foreword

PROLEGOMENON

———◆———

THE GERMAN PHILOSOPHER Walter Benjamin held an almost mystical belief in the "mission" of the translator. In *The Translator's Task,* he wrote that all books "lose something" when they are translated into another language; yet this loss is the price to be paid for a gain, because the translator's task is "to let the seed of pure language ripen in a translation."[1]

Though the patron of all translators is St. Jerome (AD 347–420), the man who translated the Bible and other religious texts word for word, the most celebrated literary translator of all remains the Roman statesman and orator Cicero (106–43 BC). As a translator of Greek texts into Latin, he elaborated a theory that greatly influenced his successors: No longer was it necessary to give the reader the same number of words as in the original text. As an alternative method, he decided to give the

---

[1][*La tâche du traducteur,* Walter Benjamin, Oeuvres I (Paris: Gallimard, 2000). A friend of Hermann Hesse and Hannah Arendt, Benjamin died under mysterious circumstances in Portbou on the Franco-Spanish border in 1940. —*Trans.*]

same *weight* to words by privileging their sense, and so achieve a better adaptation. In this way, the "real meaning" of a work would survive the transformation of the text. As a rule, modern literary translators are instructed to become totally invisible in the texts they transform. Yet in the case of my translations of Otto Rahn's *Crusade Against the Grail* and *Lucifer's Court*, I was presented with the odd temptation to abandon my phantomlike anonymity and assume the author's identity— a bit like wearing a devil mask in Carnival. The French Belle Epoque writer Raymond Roussel (dubbed the Black Sun—*soleil noir*—by André Breton) was the first to describe this magical state, which became a trap for the central character in his first novel in verse, *La doublure* (The Understudy, 1897). Curiously, the word *translation,* which comes from the Latin verb *traducere,* actually means to "to ferry across." Only after my initial passage word for word through Rahn's text did I learn a second meaning for that word. In an odd coincidence, it denotes the Cathar belief that the spirit or soul is passed on to or reincarnated in a newborn after the death of another—a process that is known better as *metempsychosis.*

In the medieval world, so rich in spirituality and yet so meager in material pleasures, this *traducianism* could be avoided only through a spiritual baptism that the Cathars called the Consolamentum. According to the French scholar Jean Duvernoy, this "would allow the spirit (or soul) to return to the heavens and resume its place in the firmament before its 'fall.'" In other words, this was a return to the morning star: Lucifer! In 1937, the recently established Schwarzhäupterverlag in Leipzig published Otto Rahn's *Lucifer's Court,* one of the most misunderstood and maligned books ever released. Although the author announced on several occasions that he intended to write the story of the German inquisitor Konrad von Marburg as a sequel to *Crusade Against the Grail, Lucifer's Court* was his second and last published work before his suicide on the Wilderkaiser in March 1939.

In this book, structured as a travel journal, Rahn begins his quest for the Grâl (Grail), a stone that supposedly fell to earth in the French Pyranees from Lucifer's crown. As he traces the story of this symbol, Rahn discovers a brilliant wisdom of celestial origin that stands in opposition to Yahweh, the demiurge of the Old Testament and God of the B'nai Israel.

Rahn's pursuit of the Primordial Tradition takes him from the land of the Cathars to pagan Europe's sacred spots: In Italy he discusses the legend of Tannhäuser and uncovers King Laurin's enchanted garden of roses, Der Rosengarten or Catinaccio in the Tyrol. At the Externsteine in Germany he recalls the legend of Irminsul, a holy ash tree that was venerated as the Tree of the World by the ancient Germans; and finally, in Iceland, he undertakes a pilgrimage to the birthplace of skald Snorri Sturlusson, the Nordic Homer who was the author of the *Younger (Prose) Edda*.

According to Rahn, the roots of Catharism can be traced to the legends of the ancient Greeks, Goths, and Germanic pagans, all sworn enemies of the Roman Empire and its successor, the Catholic Church. Like Rahn, they did not see Satan, Beelzebub, or the devil in Lucifer:[2] In the Pyrenees, he was Abellio; among the Norsemen, he was Baldr; and the ancient Greeks celebrated him as Apollo. This Luciferianism, which is rooted in the esoteric literature of Hermeticism, sees Yahweh as the manifestation of a satanic material realm, whereas Lucifer is the keeper of the highest spiritual ideals and has nothing at all to do with Satanism.

The Latin name Lucifer originally designated the brilliance of the planet Venus and literally means "light bringer." According to Roman legend, as the son of Aurora, Lucifer was the harbinger of the dawn who rode across the skies on a white charger—but he was also the evening star (Venus) who rode a dark steed. The Vulgate employs the word for "the light of the morning" (Job 11:17), "the signs of the zodiac" (Job 38:32), and "the aurora" (Psalm 109:3). Not surprisingly, it was St. Jerome who, in Isaiah 1:14, gave the name Lucifer to the devil, who must lament the loss of his original glory, when he was as bright as the morning star.

Any rejection of monotheism is generally confused with anti-Semitism, probably because Judaism, Christianity, and Islam all originated in the Middle East. Simone Weil, a French philosopher of Jewish origin, was also moved by the Cathar rejection of Yahweh, whom she

---

[2][Rahn evokes the story of the Cagots, a minority, discriminated against, who may have been the missing link between the Cathars and the Goths. Long believed to be descendants of the Goths, in a letter to Pope Leo X in 1513, the Cagots identified themselves as the last surviving Albigenses. —*Trans.*]

also saw as a God of unforgiving cruelty. Like the Bonshommes, as the Cathar *perfecti* were called, she was convinced that Yahweh was incompatible with the God of the New Testament. Weil also saw the Romans and their child, the Catholic Church, as the original source of European totalitarianism, which was so brutally employed by the Inquisition.

The main points of Otto Rahn's biography are well known: A modern Grail knight, he committed suicide by taking sleeping pills on the snows of the Wilderkaiser in 1939, after he was denounced for possible homosexual behavior and Jewish heritage. After its publication in 1933, his first work, *Crusade Against the Grail,* attracted the attention of Karl Maria Wiligut, better known as Weisthor, Heinrich Himmler's esoteric "lord" of runology. On Weisthor's recommendation, Himmler offered Rahn employment as a civilian in 1934. Eventually, Rahn formally entered the SS (in 1936) and was attached to Weisthor's department.

Few realize that *Lucifer's Court* owes its journalistic style and tone to another man: Albert von Haller, Rahn's editor and publisher at Schwarzhäupterverlag. In all likelihood, it was Henry Benrath (the George Büchner prizewinner whose real name was Albert H. Rausch), who introduced Haller to Rahn. Before he founded Schwarzhäupter, Haller had been Benrath's editor at the DEVA publishing house and was on the lookout for upcoming authors such as Rahn and Kurt Eggers for his new venture.

In 1936, Rahn finished the book in a house in Homberg/Ohm that belonged to relatives. Haller visited him there, and together they worked on the manuscript over ten days. Apparently *Luzifers Hofgesind* was Haller's title.[3] His influence on the text is easy to spot: In what today would be called an exercise in marketing, he added a chapter from *The Birth of the Millennium* (Die Geburt des Jahrtausends) by Kurt Eggers, which was the first book published by Schwarzhäupter in 1936.

Haller was also responsible for inserting an anti-Semitic statement by Arthur Schopenhauer ("We should also hope, therefore, that Europe will be cleaned of all Jewish mythology")[4] which has appeared in all

---

[3][*Luzifers Hofgesind* translates as *Lucifer's Courtiers,* but it is dialectic; in fact, the title should read *Luzifers Hodgesindl.* I have chosen the middle way by naming the book *Lucifer's Court,* which is as it appears in other languages, such as French and Spanish. —*Trans.*]

[4]["Wir dürfen hoffen, daß einst auch Europa von jüdischen Mythologien gereinigt sein wird" (Schopenhauer, *Parerga und Paralipomena II,* Bd., § 115 Ende)]

printed versions of the book. Although it is presented as proof positive of Rahn's adherence to the racist principles of National Socialism, it does not appear in the original typewritten manuscript by Otto Rahn.

There is a strange epilogue to the book's disturbing history: Four years after Rahn's death, Himmler ordered a special leather-bound edition of the book, and five thousand copies were printed. Apparently the Reichsführer-SS himself had retouched the text, but the entire edition was incinerated during a firebombing in the latter half of the war. Curiously, the manuscript that survived contains no chapters or even paragraphs. Some pages appear in boldface, which may indicate that they were added later. Many years later, when the unattributed Schopenhauer quote was read to Rahn's old friend Paul Ladame, Paul said, "Otto Rahn would never have written that." He was right.

It becomes painfully clear in *Lucifer's Court* that Otto Rahn had mistaken his enemies for his friends; like many others, he completely misunderstood the nature of the Nazi regime he had committed himself to serve. Its slogan *Ein Volk, Ein Reich, Ein Führer* (One People, One Reich, One Führer), which clearly highlighted the singular, revealed a latent monotheism. French philosopher Alain de Benoist has written in *Jésus et ses frères* (Jesus and His Brothers), "Born in Bavaria (a Catholic land par-excellence), the Nazi Party, although less monolithic than generally thought (the Führerstaat was more of an oligarchy), simply secularized the Catholic concept of the institution. It presented itself as a church led by an infallible pope (the Führer), with his clergy (the party officials), a Jesuit elite (the SS), its dogmatic truths, excommunications, and the persecutions of heretics . . ."

I would go even further: Quite clearly the racism of the biblical concept of the "chosen people" had metamorphosed into the *master race,* or Herrenvolk. In his book *Les iconoclastes* (The Iconoclasts), Jean-Joseph Goux remarked: "[T]he practical theology of [N]azism was entirely ordered by a [J]udeophobic obsession that pushed Hitler to set the German people as a rival 'chosen people' to the Jews."

In this context, although there were three well-known pagans among the Nazi elite (Himmler, Bormann, and Rosenberg) it is amazing that *Lucifer's Court* was ever published. In a statement on October 14, 1941, that debunks the fable of Nazi paganism, Adolf Hitler said in the presence of Himmler, "To my eyes, nothing would be more stupid than to reestablish the cult of Wotan. Our old mythology lost its value when Christianity took root in Germany. . . . A movement like ours should not get sidetracked with metaphysical digressions. It should hold to the spirit of exact science!"

Hitler's statement was diametrically opposed to the spirit of *Lucifer's Court*. Otto Rahn believed that the old pagan religions, based on the veneration of ancestors and nature, maintained the cohesiveness of society against the forces of intolerance. In contrast National Socialism appears as "a millenary religion of salvation." As Alain de Benoist has written, it was

> a secularized religion, of course, but perfectly recognizable as such, which aimed to achieve, through a bewitching mass liturgy, by spectacularly playing on the hopes and fears of the populace, and through the cult of a leader presented as a providential savior, the promise of collective salvation based on a total transformation of life, the absolute domination of the earth, and the initiation of a "reign" of one thousand years.

The nineteenth-century German philosopher Eduard von Hartmann explained:

> What is historical or "suprahistorical" passes little by little into history. But legends do not concentrate on recounting recent events as a historian would. To put this into perspective, we have to speak of fantastical deformation and the poetic. But this "poetry" is perhaps more true than modern historic descriptions, because legend is the veritable soul of a people which explains the decisive forces that have determined its past. Its role is to conjure images and not to describe absolute events but the fateful pressures that produced them.

This first English-language edition of *Lucifer's Court* would have been impossible without the help of many friends and colleagues. In France, Alain de Benoist, Guy Rachet, and André Douzet always did their best to steer me in the right direction; in Spain, José Maria Martorell, who is restoring of the ninth-century castle of Quermanço, where the most Cathar Perfectus Guilhem Bélibaste was held prisoner, and the well-known historian Ramon Hervas deserve special thanks for their encouragement and support. I would like to thank Rahn's German biographer, Hans-Jürgen Lange, for his help in reconstructing the history of the book, and Miriam Zoeller of Marixverlag in Wiesbaden, who provided me with her reedition of Jakob Grimm's *Deutsche Mythologie*. Of course, I must also thank Jon Graham at Inner Traditions and Sven Henkler at Zeitenwendeverlag in Dresden for their support, and my editor at Inner Traditions, Mindy Branstetter, who deserves special thanks for her patient work. Most important of all, the help and support of my wife, Eva Maria, was crucial to my task. Her advice was absolutely vital to my efforts to convey all the color of Rahn's work for my readers.

Finally, a last translation: The German word for a "double" or the mirror image of a person is *Doppelgänger*—a person who literally follows in the footsteps of another. (In German, *gehen* means "to go," but on foot.) To open the gates of Lucifer's kingdom, as Rahn once wrote, "You must equip yourself with a *Dietrich* [skeleton key]." So, nearly sixty-seven years after his death in the snow, I decided to search for a key that would open the gates to a lost world full of magic and fear. But readers should beware—as the count of Lautréamont wrote in *Les chants de Maldoror*: "Unless [the reader] applies a meticulous logic during his reading and spiritual rigor equal at least to his distrust, the deadly emanations of this book will absorb his soul like water absorbs sugar."

CHRISTOPHER JONES

Christopher Jones was educated in France at the prestigious Fondation Nationale des Sciences Politiques. He is a contributing scholar in history to Scribner's *Encyclopedia of Europe,* the editor of White Star publications' *Adventure Classics* 2006 reedition of William Bligh's *Bounty,* and author of *Vers la décroissance.*

He is the translator and editor of the English version of Robert Descharnes' monumental work about Salvador Dali's sculptures, and translated Mr. Descharnes' memoir (about Dali) as well. He is also the translator of the 2006 English publication of Otto Rahn's *Crusade Against the Grail.*

Who loves his homeland, must understand it;
Who wants to understand it, must search earnestly in its history.

JAKOB GRIMM

Prologue

THE JOURNEY BEGINS

———◆———

LUCIFER'S COURT IS BASED on travel diaries begun in Germany, continued in the south, and completed in Iceland. I had to finish this diary in advance because the events I experienced in the Land of the Midnight Sun closed the full circle in which my thoughts and observations had moved within today's scheme of things.

Like an artist working on a mosaic who piles up small stones of a particular color to arrange them later in a preconceived plan, I collected ideas and knowledge under foreign skies and in lands far from home. The sum total has produced this pageant.

Either through revisions, adding details, or underscoring—not to mention rearranging—I have prepared those chosen pages from my diary in such a way that others may scrutinize, understand, and love them. My hand shall be a lucky one!

I wrote these lines in a small town in Upper Hesse. As I looked out from my desk, spreading out before me was a countryside that is very precious—so much so that as my curiosity pushed me through difficult places in foreign lands, I was often homesick. My father is from a town that sits on a densely wooded peak that closes off the district to the south and where, as far back as anyone can recall, men and their womenfolk have cultivated the land, stood before the anvil, milled grain to flour, and sat in front of the spinning wheel in low-ceilinged rooms. Their homeland is stony and the sky is often filled with clouds. Only a few of them became wealthy.

My mother's family hailed from the Odenwald, where they had it much easier. The sun and the climate are milder there, and the earth means well for those who love it.

The ruined walls of a castle dominate the Upper Hessian town where I now live, and where I wrote this book. Not far from the castle door (the castle that still stands) is a very old linden tree where St. Boniface first preached Roman Christianity to the Chatten.[1] When I stood under it and looked north, my eyes fell upon an amazing basalt mass. There on its summit, the "Apostle of the Germans" constructed a cloister-fortress: the Amöneburg. My ancestors did not love St. Boniface, who preached the gospel of love. In a letter he sent to the pope in AD 742, he described these ancestors as "idiotic."

A few hours separate my hometown from Marburg-am-Lahn. A son of this town, the "fright of Germany," also preached for Rome. The magister and inquisitor Konrad von Marburg crisscrossed his homeland on the back of a donkey, collecting Rosenwunder[2] for the beatification of his enlightened confessor, Countess Elizabeth of Thuringia—and collecting heretics for execution. He had them burned at a place in his hometown which is still called Ketzerbach or "heretic ditch." My ancestors were pagans and my forebears were heretics.

---

[1] [The Chatten was a Germanic tribe that lived in and around the Hessian region. —*Trans.*]

[2] [Rahn is referring to St. Elizabeth of Hungary (who was Landgravine Elizabeth of Thuringia). She was known for the miraculous transformation of bread into roses. Konrad was her confessor. In German, Rosenwunder are also sea roses, *Rosa rugosa.* —*Trans.*]

For God, there isn't any devil, but for us
He is a very useful figment
NOVALIS

PART ONE

~ BINGEN AM RHEIN ~

Until the start of the the world war, I spent eight years of my childhood in this small town on the Rhine. Now, after a long absence, I am back again—for one day. The rented house where we used to live no longer exists; I am told it became dilapidated, so it was torn down. Also, the fields where I romped and played as a child have disappeared. Houses now stand there. Only the vineyards behind our garden have remained. Soon there will be a rich harvest. It is autumn.

At roughly the same time tomorrow, I will be traveling south to France on an extended journey to the lands between the Alps and the Pyrenees, maybe even to Italy and the south Tyrol as well. Many say that our homeland has more to offer than any foreign land, than countries that have so often been our curse. While this may be true, I am still going abroad to look for the ghosts of the pagans and heretics who were my ancestors. I am well aware that conventional understanding says that the future will be more tender with us than we are with the past. Although these long-gone times that I am investigating are certainly in the past, the wounds have never healed. Today, many still speak of pagans and heretics.

In this town where I am beginning my travels, a foolish woman from Grüneberg in the region of the Upper Hesse betrayed the relatives of her husband to Grand Inquisitor Konrad von Marburg, who promptly had them all burned at the stake. Shortly, I will be visiting the mother of all cloisters for Inquisitors: the abbey Notre-Dame-de-Prouille near Toulouse. The custom of praying with a rosary spread from there across Europe. The history of that Dominican cloister, which was personally established by St. Dominic, is forever linked to the destiny of the most famous heresy of the Middle Ages: that of the Albigenses, who were also called Cathars. Although the word Cathar means "pure" (Greek: *katharoi*), it became synonymous with our derogatory term in German, *Ketzer* ("heretic"; also "quarrelsome"). I am traveling to southern France because the heresy is said to have arrived in Germany from there.

I have read everything written about the Cathars, who were "so numerous, like sand on the sea, and had adherents in thousands of cities."[1]

---

[1][Caesarius von Heisterbach from Rahn's introduction to *Crusade Against the Grail*. —*Trans.*]

Oddly, they were called Albigenses only in southern France, in the lands of Provence, the Languedoc, and Gascony. In Germany, for example, they were called Runkeler or Gottesfreunde (Friends of God). They must have been very influential in Lombardy. A priest and poet of proverbs named Wernher, who lived around the year 1180 in Augsburg, wrote, "Lamparten glüet in Ketzerheit."[2]

Catholic and Protestant theologians agree happily that the Cathars had to be exterminated wherever they were found, because if they were not, European spiritual life would have been disrupted and sidetracked along un-European paths. Yet they have argued and continue to argue over how to explain the heresy's origins and from where it came. Some see in it a perversion of Manichaeism, the famous heretical doctrine from the Persian skies, and cite numerous experts and writings to back up their thesis. Others, who have remained in the minority, regard the heresy of the Cathars as an odd leftover of the beliefs of the Goths, Vandals, Burgundians, and Langobards: Under the domination of the Visigoths, Arianism became entrenched in southern France, a land that was formerly known as Gothien. Who is right? Even contemporary sources contradict each other, and it is extremely difficult to find our way through their writings. It is significant that an Inquisitor took the origins of Catharism down from old books that described pre-Christian heresies.

Catholics have assembled a long list of diabolical accusations against the Cathars, which includes: riding to nightly orgies on the backs of large crabs, kissing the rear end of a black cat, and reducing murdered children to a powdery form in order to cannibalize them more easily. They allegedly abstained from physical reproduction to prevent more souls from falling under the sway of Lucifer, the creator of all earthly things and human life, which contradicts the accusation that the Cathars venerated Lucifer. This accusation stems from the sworn testimony of twelfth-century German heretics, who recognized and greeted each other with the salute, "Luzifer der Unrecht geschah, Grüsst dich!"[3]

At this time tomorrow, I will be traveling southward to clear the darkness. May I be a worthy light bringer!

---

[2][Meaning "Lombardy glows in heresy." Lamparten is the name the Langobards gave to the northern Italian region of Lombardy. —*Trans.*]

[3]["Hail Lucifer, who was wronged! Greetings to you!" —*Trans.*]

~ PARIS ~

Shown to me were reproductions of two paintings by the Spanish master Pedro Berruguete depicting scenes from the life and works of St. Dominic. The originals hang in the Prado in Madrid.[4] In one, heretics are being burned. The pyres are beginning to catch fire; the victims are bound to stakes so that they cannot escape, and soon they will be living torches. The second picture shows St. Dominic busy burning books; already the parchments are smoldering. One book, however, rises high in the air: Having found the favor of the God of Rome, it was spared.

I bought Martin Luther's translation of the Bible in the rue de la Seine because I wanted to read the Book of Isaiah again. In it, he explains how Lucifer fell from heaven and was damned by Yahweh:

How have you fallen from the heavens, O glowing morning star; been cut down to the ground O conqueror of nations?

For thou hast said in thine heart, I will ascend into heaven, I will exalt my throne above the stars of God: I will sit also upon the mount of the congregation, in the sides of the north:

I will ascend above the heights of the clouds; I will be like the most High.

Yet thou shalt be brought down to hell, to the sides of the pit.

But thou art cast out of thy grave like an abominable branch, and as the Raiment of those that are slain, thrust through with a sword, that goes down to the stones of the pit; as a carcass trodden under feet.

Thou shalt not be joined with them in burial, because thou hast destroyed thy land, and slain thy people: the seed of evildoers shall never be renowned.

Prepare slaughter for his children for the iniquity of their fathers; that they do not rise, nor possess the land, nor fill the face of the world with cities.

---

[4][Pedro Berruguete (AD 1450–1504) was a transitional painter from Spanish Gothic to the Renaissance. He was celebrated for his depiction of St. Dominic busily burning heretics at the stake. Spain's grand inquisitor, Tomas de Torquemada (a Dominican), commissioned several works from him. The painter's son Alonso Berruguete (AD 1488–1561) became a distinguished sculptor, painter, and architect under Michelangelo. —*Trans.*]

The LORD of hosts hath sworn, saying, Surely as I have thought, so shall it come to pass; and as I have purposed, so shall it stand:

This is the purpose that is purposed upon the whole earth: and this is the hand that is stretched out upon all the nations.

For the LORD of hosts hath purposed, and who shall disannul it? and his hand is stretched out, and who shall turn it back? I am the LORD, and there is none else, there is no God beside me: I girded thee, though thou hast not known me:

That they may know from the rising of the sun, and from the west, that there is none beside me. I am the LORD, and there is none else.

I form the light, and create darkness: I make peace, and create evil. Woe unto him that striveth with his Maker! Let the potsherd strive with the potsherds of the earth. Shall the clay say to him that fashioneth it, What makest thou? or thy work, He hath no hands?

Woe unto him that saith unto his father, What begettest thou? or to the woman, What hast thou brought forth?[5]

While Martin Luther's German-language translation of the Bible refers to God as "Herr Zebaoth" or "Yahweh Zebaoth," the King James Bible translates the term into English as "Lord of the Hosts." Zebaoth or Lord of the Hosts comes from the Hebrew YHVH Tzva'ot, which is a clear reference to sovereignty and military power. Curiously, the term never appears in the Torah, although it is used in the prophetic books of Isaiah, Jeremiah, Haggai, Zechariah, and Malachi, as well as many times in the Psalms and in the Apocalypse. There is some confusion: Does it indicate the Lord of Israel, or some other cosmological demiurge? In the Gnostic scriptures of the Nag Hammadi text, Zebaoth is the son of Yaltabaoth. Perhaps this is explained by the Latinized spelling of Sabaoth, which led to him being confused with the god Sabazius.

All afternoon, I wandered along the banks of the Seine where *bouquiniers* (book dealers; there must be about five hundred of them, one next to the other) offer rare and antique books for sale. The times are over, or

---

[5][Isaiah 14. —*Trans.*]

so I have been told, when real treasures—either a precious first edition or some singular work—could be found there. Nevertheless, in one of the wooden boxes attached to the wall of the quay (as these bookstores appear), I managed to find *Aurora* by the German mystic Jakob Böhme.[6] As I turned the pages, I saw this passage:

> Look, I will tell you a secret: The time has come for the groom to crown his bride; guess where the crown lies? Toward midnight, because the light is clear in the darkness. But from where comes the groom? From midday, when the heat gives birth to and travels toward midnight, because the light is clear there. What did they do toward midday? They fell asleep in the heat, but stormy weather will awaken them, and under it, many will be scared to death.

Jakob Böhme was a Protestant cobbler from Görlitz. A contemporary of Kepler and Galileo Galilei, he died during the Thirty Years' War. I bought the book for a laughably low price. Now it is in front of me on the table—next to the Bible.

I came from the north and I will travel southward. My journey has hardly begun, but I am looking north again—toward midnight, toward a "mount of the congregation, in the sides of the north," and a crown should be there.

---

[6][Jakob Böhme (AD 1575–1625). After an initial mystical experience, Böhme embarked on a remarkable career as a philosopher. Although he continued to practice his profession as a cobbler, Böhme became known as the Philosophus Teutonicus. Strongly influenced by Paracelsus, he produced twenty-nine works, including his celebrated *Aurora oder Morgenröte im Aufgang, das ist die Wurzel oder Mutter der Philosophie, Astrologie, und Theologie aus rechtem Grunde oder Beschreibung der Natur wie alles gewesen und alles geworden ist* (Aurora or the Rosy Dawn's Rays That Are the Root or Mother of Philosophy, Astrology, and Theology from Good Sources or the Description of Nature as Everything Has Been or Should Have Been), an important example of the doctrine of Apokatastasis (in Latin, Restitutio in pristinum statum) or the universal salvation of all free creatures—including Lucifer. English followers of Böhme were known as Behmenists. —*Trans.*]

⁓ TOULOUSE ⁓

I left Paris in the afternoon during a heavy October rainstorm. Tired from the hectic life of the big city, I quickly fell asleep. When I woke up, through the window of my compartment I was welcomed by the blue of a southern sky, the stunning late summer colors of the trees, and the sparkling water of a river spanned by a high and long medieval bridge.

After nearly ten hours, I have seen all of what a traveler must see to be able to say that he has been in Toulouse. At the end of my sightseeing, I visited the cathedral of St. Sernin, a superb, Romanesque redbrick structure that reminds me in no small way of the Gothic churches of Greifswald and Stralsund, or Wismar and Chorin in northern Germany. As I approached it from the city's center, the golden rays of the afternoon sun, hidden by high town houses, illuminated the cathedral. It looked almost as if a fire was burning inside the house of God, which made the stones glow, or that the church was drenched in blood. A great deal of blood has flowed in Toulouse: the blood of the Goths and, later, the blood of the Albigenses.

As I crossed the square in front of the entry, I remembered the story of the Italian philosopher Lucilio Vanini, a Roman priest whose tongue was cut out to stop him from talking to people.[7] Finally, on February 19, 1619, he was burned alive in Toulouse, because (now unable to speak) he had begun to write his ideas. Inside the church, I noticed a sloppily rolled umbrella propped against a pillar and, close by, a peasant woman with her back pressed against another column and her arms stretched out behind her. With trancelike eyes, she stared at the crucifix before her, ignoring me and the people who filed past her. Likewise, she didn't register the clinking of coins as they dropped now and then into the metal box at the foot of the crucified figure. I withdrew and returned to the city.

Set in what is left of Toulouse's old city wall, a marble plaque records the place where Simon de Montfort, the northern French knight who was appointed generalissimo of the crusade against the Albigenses by

---

[7][Lucilio Vanini (AD 1585–1619), Italian philosopher. Vanini believed that Jesus Christ was a philosopher and a politician and that he was a strong advocate of Epicurianism and materialism. —*Trans.*]

the pope and the king of France, was killed on the day of St. John in 1216 by a stone thrown from the steady hand of a heroic Toulousaine. Even today, some Toulouse and Provençal folk spit on this spot; they haven't forgotten what Simon de Montfort did to their homeland.

I came here because of the Albigenses. Like my forebears, they made a pact with the devil. In 1275, when a large group of heretics was burned alive in Toulouse, a fifty-six-year-old woman named Angela de Labaretha was among them. The ecclesiastical authorities had extracted a very special confession from her. In the torture chamber, Angela admitted that she had enjoyed carnal relations with the Evil One and that the fruit of her womb was born a monster—apparently, it had the head of a wolf and a serpent's tail. The Evil One then forced her to steal small children in the night in order to feed them to her hideous offspring. The woman confessed to all this—under torture. By the way, Angela means "angel."

‒ *Pamiers* ‒

In a bookstore I met a young Toulousain who claims that the climate of this small town is very unhealthy. The most promising female acquaintances, he confided, are made in St. Sernin's cathedral in Toulouse at around eleven o'clock, and even *femmes legères* (women of dubious reputation) are easily found there. Finally, he advised me not to stay in Pamiers because I would die of boredom. When I told him that I was planning to continue my journey onto Foix and then to Montségur to spend several months in the high Pyrenees, he stared at me in amazement. Suddenly, a smile spread across his face—a smile that was both polite and full of pity. "Are you also searching for the treasure of the Albigenses?" he asked. When I wondered what this had to do with it, I learned of a tale of treasure that was buried seven hundred years ago in the castle of Montségur during the crusade that Rome and Paris undertook against the Albigenses, and apparently, it still lies there. Currently, an engineer from Bordeaux is looking for it with the help of dynamite, a divining rod, and other similar methods.

Surrounded by hills that block out any view of the peaks of the Pyrenees, the ancient walls of Pamiers are reflected in the crystal-clear waters of the Ariège River, which descends from the snow-covered mountains of Andorra. Among the throngs of people that crowd the old town's tiny streets, I saw many Senegalese and Arabs in uniform. I decided not to stay too long.

In the year 1207, the following events unfolded here: In response to an invitation by the countess of Foix (whose beautiful name was Esclarmonde) Roman Catholic priests, theological doctors, and monks from the cities and monasteries of southern France and the Vatican made their way to Pamiers to discuss Christian belief with the Albigensian heretics. Esclarmonde, who was herself a heretic, was worried about her homeland. She knew that the pope in Rome and the French king had already decided upon its destruction. Blood had flowed. On the orders of Pope Alexander III, Henri de Clairveaux, an abbot who had been named cardinal-bishop of Albano at the Lateran Council in 1179, had preached a crusade against the Albigenses and had assembled a horde of singing pilgrims to impose Rome's teachings by force—in other words, through bloody murder. In 1207, the infamous Innocent III mounted

St. Peter's throne. He swore to crush the head of the Albigensian dragon and prepare the heretical land for a new generation.

At the Castellar de Pamiers, Esclamonde's home during her widowhood, a theological confrontation was organized to decide who was a better Christian—a Roman Catholic or an Albigensian Cathar. Esclarmonde herself intervened in the heated debate. When she used the crusade preached by the cardinal-bishop of Albano as a charge against Rome, an infuriated priest shouted to her: "Madame, stay with your spinning wheel! You have nothing to say here!"

Although nobody truly knows anything about her, Esclarmonde de Foix was one of the great female personalities of the Middle Ages. Cursed by the pope and hated by the French king, she struggled until her last breath for one goal: the political and religious independence of her Occitan homeland. She was revered when she died—but where she is buried nobody knows. Perhaps she rests in one of the caves she had reconstructed beneath the castle at Montségur as an impregnable stronghold. One fact, however, is certain: She did not live to see the tragic end of her country. Without any doubt, those closest to her returned Esclarmonde to the land from where she came. Esclarmonde de Foix was an archheretic. Today, modern Christians would call her neo-pagan because she rejected the Old Testament, deemed that the God called Yahweh was a manifestation of Satan, and refused to believe that Jesus Christ died on the cross—hence she rejected the first possible redemption of mankind.

In 1204, Esclarmonde took her solemn vows to Cathar heresy in Fanjeaux, which is not very far from Pamiers. The patriarch of the heretical church, Guilhabert de Castres, who was a knight from the Cathar elite known as the Sons of Belissena, accepted her Haereticatio, as the Inquisitors called the heretical vow. From then on, Esclarmonde belonged to the society of Cathars.

Only a *credens*, or believer, could become one of the Cathars. They swore the following final oath: "I swear to respect God and his true gospel, never to lie, never to swear, never to touch a woman [in the case of a female heretic, this was changed to 'a man'], never to kill an animal, not to eat meat, and to live only from fruit. And I swear never to betray my belief, no matter what kind of death threatens me." After this vow, a Cathar was then a "pure one" or *perfectus*—a perfect one.[8] The new member was then dressed in a hand-woven tunic that was sometimes called a dress. By contrast, female heretics wore a sort of diadem. In the Provençal language, this ceremony was called the Consolamentum: "consolation." It was not obligatory for a simple heretical believer, or *credens,* to take this oath; he could live in much the same way as anybody else: He could have a wife and children, work, hunt, eat meat, and drink wine. A cave or a clearing in the woods served as the house of God. Their pastors were the Cathars, who were also called Bonshommes—the "good men"—as a compliment. St. Bernard of Clairveaux recounted that in southern France, all knights were *fere omnes milites,* or Cathars.

When Esclarmonde de Foix took her heretical vow, she was a widow of advanced age and a mother of six sons who were all in their manhood. Did heretical asceticism represent a conclusive passage in her life? I can hardly believe that all knights led a monklike existence.

---

[8][Curiously, the priests of ancient Egypt were also called "pure ones," or *oueb.* —*Trans.*]

~ FOIX ~

I like this small Pyrenean town. Set in well-kept, green surroundings and surrounded by commanding mountains, Foix is dominated by a picturesque castle and an attractive church. Its small but exceptionally clean streets and roads wind hither and thither. Curiously, I have seen a lot of tall, blond people here. Could they be of Germanic stock? For a long time, the Goths and the Franks were at home in Foix—as rival brothers.

The town church recalls this fraternal struggle. It is dedicated to Volusian, a relatively obscure holy man about whom the following is known: Around AD 500, the Roman Catholic bishops of southern Gaul, which was under Visigoth dominance, became increasingly unhappy with the Arian—and consequently heretical—king of the Goths, and appealed directly to Clovis, the king of the Franks, to intervene. One of the bishops—Volusian by name—opened the doors of the city of Tours to the approaching Franks. Now a renegade, the bishop was forced to flee. The embittered Goths pursued him to the Pyrenees, where he was captured and slain. After the battle of Voillé, an encounter that cost the Gothic king Alaric II his life and allowed the Franks to conquer the south, Clovis had what was left of Volusian's body gathered and declared holy. The Frankish clergy then proclaimed the cleric a martyr, and a monastery was established at Volusian's grave. A small town developed nearby over the ruins of an ancient settlement, which was reconstructed by the Frankish king Charles as a major fortified town. This became today's Foix.[9]

All the same, Foix has to thank the Phoceans for its name. In the sixth century BC, these Hellenes from Asia Minor left Phocea, their home city, because the Persian tyrant Harpagus threatened them with destruction. They settled on Gaul's southern coast. Massilia (today's Marseille), Portus Veneris (Port Vendres), and other southern French towns came into being this way. Foix is another one of them, a Phocea, or Phokis, in the European west.

---

[9][St. Volusian of Tours (b. ?–AD 496) was bishop of that city. His death at the hands of the Goths is disputed. Strangely, Rahn does not mention that Volusian is remembered for his early marriage to a violent woman. —*Trans.*]

During the era of the crusade against the Albigenses, seven hundred years ago, the land, town, and castle of Foix witnessed some dreadful events. In the name of the pope and in accordance with the desires of the French king, three hundred thousand true believers, together with the scum from all God-fearing countries, assembled in Lyon in 1209, under the command of the archabbot Arnaud de Citeaux and, shortly thereafter, Simon de Montfort. The mission of the pope, the king, and these commanders was to crush that blessed land between the Alps and the Pyrenees, Provence and the Languedoc, for three reasons: First, Roman Catholicism should reign unchallenged as Christianity's sole faith. Second, France's preeminence in the south must be firmly established. Finally, those returning from the Crusade in Palestine must be offered another opportunity to plunder, and the masses, who were accustomed to slaughtering nonbelievers, must be given the prospect of practicing their skills again. The king of France promised them rich booty. Likewise, the pope's contribution did not fail its purpose: After forty days, eternal salvation was extended to all those who took part in the war against the Albigenses and absolution was granted for all sins committed during the Albigensian crusade.

Under the patronage of the Blessed Virgin Mary, Mother of God, the hordes swarmed over the boundaries of Provence, accompanied by a psalm-singing and heavily armed legion of archbishops, bishops, abbots, priests, and monks. In an encyclical of September 1, 1883, Pope Leo XIII, one of the many Germany-haters who have sat on St. Peter's throne, declared that the Albigenses had tried to overthrow the Church with force of arms. According to the Holy Father, thanks to a Dominican invention, the heretics were thwarted with the prayers of the holy Rosary of the Blessed Virgin Mary. Either this pope was misinformed or he willingly tried to misinform. There can be no doubt: Rome and Paris started the war.

The uncrowned king of southern France, Raimundo, the count of Toulouse, made one Roman pilgrimage after another to spare his land complete annihilation—all in vain. Even as he crawled before the cross, the first cities, towns, and people were ablaze.

Eventually, the crusaders besieged Foix. Sometime before, at the Third Council of Lateran, its lord, Raimon Drut, who was one of the count of Toulouse's most loyal vassals, had accused God's vicar on earth, the pope, of watching the entire Provençal population being butchered without any regard for their belief. Already five hundred thousand had fallen victim to the murderous crusaders. The "difficult" count was then dismissed with a farewell benediction and a smug, diplomatic smile. Defying all description was what the county of Foix then suffered in horrors, confiscation of property, and persecution at the hands of the pilgrims and their successors during the purge of Albigensian beliefs (read the extermination of the Albigenses) and the presence of the Dominicans (read Inquisitors).

At the Lateran Council, used against the count was the uncomfortable fact that the sister of the count of Foix, Esclarmonde, was an archheretic who resolutely protected all Albigenses. The count considered that his sister's actions were not his affair because his sister could do what she wanted on her own property and could take care of her subjects as she thought best. Concerning her beliefs, he deemed that he had even less right to assert any and no way to force her to change. Whatever the case, he was of the unshakable conviction that every person should be free to choose his or her own faith.

When the Latin Mass was finally sung throughout the land and upstarts had confiscated the castles of the land, when the conquered territory was subjugated by France's Crown and the language of the victors—French—began to replace Provençal, the Cathar faith remained free at Montségur, protected in the highlands of Foix by the Pyrenees Mountains, where the citadel reached skyward, free until 1244, some thirty-five years after the beginning of the war. After the failure of the conference of Pamiers, Countess Esclarmonde had the foresight to instruct the best military architect of that time, Bertran de Baccalauria, to rebuild Montségur (which had formed part of her widow's inheritance) in such a way as to render it virtually unconquerable by humans. In this way, high up and so close to the clouds, a small group of loyal knights, devout heretics, and brave farmers were able to withstand the siege of an overwhelming and determined enemy.

Esclarmonde's sister Cecilia was also a heretic. She belonged, however, to the Waldenses, those followers of the Lyon merchant Peter Waldo, who, in a clear protest against Rome's arrogance and decay and ever faithful to biblical scripture, led a strictly apostolic life as a moral descendant of Christ. Even if only a few Provençal knights or burghers belonged to their faith, the Vatican had sworn to destroy the Waldenses: During the crusade against the Albigenses, it had thousands upon thousands of them killed. Yet the archheretics remained, the even-more-hated Cathars, to whom Esclarmonde's father and brother belonged. The brother was a renowned troubadour—a *Minnesinger*—and his castle was open to all traveling minstrels. In his last hours, he took the vow of the Consolamentum.

~ *LAVELANET* ~

I was hardly aware of the drive to the high Pyrenees. Since yesterday, it has poured rain; it seems that here, too, autumn wants to halt its march. In the end, I rode in the post bus. My traveling companions were farmers who were carrying their wares to market. They quickly got out of me that I am German and that I want to stay in the mountains. They wanted to show me the mountain stronghold of Montségur and how it dominates the surrounding countryside, but the clouds concealed it. "Are you also looking for the treasure of the Albigenses?" they asked in turn. Then I learned of an article about the treasure seekers that had appeared in a Toulouse newspaper shortly before.

A well-kept inn is my shelter for the night. Toward ten o'clock in the morning, the son of the innkeeper—a doctor—will drive me first to the town of Montférrier (Iron Mountain) and then on up to the hamlet of Montségur. He has some patients to attend to.

After dinner, an eighty-six-year-old townsman offered to show me his collection: For decades he has been digging in the castle ruins and caves of his narrow homeland. Without any hesitation and with shameless pride, he showed me the bones of cave-dwelling bears and lions; prehistoric stone tools; arrowheads in bone, bronze, and iron; shards; and much more. He has also searched the rubble of the citadel of Montségur, if somewhat superficially. His principal discoveries were weapons, seals, and stone balls that were rolled by the defenders onto the besiegers in the valley below.[10] Finally, with great care, he removed several small, clay doves from a shrine. He found them in the ruins of Montségur. My host could not tell me what purpose they had served. Apart from that, I learned to my astonishment that a deceased friend of his had found in the rubble of the stronghold a book in a foreign script—possibly Chinese or Arabic; he didn't remember anymore. The book with the unusual script was lost.

As I reflect upon this evening and anticipate my journey to

---

[10][Fernand Niel describes in *Montségur: la montagne sacrée* how these stone balls remain scattered about the castle of Montségur. They were used not by the defenders, as Rahn says, but rather by the besiegers, who launched them on catapults to demolish the castle walls. —*Trans.*]

Montségur with even greater eagerness, all this makes me think of a story that was told to me on the doorstep as I was bidding my hosts farewell: Sometime in the twelfth century, a powerful viscount named Raimundo Jordan lived in the vicinity of Cahors, north of Toulouse. In those days, it was befitting for accomplished knights to cultivate the *Minne* and compose poetry to honor noble ladies—in other words, to be a troubadour. Adelaide was Raimundo 's choice; she was the wife of the nobleman Baronet Pena, who knew, and approved of, this Minne. When the terrible Albigensian war broke out, both Raimundo and the nobleman took up arms to confront the enemy. Pena fell in battle and, soon afterward, Raimundo went missing. Adelaide awaited in apprehension, yearning for news of the troubadour. Believing that he had fallen in the war, she renounced her worldly possessions and retired, as the heretic that she was, to the castle in the clouds, Montségur. She wanted to pass her last days there. Nevertheless, Raimundo was still alive. Although he had been seriously wounded, he had found shelter and care with friends. After a long, drawn-out recovery, he asked to see Adelaide again and rode to Pena's castle along secret trails in the forest. He discovered that the castle had fallen to the enemy long ago and its mistress had vanished without a trace. Raimundo was now condemned as an outlaw; there was no refuge left for him other than Montségur—where he found Adelaide.

On my way home, some verses by Ludwig Uhland came to mind. As a schoolboy I had to learn them by heart. Who would have thought then that I would make my home in the "Valleys of Provence!":

> *In the Valleys of Provence*
> *Sprouted the song of the Minne, Child of Springtime,*
> *   and the Minne*
> *The holder more intimately enjoyed*

I came to this land because of the Albigenses, who, like my ancestors, were heretics. That a close relationship existed between heretics and Minnesingers was completely unknown to me before I came here.

~ MONTSÉGUR IN THE PYRENEES ~

I am living in a more-than-humble farmhouse, where I am obliged to fetch my water from a well located to the side on a pathway that leads to the so-called Camp des Cremats (Field of Fires). There, Dominican monks burned alive 205 heretics on a gigantic pyre. Not far from the well, jutting out of a stone block, is a wrought-iron cross with two swords positioned across it. Hanging from the upright beam of the cross are a whip, a cane, and a crown of thorns—as well as the keys of St. Peter. Directly behind, a colossal mountain rises; atop it, the ruins of Montségur repose in grandiose solitude.

Dizzily overlooking a deep gorge, the hamlet of Montségur has at most thirty homes. The upper part of the town has fallen down. Anyone who can pulls up and leaves for the towns in the valleys, forsaking his property. Only pasture, potatoes, and a little fruit are cultivated here. The people are terribly poor. My landlord, the village priest, complains about this. He sits over his accounts and calculates incessantly because Peter's Pence is not enough to make ends meet. Every once in a while, he visits relatives in nearby Belesta. When he returns, he is loaded with bread and sausages.

The church, a miserable construction, is frequented almost exclusively by schoolchildren. Apart from a few wizened dotards, adults visit the place only on the feast of Toussaint on November 1.[11] That is the only time in the year when this congregation comes together—to remember the dead. On my first day here, I met the engineer from Bordeaux who is looking for the gold of the Albigenses, and who lives next to the church.[12] He explained that the castle is the property of the municipality and that he has obtained their permission in a written contract, which, if his project is successful, awards to him half of the treasure (he is convinced that it is gold and silver). Furthermore, he hopes to find the authentic Book of Revelation, the Apocalypse According to John, which should contain the true message of Jesus Christ and was believed to be in the possession of the Albigenses. The Cathars believed that the Church of Rome wanted to destroy the only

---

[11][All Saints Day. —*Trans.*]

[12][His name was Arthur Caussou. —*Trans.*]

true message of the Son of God because the Catholics had falsified it.

How does he know all this? I asked. He made it clear that he couldn't tell me because he belonged to a secret association that demanded silence from its members.[13] Even though the Albigenses were exterminated almost to the last man by the Inquisition and its executioners, the true Book of Revelation was placed in a safe resting place inside the mountain, which is hollow. Long after the castle had fallen, the Roman Catholics were still digging up the place in their search for the holy scriptures of John—but in vain. In addition, he told me that he knew the location of Esclarmonde's grave. A man with a divining rod had revealed the place to him, and thanks to the way the rod turned, he was able to describe the sarcophagus: It was stone with a golden dove decorating the top. I had to stop myself from smiling.

Never before this morning have I seen such a stunning view from the summit of the castle mountain. From Carcassonne, where the Visigoth kings once held court, to Toulouse the plains were free to the eye. To the east, I thought that I could make out the sea somewhere between Montagne Noire and Alaric's Mountain, where I noticed a silvery glimmer. Toward my feet, I could see the rich flora of the abbey of Notre-Dame-de-Prouille, the mother monastery of the Dominican order, home of the Rosary of the Blessed Virgin Mary and cradle of the Inquisition. After his vision of the Mother of God on the occasion of her celebration day (when she ordered the invention of the Rosary and the annihilation of the heretics), St. Dominic founded the abbey to keep an eye on Montségur. Yet he never visited the heretical mountain. Before the citadel fell, his eyes closed forever and, if the Church is right, he entered into the company of saints. But St. Dominic had a lot of lives on his conscience . . .

Northeast from Toulouse, a light mist hangs in the air where lies Albi, the town that gave its name to the heretical movement because so many Albigensians lived there. I noticed the town of Mirepoix very clearly at my feet. In pre-Christian times it was called Beli Cartha, the "city of light," because Belis and Abellio were names for the gods of light. Between the peaks, directly north perhaps four hours from here, I

---

[13][Rahn is referring to the Polaires, a secret theosophical society based on the Hyperborean tradition, whose members included the writer Maurice Magre and the countess Miryanne Pujol-Murat. —*Trans.*]

could make out the castle of Foix. Its towers reflected the morning sun. In the west and the south, the Pyrenean peaks stretched toward the sky, one more proud and bold than the other: Canigou, Carlitte, Soularac, and the majestic St. Bartholomew's Peak—the Tabor, as the farmers call it. But is it a mountain of enlightenment, like the Palestinian Tabor? Its almost three-thousand-meter summit[14] is almost always enveloped in clouds.

Over the course of thirty years, the pilgrims and soldiers of the crusade against the Albigenses, and later the Dominicans, united with the French who hurried to Montségur. Behind its thick walls, as we know, the last free heretics and Occitan knights had found refuge. They managed to hold out until Palm Sunday of 1244. Then, shepherds who had taken Catholic money pointed out a stone ridge from which the besiegers could reach the summit without any fear. Sole access to the castle was on the western face of the mountain, which was less steep but, thanks to defensive works, was well protected. Yet here, too, danger threatened the besieged inhabitants of the citadel. The aggressors constructed a machine called a *gatta,* a siege tower, which, day after day, crawled a few feet closer to the summit to menace the castle walls.[15] The betrayal of the shepherds caused the collapse of resistance inside the citadel. All who refused to recognize the supremacy of Yahweh, the authority of Peter's keys, and Rome's dogma were burned alive on Palm Sunday on a gigantic pyre erected at the foot of the mountain. Among the 205 victims were the castellan's daughter, Esclarmonde de Belissena, a relative of Esclarmonde de Foix. The other prisoners, about 400 in total, were thrown in the dungeons of the fortress of Carcassonne, where the vast majority perished in misery.[16]

---

[14][Approximately ninety-eight hundred feet. —*Ed.*]

[15][Rahn has based his version of the siege quite clearly on Napoléon Peyrat's monumental six-volume *l'Histoire des Albigeois.* But as historian Fernand Niel has pointed out in *Montségur: la montagne sacrée* (Paris: Editions La Colombe, 1954), Peyrat mistranslated the word *machina* into the so-called gatta, or siege towers, that were used in the assault on Jerusalem. In fact, the besiegers of Montségur used catapults, which were known as *trebuchets.* These machines launched stone balls against the walls of the fortress. To this very day, nearly 750 years later, the vicinity of Montségur is littered with these neatly chiseled stone balls. —*Trans.*]

[16][Many served under Louis IX by converting to Catholicism. —*Trans.*]

I decided to rest alongside a shepherd I encountered on the Pic du Soularac. He gave me some of his cheese to eat, and I let him drink red wine from my *gourde* (a sort of flask made from animal hide), which I carried in case I lost my way. Even if the sun glowed from a cloudless sky, a southern storm howled. The shepherd and I talked of Montségur and the treasure of the Cathars.

My shepherd had wanted to know the truth—if the Grail had really been kept at Montségur—so he began to tell me a story: When Montségur's walls were still standing, the pure ones kept the Holy Grail there. But the devil's followers coveted the Grail for a reason: They wanted to restore it to their lord's diadem, from which it had plunged to earth during the fall of the angels. The castle was threatened—Lucifer's armies had camped beneath its ramparts. In this great emergency, a dove flew down from the heavens and split open the mighty Tabor with its beak. At that moment, Esclarmonde, who was the keeper of the Grail, threw the precious relic into the mountain gorge, which then closed upon it again. In this way, the Grail was saved. When the devils finally forced their way into the castle, they were too late. In a frenzy, they burned all the pure ones not far from the castle mountain at the Camp des Cremats, the Field of Fires. All were burned, except of course Esclarmonde. When she realized the Grail was safe, she climbed to the top of the Tabor and became a dove; then she flew off to the mountains of Asia. In this way, Esclarmonde escaped death and still lives on in Paradise. That is the reason, said my shepherd, why her grave will never be found.[17]

When I asked him what he thought of the man with the divining rod and his description of Esclarmonde's sarcophagus, he snarled, "*Ce sont tous des fumistes!*"—"They are all crazies!"

Together with the priest's nephew and a few farmers, I sat at the fireplace in a low-ceilinged kitchen. In the next room, young fellows were playing cards loudly. It was dismal outside; the castle and the hamlet of Montségur were enveloped in clouds. Even today, three days later, they have still not given way. It is autumn and bitter cold. Everyone knows that Montségur was the castle of the Grail. The whole region of Foix

---

[17][Perhaps this tale lies at the heart of Rahn's fascination with the Grail, and the Cathars. In fact, the legend, as it is told by the shepherd, appears almost entirely in Wolfram von Eschenbach's *Parzival*. —*Trans.*]

thinks so. The engineer scoffed when they spoke of it with him. That is why they didn't mention it to me.

Because of my enthusiasm, our talk became bolder and I learned more: The engineer will never find his treasure. It lies in a cave in the Tabor forest. A massive stone block protects the cave's entrance from intruders, and the treasure itself is guarded by hundreds of vipers inside. Whoever wishes to enter can do so only during Mass on Palm Sunday—on the Fête des Rameaux. That is the moment when it is possible to lift the stone slab, because the snakes are fast asleep. But God help the person who has not left the cave before the priest has sung *Ite Missa Est!* At the end of Mass the slab closes again, and the intruder suffers a terrible end as he is bitten to death by the newly awakened vipers.

One of the fellows in the circle said that his grandfather, who was a shepherd, had found, deep in the forest, just such a stone slab with an iron ring. It was so heavy, however, that it was impossible for him to lift it. So he hurried back to town for help, but then he couldn't find the spot again. Strange country!

Winter has arrived; it has snowed for eight days straight. When I left my home in the north, I would never have dreamed that in order to get my meals, I would have to shovel my way to the small inn through a snowdrift. Were it not for the southern French farmhouses, I could easily forget that I am residing in France's most southerly region, only a few hours from Spain—a region that we erroneously think is a garden filled with lemon and orange trees. Instead, there are colossal mountains that look like they belong in the Bavarian Alps, snow-covered elm trees, and pine forests—so "northern" is this south. Until now, I had never before seen the blue of the sky and the clarity of the sunlight. The nights are brutally cold, and the stars are so close that you could easily think that you might grab them with your hand.

I am shoveling one log after another into the fireplace, only to realize that though it is glowing hot near the fire, a few steps away, you can freeze to ice. If you sit in front of the fireplace, you are covered in gooseflesh and sweat at the same time. I, like the country folk, prefer to stay in the innkeeper's kitchen, where an oven spreads the heat evenly. The kitchen has become the innkeeper's dining room.

It is impossible to climb the castle mountain. I tried, but the snow is far too deep. When I finally could get through, I discovered to my astonishment that the northern slope under the castle had become an unassailable wall of ice—but I could hardly get through against the storm that swirled around the mountain. Faced with this, I decided to have a few books sent from Germany: *Parzival,* the epic of narrative poetry by the German Minnesinger Wolfram von Eschenbach; the ode *Der Wartburgkrieg;* and French and German works on the Grail legend and the Minne. Wolfram's poetry fills me with unbridled joy. Isn't every man who seeks justice just like Parzival? Isn't every mother who must commend her son to the demands of life just like Herzeloyde? Isn't every forthright man who seeks the beacon of truth drawn irresistibly to the land of the Grail?

I am not so attracted by the narrative of *Der Wartburgkrieg,* which was written anonymously.[18] It does not have the resolution, timelessness, and profound strength of Wolfram's work. Nevertheless, significant passages of the book illustrate perfectly those troubled times of the thirteenth century of the Christian era. The cry "Free from Rome!" found an echo here. Although it is bound by its time, the book earned its place in German literature.

The object of Parzival's longing is the Grâl (Grail), a stone of light. Compared to it, earthly brilliance is nothing. The Grail represents the fulfillment of all worldly desires: in other words, Paradise. He who beholds it will never die. Hercules, Alexander the Great, and other heroic figures of Greek antiquity knew of its existence. Moreover, a "pagan and astrologer"[19] read its name among the starry lights, and announced its coming to mankind. How the Grâl fell from the star-filled heavens to earth Wolfram doesn't say. But the stone remained: "[A] troop left it on earth, and then rose high above the stars, if their innocence drew them back again." Since then, the Grail has been kept in a castle called Muntsalvatsche, guarded by Grail knights and a king who is attended by Grail maidens. Only their leader may carry the precious stone. A

---

[18][*Der Wartburgkrieg,* or *Sängerkrieg auf der Wartburg,* was composed around 1206 and describes a contest of Minnesingers at Wartburg Castle, which belonged to the landgrave of Thuringia. Built in 1070, the castle is remembered as the place were Martin Luther hid after the Diet of Worms and translated the Bible into German. —*Trans.*]

[19][Flegetanis in *Parzival.* —*Trans.*]

young hero, Parzival, sets off in search of the Grâl. Leaving his mother, Herzeloyde, he seeks knighthood; then, as a knight of King Arthur's Round Table, Parzival continues to seek the highest earthly reward: the Grail. He finds it at the castle, and becomes the Grail King. When Parzival's son Lohengrin comes of age, he becomes the Grail's herald, traveling in a boat pulled by a swan to all people suffering injustice.

The publisher of my *Parzival* edition believes that Wolfram's Grâl Castle must lie in the Pyrenees.[20] References to places such as Aragon and Katelangen (Catalonia)[21] must have led him to this conclusion. So my Pyrenean farmers are not wrong after all when they call the ruins of Montségur the castle of the Saint-Graal, and the snow that Parzival's steed trots upon to the holy castle is very probably Pyrenean snow. Muntsalvatsche, which was the only name Wolfram gave the Grail Castle, means, as many accept, "wild mountain." The French word *sauvage,* or "wild," is based on the Latin *silvaticus* (from *silva,* or "forest")—and there is no lack of forests around Montségur. In the spoken dialect of the Pyrenees, "wild mountain" translates as *mont salvatgé,* contradicting Wolfram. On his authority, Richard Wagner, the composer of *Lohengrin* and *Parzifal* called the Grail Castle by the name Montsalvat, which means "mountain of light." Both Montsalvat and Muntsalvatsche can translate as *mont ségur,* "secure mountain" or "peace mountain." In this regard, Montségur, that ruin with which I live, is present also in the much-sought-after Grail Castle.

Only in Wolfram's epic can you find the name Muntsalvatsche. Other early medieval Grail poets, and there were many, selected different designations. In an Old French novel, the goal the Grail knights were striving for is the paradisal Eden—Eden, Chastiax de Joie, joy, togetherness, or *chastiax des armes* ("soul" or "togetherness"). Poetry is the final goal of the Olympians themselves. Therefore, the seekers of the Grail became Olympians, as the Greek gods and heroes were. In all the great literary works of the early Middle Ages, the mountain and castle of the Grail were regarded as sources of light and as a place of enlightenment. Perhaps this is the reason why the Pic du Saint Barthélemy, on

---

[20][Wolfram von Eschenbach, *Parzival,* trans. A. T. Hatto (New York: Penguin Classics, 1980). —*Trans.*]

[21][Cataluña in Spanish. —*Ed.*]

whose easternmost outpost stands the castle of Montségur, carries the name Tabor, as the biblical mountain of the enlightenment is called.

A sharp, multicolored picture representing Jesus Christ on the Mount of Olives was hanging on the wall of my room until now. It depicted a winged angel, emerging halfway out from a cloud and holding out to the faithful a monstrous cup. I have removed the picture and replaced it with a sheet of my best writing paper, upon which I wrote, as carefully and beautifully as I could, some verses of Wolfram von Eschenbach: "The authentic tale with the conclusion to the Romance has been sent to us in German lands from Provence: When Lucifer made his descent to hell with his following, humans developed. Consider what Lucifer and his comrades achieved! They were innocent and pure."

I prefer to believe that Satan's, not Lucifer's, armies stood before the walls of Montségur to steal the Grail, which had fallen from the Light Bringer, from Lucifer's crown, and was kept by the pure ones. These were the Cathars, not those clerics and adventurers who, cross on chest, wanted to prepare the Languedoc for a new caste—their own.

— AGAIN, LAVELANET —

I left the hamlet of Montségur a few hours ago. A mule cart carried my luggage down into the valley. My workbench is located in the front garden of the small hotel beside a fig tree. In the large and famous weaving mills, the sirens howl. It is shift change. I am told that nearly half of all inhabitants of this small town are weavers, and the spinning wheel is domestic from primeval times. The Cathars were also called Tisserands—the Weavers . . .

I was again the guest of the eighty-year-old Monsieur Rives, as I prefer to call him. I found out some important details: Minnesingers and heresy belonged together even before the time of the Albigensian crusade. He confirmed that the Cathars constituted a gleyza d'amors, or a church of the Minne, and that the ritual in which a troubadour swore fidelity to his lady was called, in German, the Consolament-Tröstung, the same name as the well-known ritual in which a heretical believer, or *credens,* was ordained a perfectus. In the same way, a singing and minstreling *chevalier errant,* or wandering knight, could aspire to become a *chevalier parfait,* or a perfect knight; either bitterly or gently, a *pregaire* could become a *trobador,* a finder.[22] The level of chevalier errant was the same as that of a heretical believer, and a chevalier parfait was equal to a heretical perfectus. All these Latin designations were introduced by the Inquisitors, who took down the confessions of the heretics in that language. Regarding the *Table Ronde,* or Round Table, whose miracles were exalted in most of the literary works of the Middle Ages, it has the perfect form: a circle, the symbol of the community of the perfecti and the chevaliers errants.[23] The Arthurian and Grail legends must be treated as the culmination of the exalted, poetical world of the Cathars.

When I asked him if he believes that Montségur was the legendary Grail Castle and whether he takes seriously this assessment, Monsieur Rives gave me a frank answer: yes. In schools and universities, he con-

---

[22][Once a troubadour had chosen his "lady," there were a series of "levels" that defined his relationship with her. The first grade was *feignaire,* which meant that the troubadour dared not approach his lady directly; a pregaire was a supplicant who received discreet encouragement from her; an *entendaire* had achieved an understanding with his lady and a *drutz,* a friend who had a right to a kiss. —*Trans.*]

[23][Curiously, here Rahn touches on the subject of the Grail and anti-Grail shapes. —*Trans.*]

tinued, we learn that the troubadours were a sentimental, effusive group of unattached males who left the concerns of everyday life to their patrons and sponsors; they had no interest other than winning the favor of a lady, often a married woman, through songs, and *courtoisie.* That Rome consciously distorted the truth after the Albigensian crusade is fact. Anyone who reads the verses of the early Provençal Minnesingers must admit that a troubadour never called his lady by name—rather he sang the praises of the "blonde lady," or the "lady with the beautiful face," or the "light of the world." These idealized ladies were nothing other than the symbolic embodiment of the church of the Minne. For example, when troubadours celebrated their "blonde lady from Toulouse" or their "lady from Carcassonne," it meant nothing other than the Cathar community in Toulouse or Carcassonne. When, through the threat of the stake, Rome's Inquisitors finally imposed the cult of the Blessed Virgin Mary and, through force, the custom of the Rosary, the troubadours dutifully addressed their verses to Maria. Secretly, however, they were referring to their church of the Minne. This is revealed quite clearly in the documents of the Inquisition: The *domina,* or "lady," of the Minnesingers was a "goddess" whose divine wisdom was praised in song. She was not a human being. It was initially the upper (north of Rome) Italian Minnesingers known as Fedeli d'Amore (greatly influenced by the Provençal Minnesingers) who, with fervent praise, pledged their loyalty to the Madonna Intelligenzia: Lady Wisdom.

Upon examining the biographies of the troubadours, I note that if a domina or madonna was married, her knightly husband is always mentioned—but never by his full name or with any indication of his residence or sphere of influence. This married man (which can be easily proved from contemporary sources) was generally recognized as the protector of the Cathar community within the sovereignty of his area. In the sad story of Lady Adelaide (that is, our name Adelheid, "noble nature"), which was told to me during my last visit, the woman was protected by Lord Pena (his full name does not add anything to the story), who protected and promoted the Cathars in his Albigensian district. Adelaide's admirer, troubadour Raimund, composed his *minne* in her honor with the full knowledge and approval of Lord Pena. That means that she gave him the Consolamentum: On his knees, the troubadour had to swear loyalty to her unto death, and she then gave him a ring or garment as indication of her acceptance of his Minne.

I aked my host why the German word *Minne* doesn't appear in Provençal Catharism and the songs of the minstrels. I was mistaken, my host answered. The word for the ceremony of Consolamentum contains the word *manisola* in the language of the Albigensians. In the festival of the consoling Mani, the word *mani* has the same root as the German word *Minne*—the cognate Gothic word *munni*, which is what we call "memories." The Minne was never absolute love! It meant a "memory of love." In addition, in Sanskrit, the written language of ancient India, it has the same meaning and designates a legendary stone that allegedly illuminates the world and drives out the night of terror. It is perhaps a well-known fact that many seekers of this stone, who usually see it as a stone table that provides food and drink, regard it as the archetype of the image of the Grâl, since the powers of the gral are many and include providing both food and drink. Finally, I asked my host whether Provençal minstreling was of Germanic inspiration. My question was answered: The manisola and Consolamentum were reflections of Germanic Minne, and because they were celebrated in May, they are related to the custom of the Germanic May dances. Since west Gothic times, the custom remained here in the Land of the Goths—the Languedoc.

Before I said good-bye to Monsieur Rives, he gave me a book that would expand on his points. He also pressed my hand heartily and said: "Don't forget that the troubadours practiced a *gai saber*, 'the joyous wisdom' that should be cherished!" My head spun. If what I came to learn now applies, I must throw onto the garbage heap all my previous beliefs. I would have to unlearn and relearn, as it is said.

So it is!

Our word *Minne* does not mean "love," but "remembrance" and "commemoration"! Because my ancestors were thinkers and romantics and poets, I myself want to be a poet of the Minne. I am seeking. I would like to be a *trobador*—a finder! My "knowledge," which sometimes may seem hard or arbitrary, should be cheerful and should make mankind happy—but at the right moment; I don't want to make it easy for those who will read this book.

— CASTLE L. IN THE TOULOUSE REGION —

I am a guest of Countess P., an elderly lady.[24] Nobody knows the history, legends, and customs of her homeland better than she. Her library is unusual in its uniformity and completeness. The countess frequently visited me at Montségur. Now I am returning the visit.

Today, we spent the late afternooon at the Mediterranean coast. As we returned leisurely in the early evening, we passed by Mont d'Alaric, a melancholy and bleak mountain that owes its name to the Gothic king Alaric. On the right-of-way was a covered wagon in the shade of a tree, and before it stood a slim man with snow-white hair. Beside him, a young blonde woman sat on a stone. With bright eyes, the old person urgently looked at us. "That is a Cagot," exclaimed my companion, "a nomadic Cagot. There is also a permanent population of them high up in the Pyrenees. If you ask the farmers about them, they usually reply that they are poorly regarded people. The name Cagot is probably a mixture of Cathares and Gots, or Cathars and Goths. We just saw a descendant of the last Albigensian."[25]

In the evening, we sat before the fireplace. The countess knitted. I read from a book the fact that graves from the Albigensian era were found in the area of the Montagne Noire.[26] One of them was a mass grave. Twelve skeletons lay in such a way that they formed a kind of wheel: The heads were grouped together at the hub and the bodies formed the spokes. The author's reckoning that this suggests sun admiration was probably correctly.[27]

Then we talked. My hostess was raised with the legend that identifies Montségur as the Grail Castle. She is convinced that the Grâl was kept at this castle and that her ancestors had been Grâl knights who laid down their lives in defense of the Grâl. Many of them fell in the siege of Montségur; some were even burned. Finally, she offered this: "The great Esclarmonde was my bloodline. I am proud to see her in spirit on the platform of the keep of Montségur, gazing into the stars. The heretics

---

[24][Comtesse Miryanne Pujol-Murat. —*Trans.*]

[25][Cagot or Canis Gothi were also called Chrestians. —*Trans.*]

[26][Black Mountain. —*Trans.*]

[27][The book is *Magiciens et illuminés*, by Maurice Magre (Paris: Fasquelle, 1930). —*Trans.*]

loved the stars. They believed that after death, a soul wandered from star to star until it approached the stages of divinization of the spirit. In the morning, the heretics prayed to the rising sun. In the evening, they turned devoutly about-face at its departure. At night, they turned to the silvery moon or the north, because the north was holy to them. They regarded the south as the dwelling place of Satan. Satan is not Lucifer, because Lucifer means "light bringer"! The Cathars had another name for him: Lucibel. He was not the devil. First the Jews and then the papists downgraded him to that. The Grail was a stone that fell from Lucifer's crown. This made the Cathar church, as they themselves stressed it, a Luciferian-Christian one.

"If Montségur was the mountain of the Grail Castle, then Esclarmonde was the lady of the Grail. After her death, the destruction of Montségur and the extermination of the Cathars orphaned both the Grail Castle and the Grail. The Catholics who waged the crusade against the Albigenses, which was a war of the cross against the Grail, did not fail to acquire the non-Catholic symbol of faith for their own purposes. But it was not enough that they proclaimed the Grail to be the cup from which Jesus gave his disciples the last Communion and which caught his blood on Golgotha. They even declared the Benedictine cloister Montserrat, conveniently south of the Pyrenees, to be the temple of the Grail. After it became known that the Cathars, who were often called the Luciferians by inquisitors, had kept the Luciferian Grail stone north of the Pyrenees, Catholic monks claimed to keep it south of those same mountains—but they made it into a relic for the believers of Jesus who vanquished the princes of hell."

We both fell silent. Then the countess continued: "I do not need to remind you that the Basque Ignatius of Loyola was the founder of the Society of Jesus. Did you know that he invented the Jesuit Spiritual Exercises, the organization of the Jesuit order and, if I do not err, the adoration of the bleeding heart of Jesus on Montserrat near Barcelona? You should follow up these connections."

My hostess gave a few books to me as a gift. I am especially pleased with a German book, published seventy years earlier, with the title *Caesarius von Heisterbach*. The author calls it a contribution to the cultural history of the twelfth and thirteenth centuries. Perhaps I will place in my next book a sentence from St. John the Evangelist that appears at the beginning: "Gather together the pieces (hunks, scraps, tidbits); on that nothing dies!"

My ancestors were heroes and my relatives were heretics. For their vindication, I am gathering the pieces that were left by Rome.

⁓ CARCASSONNE ⁓

Thirty-five years before Montségur's fall, on August 15, 1209, the day
that commemorates the Virgin Mary's ascension to heaven, this city fell
to the pilgrims of the Albigensian crusade—thanks to the intervention of
the Blessed Virgin, as one chronicler noted.

A long siege had preceded the event, and terrible scenes had taken
place; Carcassonne was confronted with the most dreadful of all deaths:
Before its gates, "Christ's soldiers" lay ready to ignite execution pyres,
and within its mighty walls, the accumulation of people and their livestock seeking refuge had caused an outbreak of the plague, which rav-
aged Carcassonne's beleaguered inhabitants, probably as a result of
hunger, clouds of mosquitoes, and a lack of fresh water.

Two days before the fall, an envoy of Rome appeared at the
eastern gate. He asked Viscount Raimund-Roger Trencavel, lord of
Carcassonne, to begin peace negotiations within the crusader camp,
swearing before God the almighty that free passage was assured the
people within the town's walls and would be respected. After a short
discussion with his barons and consuls, Trencavel decided to accept
this request. He hoped to save his city. Accompanied by a hundred
knights, he went to the tent of the leader of the crusaders, the archabbot Arnauld de Citeaux. There he was taken by surprise, and captured
with his companions. The archabbot allowed only a few knights to
escape, so that they would bring the news of the capture of their prince
to the city's inhabitants.

The next morning, Arnauld expected Carcassonne to surrender. But
the drawbridges were not lowered and the gates remained locked. The
crusaders, suspecting a ruse, approached the walls distrustfully. They
listened. No noise. Then they rammed open the east gate. The city was
empty. Ghostlike, the footsteps of the intruders echoed in the deserted
lanes. What had happened? The besieged had saved themselves by fleeing to the mountains through an underground tunnel. The crusaders
found in cellars only five hundred old men, women, and children for
whom escape would have been too arduous. Hundreds of them, who
confessed to the Catholics out of fear of death, were stripped to their
skin and then let loose, "clad only in their sins." The others, however,
were condemned to death at the stake because they refused to swear off

the heresy. As the crusaders celebrated a thankgiving service to God in the Church of Saint Nazaire, the screams of the burning heretics could be heard. Incense mixed itself with the smoke of the pyres. When the howls of the victims had faded away, the archabbot of Citeaux read the Mass of the Holy Spirit and recounted the birth of Jesus Christ. After the northern French knight Simon of Montfort was selected as the new secular lord of the conquered country "under the obvious influence of the holy spirit" and "for the fame of God, the honor of the Church, and the fall the heresy," Montfort had Viscount Trencavel poisoned. In this way, the cross triumphed in Carcassonne. It was raised on the highest tower of the city as a sign of their triumph . . .

Beautiful and solemn Carcassonne! Nowhere in the Western world is there anything comparable. The massive walls of your towers and parapets rise up defiantly, and they speak.

I stood today at the Tour de l'Inquisition—Inquisition Tower. Within its walls, the Albigensian drama was played out to its bitter end. This is where the inquisitors imprisoned those defenders who had not been burned on the funeral pyre at Montségur—four hundred in total. Among the prisoners was a knight who had once proclaimed in full view of a cross that he never wanted to be saved by that symbol. Which holy symbol would he have preferred to the cross? The Grail?

I stood before the Tours des Visigots, the Visigoth Towers, and the Tour du Trésor, Treasure Tower. Perhaps this Visigoth structure once housed the Grâl. As old romances recount, it formed part of a famous Gothic treasure that had a strange destiny. The Goths stole it from the Romans, and it remained in their possession until the Visigoth king Alaric founded Carcassonne. Then the Ostrogoth king Theodoric, also named Dietrich von Bern, had it transported to Ravenna about a hundred years later.[28] Part of the treasure, however, remained in Carcassonne.

Mysterious Grail!

It is night. Sultriness weighs on city and country. Over the Pyrenees lightning flashes, and there is low thunder. A thunderstorm seems to be approaching. One star after the other is wiped away by the racing

---

[28][Theodoric the Great (AD 454–526), king of the Ostrogoths, appears in the *Niebelungenlied* as Dietrich von Bern. —*Trans.*]

clouds. A scorching wind from the south floors me. I would like to work and am not able to do so. My explorations suddenly seem useless to me. Secretly, I scold myself as a foolish dreamer.

In three hours I travel farther—to Saint-Germain in Paris. I must note a few things, so that they are not lost.

First, Wolfram von Eschenbach named the Grail seeker and Grail king Parzival, a name that means "cut well." (The old Provençal words *trenca vel* mean exactly the same.) In this way, Wolfram anointed Carcassonne's viscount Raimund-Roger Trencavel as Parzival.

Second, Trencavel's mother was named Adelaide. She was the model for Wolfram's Herzeloyde. Before her marriage to Raimund-Roger's father, she was courted by the king of Aragon, Alfonse le Chaste. This "chaste king" must have been the model for Wolfram's deceased king Kastis, who was first engaged to Herzeloyde.

Third, Adelaide and her son were devoted to the Cathar heresy. They rejected the cross as a holy symbol. As Wolfram von Eschenbach notes several times, the Grâl was the symbol of the heretical faith left on earth by pure ones. He meant the Cathars, because the Cathars are often called pure ones.

Fourth, Wolfram von Eschenbach calls Anfortas (the Grail King whose suffering is ended by Parzival) *guotman* and *guoten one*. The Cathars were honored by their followers and patrons with the name Good Men, or Bonshommes.

Fifth, Wolfram von Eschenbach asserts that the true legend of the Grail came to Germany from Provence, thus from southern France. The minstreling poet Kyot of Provence recounted the tale. Around the turn of the twelfth century, a troubadour named Guiot of Provins stayed at the Carcassonne court as a guest of the house of Trencavel. This wandering Minnesinger was none other than Wolfram's Kyot. As was common at that time, to express his thanks to his hosts of the house of Trencavel, the Minnesinger composed a tale in which Adelaide and her son, Raimund-Roger Trencavel, appear as Herzeloyde and Parzival, respectively. Wolfram simply merged Guiot into his Kyot.

Sixth, Adelaide of Carcassonne and her son Trencavel were closely related to Esclarmonde de Foix, the mistress of Montségur Castle, or the Grail Castle of Munsalvat! In Wolfram's *Parzival* she appears as

Repanse de Schoye, the only person permitted to carry the Grail. She is also Parzival's cousin.

Seventh, Wolfram von Eschenbach and troubadour Guiot of Provins may have met one another in Mainz, because both were there when Frederick Barbarossa organized a chivalric celebration. Therefore, the characters of Parzival and Herzeloyde are not the creations of Kyot-Guiot, because the tales of the Grail and Parzival were uncommonly popular and beloved at that time. The legends are probably much older than seven hundred years. I can say only that Kyot-Guiot made his hosts into the characters Herzeloyde and Parzival.

Eighth, although Rome destroyed the writings of the Cathars, we possess in Wolfram's *Parzival* a literary work that was certainly dictated by Cathars!

‑ SAINT-GERMAIN-EN-LAYE ‑

I have been working for weeks now at the Bibliothèque Nationale in Paris because the records of the Inquisition are kept here. They give a clear picture of Montségur's tragic end. Now I know that during that Palm Sunday madness when Montségur was betrayed, four heretical perfecti wrapped in woolen sheets were secretly lowered on ropes from the summit of the castle rock into the abyss to save the heretical treasure.[29] The project succeeded. They were able to hand over their precious property to Pons Arnaud, a heretical knight who was the lord of the small castle Verdun in the Sabarthès.

The canyon west of the Tabor range is called the Sabarthès. A mule path—the Route des Cathares, the pathway of the pure ones—leads there from Montségur. If the mysterious Cathar treasure was indeed the Grâl, which according to legend can be recovered only when the congregation is attending Mass, then we must look for it in the Sabarthès. Soon, spring will come, and I will travel again to the land of the Albigensians—and this time also to the Sabarthès!

Thanks to my research in the Nationale (as Frenchmen call their state library), I discovered hitherto new and strange aspects of the Cathars and troubadours, who formed a single "community of the Minne." For instance, the German Cistercian monk Caesarius von Heisterbach, who was their contemporary, wrote that if the Cathars had recognized Moses and the Prophets, they could not have been considered heretics; that the Albigensian error was so popular that it would have affected a thousand cities within a short time—and all of Europe would have been poisoned had the sword of the believers not smashed it. It became a conflict between so-called orthodox Christianity and the world of the Cathars. In reality, the crusade was the enforcement of the bigotry and intolerance of the Old Testament.

Furthermore, twenty years ago, the Catholic University of Louvain published a thesis of Edmond Broeckx, a theology professor who presented it during a short seminar at Hoogstraten. Dedicated to Cardinal Mercier, the dissertation was entitled *Le Catharisme,* The World of

---

[29][The names of the four perfecti were Poitevin, Hugues, Amiel Aicart, and Raimundo de Alfaro. —*Trans.*]

the Cathars. In it, the author asserts that only a few heretics practiced monkish asceticism, which was an exception. (I probably do not need to worry about exceptions!) Broeckx wrote in his thesis that some heretics had practiced the trade of butcher, and gave as an example the story of a man from Salsigne who was not required to give up his occupation. Concerning killing in general, a heretical perfectus named Guilhelm de Belibaste was permitted to kill not only animals but also Catholics as soon as they began hunting heretics! More important, however, was another discovery that I made in this book and which consists of only one sentence: *La secte possédait écrits et chants nationaux.*[30]

All these writings and songs were destroyed in a fate similar to that of those who wrote them. That painting hanging in the Prado in Madrid, which shows St. Dominic burning heretical books, says enough.

The Grail legend, which came "from Provence to German lands" and, in the land of the Franks, "was sung in the German language" by Wolfram von Eschenbach, is one of these national songs. Wolfram wrote in his *Parzival* that *peregrini* burned Provence—that is, the pilgrims of the Albigensian crusade, *innumerabiles cum ingenti gaudio* (innumerable ones with tremendous joy). This terrible sentence can be found in the writings of Pierre de Vaux Cernay in *Hystoria Albigensis.*[31] In addition, we can find the more pleasing fact that "nearly all the barons of the country were protectors, and harborers of the heretics. These men sincerely loved and defended them against God and the Church." Wolfram von Eschenbach was a courageous man, otherwise he would not have conceded that the true tale came from Provence!

Bernard of Clairvaux once said that there were no greater Christian sermons than those given by the Cathars, because their morals were pure and their actions were in harmony with their words. Nevertheless, he was careful to add that he wanted to have all heretics burned at the stake. I am really not qualified to say if the Cathars held proper Christian sermons, as the French Dominican Jean Guiraud maintained in 1907, or that heretical rites agreed with the Liturgy of early Christianity. It certainly seems, however, that the Christ of the Cathars was completely different from the one who grew out of the Bible. In the Inquisition

---

[30][The sect possessed national writings and songs. —*Trans.*]
[31][Albigensian History. —*Trans.*]

registers, we can read: *dicunt Christum phantasma fuisse non homi-nem*. They stated thus that Christ was a ghost, not a human being! In another place, I found that Christ taught that he was "held in the stars of the sky." The Cathars must therefore have confessed (like that recently deceased and hard-struggling German Arthur Drews)[32] the point of view that Christology is nothing other than an astral myth gathered from the course of the stars.

The heretics loved the stars, an old woman whose ancestors were Cathars recently said to me. She told the truth. I visited the local palace museum. Approximately three hundred years ago, Henry IV, the so-called Huguenot king of France from the noble House of Foix, resided here. In a large hall are displayed prehistoric finds from the Pyrenees. Hardly an article is without a swastika, the age-old symbol of the sun and salvation. It makes me think of Germany.

---

[32][Arthur Drews, a professor of philosophy and German at the University of Karelsruhe, provoked a great deal of controversy during his lifetime because of his unorthodox ideas on religion and because he disputed the notion of the historical Jesus. —*Ed.*]

~ CAHORS ~

I am again in southern France. Cahors is the town in which, from my express train window on my first trip to the land of the Albigensians and the troubadours, I saw a bridge that spanned a river. I wonder: Why do they call the pope *pontifex maximus,* a "great bridge builder"?

Viscount Raimundo, a troubadour who hailed from this area, was crazily in love with the heretical Lady Adelaide of Pena. Separated during the Albigensian wars, they were reunited in the castle of Montségur, where he finally found his lost lady. And what a strange coincidence: The German Cistercian monk Caesarius von Heisterbach, to whom we owe so much information about the Albigensians, made a pilgrimage here around the year 1198! Already sometime before, St. Engelbert, who was the archbishop of Cologne and a notorious heretic-hater, had undertaken this pilgrimage—twice, no less. It seems to me that these were actually study trips. Once, Caesarius observed how a Spanish heretic was incinerated. This experience became useful to him when some heretics were burned near Cologne's Jewish cemetery. I will return to this another time.

Caesarius once explained how and why he entered the Cistercian order:

> Once, I went to Cologne with the Heisterbach abbot Gevard. Along the way, he exhorted me urgently in conversation, and told of that wonderful appearance in Clairvaux, during harvesttime, when the brethren cut sheaves in the valleys. In bright clarity, the holy bearer of God, her mother Anna, and holy Mary Magdalene came down from the mountains into the valley and dried the monks' sweat, fanning and cooling them. That impressed me so much that I promised the abbot that if God would give me the will, I would enter no other monastery than his. At that time I was still bound, because I had vowed a pilgrimage to holy Maria von Rocamadour. When I had completed this pilgrimage at the end of three months, I betook myself, without any of my friends knowing about it, for the valley of the holy Petrus behind Heisterbach . . .

So Caesarius became a monk. He then wrote his famous *Dialogus miraculorum* (Miraculous Dialogue), which Roman theologians and historians declared dangerous for the Church, because he makes genuine miracles appear suspicious and ridiculous. He also wrote *Vita S. Elisabethae Landgraviae;*[33] *Ad petitionem Magistri Joannis*[34] (John was a real *tortor haereticorum,* "torturer of heretics"); and finally the essay *Contra haeresim de Lucifero* (Against the Heresy of Lucifer).

As I read again those verses of the Prophet Isaiah in the Bible that herald the damnation of Lucifer and his children by Yahweh, the God of the B'nai Israel (Children of Israel), I decided to give this book—for which I am traveling, thinking, and writing—the title *Lucifer's Court: A Heretic's Journey in Search of the Light Bringers.*

In this way, I am hoping my readers will appreciate the story of those who sought justice regardless of the Mosaic twelve commandments and from their own sense of justice and duty; those who, rather than arrogantly expecting assistance from Mount Sinai, went to a "mount of the congregation, in the sides of the north," in order to bring solace to their kind; those who placed knowledge above faith and existence above the light; and, not least, those who recognized that Yahweh could never, ever be their divinity and Jesus of Nazareth could never, ever be their salvation. In Lucifer's house there are many dwellings. Many paths and many bridges lead to him.

---

[33][Life of Holy Landgravine Elizabeth of Thuringia. —*Trans.*]
[34][Upon the Request of Master John. —*Trans.*]

— ORNOLAC IN FUXEAN COUNTRY —

The Sabarthès, where I am living now, is a narrow valley enclosed by enormous limestone cliffs and the wild waters of the Ariège River on the east. This crystal-clear river, leaving beautiful waterfalls in some places, cascades down the valley over boulders from the Col de Puymorens to where the road from Toulouse forks at a much transited pass that leads into Catalan territory and Andorra. Finally, it reaches Ax-les-Thermes, an age-old resort. Roman centurions healed their scars in its sulfurous waters. In the Middle Ages, Crusaders returning from Palestine looked to restore their gaunt and exhausted bodies in its waters. The Church had assured them as long and vital a life as possible.

Turning northwest from Ax-les-Thermes, the still-gushing Ariège inundates a dark ravine that separates the foothills of the Pic du Saint Barthelemy from those of the Pic du Montcalm. We can find here the villages of Verdun, Bouan, and Ornolac and the resort Ussat and the small picturesque town of Tarascon (not to be confused with the more well-known Tarascon on the Rhône). Also found here is Sabarat, which in former times was a place of pilgrimage. It lost its fame when Lourdes blossomed in the last century. Sabarat gave its name to the Sabarthès. After this, the Ariège turns in a northerly direction toward the cities Foix, Pamiers, and Toulouse, to unite with the Garonne. Together they flow to the Bay of Biscay.

I went in the opposite direction of the same road where, on Palm Sunday of 1244, four sturdy Cathars rescued the mysterious treasure of the church from the besieged castle of Montségur.

Still called the Route des Cathares, the Pathway of the Cathars begins at the small village of Ornolac, where I live, and climbs, detouring to the Plateau de Lujat, a sort of plateau on the mountain. In some places, the Pic du Saint Barthélémy falls perpendicularly to the Sabarthès. On the plateau, which is covered with thick hawthorn bushes and wild blackberry hedges, I found an arch built into the mountain. What purpose it once served I cannot say. I could imagine, however, that it was a kind of wayside rest area for those Cathars who traveled from Sabarthès to Montségur. They needed such a place, because here begins a grandiose high mountain world: Rock and more rock piles itself higher and higher until it reaches a summit nearly three thousand meters high.[35] The Pathway of the Cathars is admirably and safely built. Often, when a sudden abyss opens up and you are sure that this is the end, strong tree trunks joined by planks cross the gorge. Anyone who isn't afraid of heights and is persistent can arrive on the summit of Tabor after a climb of several hours.

The Pyrenees farmers call Tabor the Pic du Saint Barthélémy. Up there, if no clouds obstruct the view, you can see the castle-crowned peak of Montségur, the path's goal, and, in the far distance, Sierra Maladetta. On the Tabor summit lie the remnants of a sacred site, which include a bell tower and a weather station. This station, built on the remains of the temple, was destroyed by a storm. Only the foundation walls and some smooth, polished stones are left here.

As I further explored the Val de l'Incant (Enchanted Valley) near Montségur, I had to kill a dangerous viper on which I had negligently stepped. It had already pulled itself up to bite.

Among the many partly fortified Sabarthès caverns, I want to give priority to two: the Lombrives Cave and the cave of Fontanet, also called the Font Santo, the Holy Well. Each bores miles deep into the limestone mountain. Wonderful stalactites decorate them; marble and crystal glitter and sparkle in the light of a miner's lamp (to which I have managed to accustom myself). Bizarre shapes and designs and inscriptions and indications of paths can still be found on the cave walls; and from deepest depths roar the sprays of underground rivers, carving out channels in the mountain. Sometimes a yawning ravine obstructs those who walk in the caverns. It is better to hesitate and proceed with caution, so that a wrong step does not crush human bones. Since the time when man produced devices and weapons from stones, people slept here. The cave of Lombrives, the largest and most branched, contains an enormous hall—known as the cathedral—that is more than eighty meters[36] tall in its interior. It is the most enormous underground *gleyso*, or church, as a cave cathedral of the Albigensians is still called today. The cave of Fontanet must have likewise seen cult activities of the Cathars. It is also a gleyso, and in it stands the so-called altar, a stalagmite of inde-

---

[35][Approximately ninety-eight hundred feet. —*Ed.*]
[36][About 260 feet. —*Ed.*]

scribable beauty. The bright walls of the hall in which nature placed it are smoke-blackened. These traces of smoke, which start at approximately a man's height above the ground, could have been made only by torches. Thus the following explanation may pertain to this place: The Provençal heretics conducted their highest consecration ceremony, the Consolamentum, by torchlight in these caves.

Wolfram von Eschenbach also describes a cave: Before his hero, Parzival, finds the light of the Grail, he stops in the cave of the hermit Trevrizent by the Fontane la Salvasche. There Trevrizent leads him before an altar, where Parzival is dressed in a tunic, just like a Cathar (who put on tunics before heretical ordinations in Fontanet). The correspondence is surely unambiguous!

In a similar way, the cave of Lombrives can be linked to the Grail legend. A set of stone stairs leads from the cathedral to another part of the tremendous labyrinth. Suddenly, a ravine hundreds of feet deep opens up. Overhanging it is an enormous boulder from which the dripping water has conjured a club. The farmers call it the tomb of Hercules, and Wolfram also mentions Hercules as a prophet of the Grail. The rural legend tells it thus: In times long gone, King Bebryx ruled from an underground palace in the Lombrives. One day Hercules came along. He was welcomed by Bebryx, who had a daughter called Pyrene. Hercules and the king's daughter fell passionately in love. Soon after, the adventurous warrior was called far away, and he left King Bebryx's palace. Pyrene, however, was carrying his child and followed him out of fear of her father's scorn and longing after her true love. Wild animals pounced upon the helpless princess. Screaming, she called for Hercules to help her. Hearing the distress call, he ran to her aid, but it was too late. Pyrene was dead. Hercules cried, and the mountains roared, echoing his misery against rocks and caves. Then he buried Pyrene, but she can be never forgotten, because the Pyrenees bear her name until the end of time.

Three other stalagmites in a lake in the midst of the cave form what are called the Throne of Bebryx, Bebryx's Grave, and the Grave of Pyrene. There the water runs incessantly, as if the mountains are weeping for the dead king's daughter. Her petrified garments that she wore in her life hang on the wall and ceiling. Pyrene is also supposed to have been the goddess Venus. Because this Sabarthès cavern is more beautiful, larger, and more mysterious than the others, if I wanted to relate all the experiences I had in it, then I would fill many, many pages. Quite often, I dangled in mortal danger, but I always found my way back in one piece. I almost never came home without discovering something. If you visit the Sabarthès, explore Ornolac. Other discoveries there are very close to my heart—in particular, designs and inscriptions. Some are age-old, while others are from our time. The most recent inscription may be the question asked by a young man: Why did God take his wife and the mother of his children? Another, from the year 1850, demands an answer: "What is God?" And another offers: "*Je me cache ici, je suis l'assassin de Maître Labori Labori.*"[37] (Maître Labori was the man who defended Emile Zola, the writer who wrote the famous novels *Rome* and *Lourdes,* and, if I am not mistaken, was wounded in Rennes in 1899.) Even Henry IV, the French Huguenot king, wrote his own name on the cave wall in 1576. Four decades later he was murdered by the fanatical Catholic François Ravaillac.[38] Henry was a descendant of Esclarmonde de Foix. Her burial place could very well be in proximity to these stone objects, where Hercules and Pyrene slumber in death.

The inscriptions from the Albigensian era deeply impressed me. There are many, but they are difficult to find. A whole year had gone by until, on the marble wall in the eternal night of the cave, I finally saw a ship drawn in coal by a Cathar hand many hundreds of years ago. The sun serves as its sail, life-bringing and reviving after a long winter! In the vicinity of this drawing, I excavated human bones from the sandy soil. They were charred. I asked myself if the Cathars burned their dead. These could not have belonged to the victims who were put to death on funeral pyres by Rome's Inquisition, because the inquisitors threw to the four winds the ashes of burned heretics.

Last but not least, I became aware of a tree of life, also drawn with coal, and the design of a dove hewn into the stone in a very mysterious cave. The dove is the symbol for God's spirit and is the coat of arms of the Grail knights.

---

[37][I am hiding here; I am the killer of Maître Labori. —*Trans.*]

[38][François Ravaillac, Henry's assassin, was drawn and quartered. —*Trans.*]

With nostalgia, I pack my bundle to leave the Sabarthès. I must also leave a cat that had approached me the previous year and had become my constant companion, even in the caves. She was faithful to me, and with her loyalty, she, an animal, chastised the lies of those medieval monks who said that the heretics are "wrong like cats."

As I reflect on this time of my life on Montségur and near the Grail Castle, I confess openly that I would gladly have found the Grail that could have been the heretical treasure which I read about in the Inquisition's register.

~ MIREPOIX ~

I am not a Bible expert, nor would I wish to be one. Nevertheless, for
me it is clear: The Old Testament and the New Testament do not speak
of different or opposing Gods. For me, the Gods in both are one and the
same. The Old Testament curses the "beautiful morning star"; yet the
New Testament reveals in the Apocalypse of John a "king and angel of
the abyss," who has "in Greek the name Apollyon."[39] Apollyon, angel
of the abyss and prince of this world, is none other than Apollo, the light
bearer. My belief that the "morning star" of the Old Testament and the
figure Apollyon, who appears in the New Testament, are one and the
same is based on the fact that in Greek, the morning star, or Phosphoros
(this name also means "light bringer"), is the constant companion, messenger, and representative of the sun god Apollo, as the supreme Light
Bringer was then called. Further, the beautiful "star of the morning" is
a reference to the sun.

Significantly, I have selected the small Pyrenean town of Mirepoix as
the appropriate place to write these lines. It is located at the foot of that
great pyramid that dominates the Grail mountain of Montségur, some
two hours away from the hamlet at the foot of the castle rock. I was
again up there at Montségur Castle. The engineer from Bordeaux is still
looking for the true gospel of John for his secret society. The principal
reason for my being here is this: In pre-Christian times, Mirepoix was
called Beli Cartha, which means "city of light"; Belis and Abellio were
the local names of the light god, Apollo.

Once every year, Apollo, son of Zeus, returned to the south from
blessed Hyperborea, that mythical country "beyond the north wind,"
only to soon head north again on a predetermined course. The Greeks
celebrated the day of the spring equinox as their holiest festival. Apollo
was the rising sun—a majestic and unalterable light. Times set for the
sun god when Helios, who was initially admired as the main god only
on the Isle of Rhodes in the seas off Asia Minor, assumed Apollo's place
or both became one with him.

---

[39][Apollyon corresponds to the Egyptian falcon-god Horus. In fact, the names are sometimes run together—Horapollyon is the subject of the first treatise of Nostradamus in
1541. —*Trans.*]

In the beginning, Apollo brought light to the Dorian and Ionian hunters, herders, and field farmers who migrated from the north to Hellas, after the long winter night. They were the guardians of the fields and pastures and the herds and bees and everything else that tugs at the heart of a farmer. Therefore, the herders celebrated a festival in his honor with a ram, and the farmers honored him with their harvest celebrations. In their songs, they sang how he had slain the winter dragon Pythos and begged the light not to stay too long in the north with the lucky people of Hyperborea.

Because spring and summer drive out the diseases of winter, Apollo was raised to a god who defends against all evils and was celebrated as the father of the semidivine physician Asclepios, who was a part of Apollo. One was known as a savior and the other, a rescuer. The cock, which announces the morning light, was holy to them. Therefore, when Socrates had to empty the deadly cup of hemlock, he told his pupils not to forget to sacrifice a cock to Asclepios. With absolute trust in Apollo, the savior, and in Asclepios the redeemer, Socrates confidently awaited the new morning.

In addition to the farmers and herders, Apollo was beloved by wayfarers and sailors. He accompanied them over the mountains and seas, the flatlands and islands, so that they could reach their destinations safely. Near the northern Greek mountain called Parnassus, where the famous temple of Delphi was located, on the seventh day of a spring month, Apollo's birthday was celebrated on the island of Delos in the Aegean Sea. He was most beloved on this island. The myths say the earth laughed on his birthday, and immediately the cherub's voice resonated: "A lyre would be better, and a curved bow. I will announce Zeus's infallible advice to mankind!" Then Apollo jumped out of the circle of the "goddesses" who had assisted his mother as midwives, and high over the clouds, he announced Zeus's law to mankind, and taught songs and how to play the lyre. In this way he became a god of poets, for whom verse and prayer were one.

When Apollo appeared, the earth was said to have laughed. Did she know that she would be granted a merry science? Delphi, which was located, along with Delos, in the landscape of Phokis at the foot of the Parnassus Mountains in the country of Phokis, became the main place of worship of the god. It is in Delphi where Apollo, a Hellenic Sigurd-Siegfried, is supposed to have defeated the dragon of winter and darkness, Pythos, and buried him under a stone. Here in Delphi, Pythia sat on a tripod and spoke wisdom over a chasm from which rose a cold and numbing steam. Here the Castalian spring poured the cleansing waters that were essential for a dialogue with God, a *katharsis*. In the spring, Apollo returned from the sun country of the Hyperborea, which was beyond the north wind commemorated here.

Whoever admired Apollo would never forget to dedicate sacrifices and prayers to his twin sister, Artemis, who is beloved in the Pyrenees under the name of Belissena. Like her brother, she governed a star: She was the law of moon and its natural light. The moon receives light from the sun and goes through the same zodiac, only faster. Artemis was accompanied by her nymphs on quiet solo hunts of animals in field and forest, but she was also the animals' gamekeeper in addition to being their hunter. As the goddess of the dew, which falls more plentifully on moonlit nights, this goddess and her light-bringing brother fed the plants. The monthly flow of women is subject to the rule of the moon and is under her special protection. As a rule, a woman stays away until Artemis comes unnoticed as Eileithyia. A midwife to women in childbirth, she assists them in childhood emergencies. The Romans, who admired her as Diana, imagined her as the moon, the *familiarissime lumen,* the most trustworthy star in their firmament. As the goddess of birth, she is also the goddess of fertility—but this fertility goddess was not conceived in voluptuous Asiatic sensuality. Virginal, she chastely awaits her beloved, who blesses her and makes her a mother, the highest goal of femininity.

The Greeks also venerated a maternal and terrestrial Artemis who resembled the mother of the earth, Gemeter or Demeter. Once I had learned the ancient Greeks' basic principles, I can assert the following with some degree of confidence: They did not pray to personal gods, but to powers and forces that prevail in the universe above this world and in the underworld, to the Great Father and the Great Mother. In his *Gallic Wars,* Caesar said that the Germanic tribes venerated only those gods whose power was obviously manifested: The sun and moon and fire composed almost literally the religious concepts of the north in general and northern Greece in particular. The Greeks also believed that the universe was ruled by the sun, this world was ruled by the moon, and the underworld was ruled by fire. This threefold pattern corresponded in turn to their three genders: the male, the female, and the neuter. Fire was imagined as neutral (or androgynous), the earth and the moon were feminine, and the sun and the sky were male. This group of three coexisted in various relationships with each other, which led the ancients to give these natural forces a divine appearance, helping to bring them into harmony with one another. (An example: From the sky in which the sun rises, lightning flashes to earth and ignites a fire. Very probably the Greeks would have said that the sky and the earth had ignited the fire.)

I spoke of the goddess Artemis, who is known in this country as Belissena. She is the female moon. At night, she can never be touched by the sun-male—to whom the day belongs—and so remains untouched, for in many respects she is similar to him; she is often imagined as his twin sister! The godlike woman is also the female earth, who must be fertilized by the sun-man in order to bear earthly children, which is an expression of love itself and for which she awaits the sun-husband. In former times, the Greeks felt that the goddess of love had remained in the sky, where she developed a special personality. This easily explains the fact that several goddesses are derived from the god woman: Hera, the mother of the sky; the virgin Artemis; the beloved Aphrodite; and Demeter, the mother of our earth (which were called by the Romans, respectively, Juno, Diana, Venus, and Ceres). The much maligned polytheism of the pagans looks completely different in this light. We have either misunderstood them or, as I believe, wanted to misunderstand!

In the heyday of Catharism, a famous hermit named Joachim de Flora lived in Sicily.[40] He was considered the best commentator on the Apocalypse of John. When the ninth chapter of Revelation speaks of grasshoppers, Joachim believed it referred to the Cathars: "Some with the strength of scorpions will come out from the bottomless depths of the abyss." Joachim lamented that these Cathars were the personification of the Antichrist. He believed their power would grow and their king was already selected. In Greek, this king's name is Apollyon.

Apollo cannot be any other than Lucifer, who was called Lucibel

---

[40][Joachim of Flora (1132–1202), Cistercian abbot and mystic. —*Trans.*]

by the Provençal heretics. They believed that an injustice was done to Lucifer. The Cathars interpreted Lucifer's fall as "the illegitimate usurpation of the firstborn son of God—Luzifer—by the Nazarene." Some of them—who were the exceptions—considered Lucifer equal to the lost Son of the Gospels and one who strayed from God the Father through overconfidence and pride. They believed that he would fall on his knees before the Almighty on Judgment Day and ask him for forgiveness. This cosmogonical myth (it should not be seen as anything else) assumed that the world was a suffering place far from God that could aspire to perfection only when the eternal God-spirit spiritualizes, sanctifies, and releases it from the perishable and nonspiritual. For those heretics who formed the exception, the Christian concept of redemption, although practiced in an un-Roman way, worked its weakening influence. We do not need to worry about these exceptions.

The cornerstone of Christianity is the belief in the personification of God through Jesus, the son of God who became a human being. The Cathars cryptically stood in contradiction to this concept. They said: We heretics are not theologians, but philosophers who seek only wisdom and truth. We have already recognized that God is light and spirit and strength. Even if the earth is material, it exists in a relationship with God—through light and spirit and strength. How could we and this world live together if the sun did not give us life? How could we think and recognize if we had no minds? How could we recognize truth and wisdom, which are so difficult to find, to seek, and, despite all obstacles, seek again and again, if we had no strength? God is light and spirit and strength. He works within us. God is law and gives laws; however, these are not the ones that Moses brought down from the summit of Mount Sinai and annouced to the B'nai Israel. For us, God's book of laws is made up of the starry sky and the earth, which is filled with living creatures. By the same law, the sun goes through its preordained rotation, from its rise to its setting, through the twelve signs of the zodiac or between winter and summer and back again to winter. The sun leaves mankind in the evening, and then God's law allows the moon and the countless stars to radiate out along their prescribed path in the sky. We are not saying that the sun or another star is God. They are divine messengers and only bring him closer to us.

The Cathars said: Divinity is multifaceted, but there are not several Gods, as we are often accused of believing. With our senses we can grasp only one part: nature. This is composed of ourselves, because we are perishable material; the thousandfold faulty world in which we have to live our lives; and the starry sky, days, and nights. Nature is not God the Father, who is absolute light and spirit and strength. She is God's child, a creation of that light, spirit, and strength. She governs herself according to the laws given by God the Father. Therefore, we find it foolish to request from God the Father rains or beautiful weather or health or money, as many Christians do. No miracles can break the law.

The law alone is miracle enough. If anyone tries, anybody can achieve miracles. A physician (the Cathars were so renowned as physicians that even Catholic bishops allowed themselves be treated by them in order not to leave this wonderful world just yet) can achieve the miracles of healing only if he knows the prevailing laws of the human body so well that he is able to restore the disturbed order. Nature is not God, but she is divine. She is not absolute light, but is the bringer of light. She is not absolute strength, but is strength's distributor. She is not absolute spirit, but from our birth she obtains an effective spirit in the law of realization that leads to God. This is the only real redemption. Our supreme light bringer is the sun. The leaders of the heavenly host, which some call angels, are nothing other than the stars. They all are subject as well to earthly laws. Thus, we can recognize humans if we search and observe the sky carefully for the laws that reign up there and arrange our lives in such a way that we do not break divine law, but fulfill it. We must be children of the Light Bringer's sun!

A subject and relative of the House of Foix lived in Mirepoix at the time of the Albigensian crusade. This knight, Peire-Rotger de Mirepoix, was a member of the radical Cathar group known as the Sons of Belissena. When the fortress of Montségur was besieged in his territory, he became the citadel's commander. When the situation was most grave, on his instructions the treasure of the church was taken to the Sabarthès by four heroic Cathars. Before Rome and Paris had carried out their long-planned crusade against the Albigenses, his castle at Mirepoix had been a place of assembly for courtly life: At any time, troubadours and wandering knights could enjoy his hospitality there, and they were not conscripted without receiving substantial provisions for their journey. Most Minnesingers were bitterly poor. Many of them came from the common people. To cite one of many examples, Bernard de Ventadour was the son of a baking-oven stoker. In no way, however, did poverty and humble origin block their way to chivalry. The eloquent farmer or the composing craftsman was ennobled when he sang to chivalry. A song written by troubadour Arnold von Marveil, he who was not distinguished by birth, might nevertheless be suitable, because everyone—citizens and craftsmen and farmers alike—had virtue and a sense of honor. The poet felt that cowards and fools were not worthy of his attention, let alone his verses. He spoke from the heart.

Much was required of a troubadour: He must have "an excellent memory, and comprehensive historical knowledge"; he had to know all myths and legends of his homeland; and he had to be "cheerful and kind, full of spirit and adroit, attracted by gifts of the spirit and the heart, courageous in war and tournament, and receptive to all who were great and good." Every genuine troubadour had to possess—to express it in today's scholarly language—an encyclopedic knowledge. Perhaps the time of the Minne has come again in our age, which strives for summary thinking. It is true that the way of thinking of that long-ago age may be appropriate for us. Without reservation, we can affirm its "sincere desire for the expression of beauty in life and for tasteful education in accordance with a joyful artistic existence and with its ideal of the internal nobility of mankind." Provençal chivalry did not have anything to do with the infamous feudal system!

Paris and Rome were white with hate and looked with envy upon the Provençal world of the Minne. At the height of its power, the French Crown had long desired access to the Mediterranean and domination over the richest part of old Gaul. And why did the the throne of St. Peter express such hatred? Like the Cathars, the troubadours (since that time, we have lost the usual distinction) were condemned by the Roman Church as slaves of the devil, intended for eternal damnation. Often, papal legates intervened against individual troubadours with prohibitions—but to no end, for the Minnesingers abruptly rejected all Catholic theological concepts, terms, teachings, and legends. They sang not to Jehovah or Jesus of Nazareth, but to their hero Heracles or the god Amor. And this god was deeply hated by the vain Roman Church, which was rejected by the Cathars as "Satan's synagogue" and a "basilica of the devil."

The famous troubadour Peire Cardinal believed that God-Amor can be experienced by a strong spirit whose eyes have been cleared by faith. So sang the no less famous Peire Vidal, but he added that God appears only in springtime, and to catch a glimpse of him, we must go farther into his house, which is newly blossomed nature. This God looks like a knight: He has blond hair and rides on a light horse that is black like the night on one half and dazzling white on the other. A garnet on the reins shines like the sun. In this knight's attendance is a paladin whose name is Loyalty.

The Bible tells that a person should be faithful until death so that God can bestow the crown of eternal life. As far as Rome was concerned, however, the troubadours were the serfs of the devil because they had sworn loyalty to the god Amor. As innumerable examples of their poems show, they sang of the wonders of a stone that fell from Lucifer's crown—thus, if we use the language of the Bible, the "crown of eternal life" could be construed to be Luciferian, and if we spin the thread further, God-Amor seems to be the incarnation of Lucifer. This becomes certain if we tie the thread differently: God-Amor is the god of springtime, and Apollo is this god. Therefore, both Amor and Apollo are the god of the spring. He who restores the sunlight of the spring to earth is therefore a light bringer—a Lucifer. As we have read in Revelation, Apollyon (or Apollo) is equated with the devil. Therefore, according to the dogma of the Roman Church, which is based upon the Bible, and the writings of the Fathers of the Church, Lucifer is Satan. Consequently, the Church believes that the God of spring, who is Apollo-Amor, is Satan or the devil. Following this line of thought, it is easy to understand why Rome labeled the troubadours slaves of the devil and why Joachim von Flora cried woefully that the Cathars were anti-Christian because Apollyon was their king. From now on, I probably need to make no more distinction among the Cathars, the troubadours, and the stewards of Lucifer's court.

Peire Vidal, who was the son of a Toulouse furrier as well as a knight and troubadour, calls his paladin Loyalty. As result, loyalty is conditioned by a law that can be both external and internal. As such, the troubadours were subordinate to the law of the Minne. Its highest clause declared that *amor* has nothing to do with carnal love. All troubadours, however, were so-called *chantres d'amor,* "singers of love." We find an easy way out of this dilemma if we use the centuries-old German translation for this: Minnesinger. Provençal amor is the courtly love of Germany. Originally, this courtly love had nothing to do with physical love, because as Walther von der Vogelweide very probably knew, "neither man nor woman" has "soul nor body" without spiritual strength, and what fortifies the spirit is loyalty. That is also Wolfram von Eschenbach's opinion: True love is true loyalty!

The laws of the Minnesingers consisted of several clauses known as *leys d'amors.* The first troubadour found the laws in the boughs of a golden oak, where a falcon had left them. Therefore, he is a *troubadour,* a "finder." He was also called "savior."

As the pilgrims of the Albigensian crusade (which the Jesuit historian Benoist called "the most just thing in the world") eagerly implemented the pope's orders to subjugate the land for its new masters because the Church had promised them eternal life and booty, the troubadours sang of the loyalty required "in the service of their threatened princes, and their politics against the Church, Frenchmen, and the Inquisition of the Dominicans."[41] So they sang—and fought. When the magnificent castles of their sponsors lay in ashes, they fled to foreign lands, over the Pyrenees or over the Alps. From then on, guilty of heresy, dispossessed of their lands, they were known as *faydits:* outlaws. Now they were a wandering people, and their real homeland became at first the forests and the highways of Germany, northern Italy, and Spain. I recently read in a Welsh researcher's book that some troubadours were supposed to have been found in Iceland.

But the Light Bringer Apollo, god of protection for poets and wanderers, did not leave his people in their emergency. He also had become an outlaw; he had even become the devil himself. Because he was not the Evil One, however, he remained faithful to the heavenly laws and reigned over the forests, and roads. He let the garnet on the bridle of

---

[41][From de Benoist's tome on the crusade dated 1691. —*Trans.*]

his light horse shine like the sun. If a singer died, then Apollo carried him over the clouds to the "mount of the congregation, in the sides of the north"—to the farthest northern point. Why were his children not allowed, like others, to inhabit cities, and be buried like them? There is light in the Light Bringer's house—more light than in all the cathedrals and churches and places of worship, where Lucifer is nowhere to be seen among Jewish prophets and apostles or Roman gods and other holy ones on dark glass panes. His forest is free!

Far from the heavenly law, Apollo's garnet could not shine, and the devil's grandmother came—the grandmother who reigns over the earth and the moon.[42] Under cover of darkness, she gave outlaws a meal of her game—for she was the gamekeeper—and a drink of her dew, which she dispensed, and she pointed the way with her silver rays, for when the devil and his grandmother were not at home or could come only later, they sent a representative, or a messenger. Lucifer sent the morning star and the grandmother sent the evening star. The same star is called Lucifer or Venus. By no means has it fallen from our sky!

---

[42][The garnet is the carbuncle or shining stone, the grandmother earth is a pagan idea. —*Trans.*]

~ PORT VENDRES, ROUSSILLON ~

From early morning until late in the evening, and often even throughout the night, life never stops along the wharves. Time flies there. Fishermen ask me to go out with them—they tell me that we'll be back by sunrise—then they have second thoughts: Because the sea is still rising these days, they think I should wait a bit.

Today, a big steamer left for Africa with a great number of English tourists on board. I am told that the French Mediterranean coast no longer has the mild weather that it once had in winter, and so North Africa has become its rival.

Located at of the base of the east Pyrenees, this port town is ancient. The Phoenicians, sniffing gold in the mountains of Pyrene, established an important trading post here. Expelled by the Greeks, however, they had to abandon their settlements. Portus Veneris, Port of Venus, is the old name.

In the gray days of prehistory, roving seafarers traveled across the seas. They were Greeks whose hometown was Argos,[43] and they landed in a Port of Venus. Their journey had a singular purpose: They wanted to take the wool from a sacred ram—the golden fleece—back to the sun island Aea. Many adventurers had attempted it. These seafarers encountered a fierce struggle with a Bebrycian king, who had challenged all strangers in his country to a fistfight and had killed every one of them. Finally, however, the hostile king was slain. After they arrived in the Port of Venus, the Argonauts, as these Viking-like Greeks were called, were permitted to take the golden fleece from where it hung on the branches of a holy oak.

The Argonauts were led by Jason, the Thessalonian. His name means "savior," and his twelve (or fifty-two)[44] companions were heroes and singers and the sons of gods of old Greece: Hercules, Castor and Pollux, and Orpheus, just to mention the most famous names. The goal of the Argonauts was, as I've said, to capture the golden fleece. According to old myths, it was to be found beyond a great sea in the north; and the

---

[43][Actually, they were named after their ship, the *Argo,* which was named after the the shipbuilder Argus. They did not come from a hometown called Argos. —*Trans.*]

[44][There may have been 12 or there may have been 52—versions/translations are different, hence different numbers. Usually, they were said to number between 40 and 50. —*Trans.*]

Argo, the sailing ship of the Argonauts, sailed "with northern hoist." To find the sun isle lying toward midnight, they set an oracular piece of wood into the prow of their ship. This wood of Dodonian oak was taken from Greece's holiest tree.

In my homeland, Rome's envoy Bonifatius took an ax to the holy oak at Geismar. It had been dedicated to Thor-Donar and was called by farmers the "strength of God." At the supreme sanctuary of the Greeks in Dodona, this Dodonian king stood under the tree. The ancient Greeks believed that they could hear God speak when the leaves of this tree rustled in the wind. During their travels, they did not have the ability to listen to the gods' trusted voice, so the Argonauts handcrafted a plank of Dodonian oak and inserted it into the prow of their ship, the *Argo.* This wood told them to turn to the north, where the oak is at home. Up until AD 1000, the Norsemen still consulted an oracular piece of oak wood consecrated to the god Thor. After the Norwegians began to feel the limits of their traditional liberty, they sailed to faraway Iceland, to settle there. Once in sight of their new homeland, they threw a hide-covered oak pillar into the sea. If their God allowed their holy wood to [wash ashore in] the country, they would establish themselves there.

The troubadours, those Provençal Minnesingers, had not forgotten the tree's holiness: It was present in the knowledge of courtly love and the Minne, the so-called leys d'amor, and in the the fact that the first troubadour, the redeemer, is supposed to have received the law from an eagle or a falcon that sat on the branch of a golden oak.[45] *Troubadour* means "finder." The first troubadour found the law of courtly love and the Minne in the boughs of an oak. The Argonauts, also finders, took the golden fleece from an oak when they finally reached the goal of their long odyssey. To a certain extent, they were chevaliers errants, wandering knights who became poets, because originally the Greek word *Argonauts* also meant "finder." Goethe also believed that the golden fleece had made his Finder a poet, and on the classical Walpurgis Night,

---

[45][Horus, the ancient Egyptian god, was directly associated with Apollyon. Horus is always depicted as a falcon; the troubadours received their leys d'amors from a falcon; Apollyon was the corresponding god in Greek mythology. By the way, there is a town in the Pyrenees that is called Orus; interestingly, Egyptian statuary of the goddess Sekhmet has been unearthed in the Pyrenees. —*Trans.*]

Faust learns from the healing centaur Chiron of "the beautiful circle of the Argonauts and all that built the poet's world." Chiron, half human and half horse, answers:

> In the noble Argonauts circle
> Everyone was brave in his manner;
> And with the strength that inspired him,
> He could be sufficient where it was lacking in others.

Were the Argonauts inspired by the power of courtly love? Whatever inspired them, it was a divine search founded on a strength that moves mountains and allows seas to be crossed.

One of the Argonauts was Hercules. As the Greek historical writer Herodotus reported in the fifth century BC, Hercules was doubly admired: as a human hero and as a god. Although Hercules had once been human, he was, as an age-old Maltese inscription states, a proto-leader to the Greeks who subsequently became a god. His myths can be found in the songs of the ancient Greeks: tales of strength of will and redemption through one's own strength. His was the will of the strong who rose against fate and thus fate itself. He made himself into a sun hero who won out over the night of calm and inertia. He sought God and found God in himself. Therefore, he himself became a god.

Hercules was a rebel: He wanted to be akin to the greatest of all. In addition, he was a silent sufferer: He patiently suffered the fateful law that ordered and fulfilled the cosmic universe. In this way, he became an Olympian. It was Hercules who found the golden fleece on the sun island Aea. Medieval men felt that this fleece, symbol for god-making, in reality had been the stone of the wise.

Did Hercules find the Grail, the stone of light? Was he a Hellenic Parzival? I believe so. Wolfram von Eschenbach writes that "Heraklius had known the stones." Thus Hercules also knew about the stone that fell from Lucifer's crown—the Grâl. In an Old French literary work, Olympus is cited as the final goal toward which the Grail knights strove. So, Hercules enters the tale of the Grail and Parzival seated himself at the gods' Olympian table to partake of nectar and ambrosia.

As admitted by a pious Belgian theologian, who was also a useless historian, the Cathars cherished and cultivated their national writings and songs. Although Roman Catholicism had destroyed everything in Provence, Lombardy, and Germany, it was not totally successful in silencing the songs. Lucifer's court still sings—albeit quietly—ancient and even new songs. In the Languedoc, the Pyrenean peasants, those worthy descendants of their ancestors, cultivate these songs. In the mountains and forests *oun au descoubrit Apollon,* where Apollo is discovered, it is still possible to hear in the rushing water and trees the long lost and courageous lore of the old gods who were made into idols and devils. These precious songs and legends were passed on to grandchildren, from father to son. Just as before, the gods—gods who were actually only one God—continued to live on sun-drenched summits or in the eternal night of the caves. The manes of ancient warriors and heroes are still woven among the ruins of their castles. I know a few such songs. Into the harbor of Venus came the Argonauts. Perhaps this harbor that we know as Port Vendres was where they anchored. Perhaps a Bebrycian king overcame the Dioscuren and the Sabarthès farmers who buried him in the cave of Lombrives.

Wolfram von Eschenbach received the tale of the Grail from Provence. The mountains of Provence are home to the Grail Castle. According to Wolfram, Hercules was a prophet of the Grail. The farmers of Ornolac believe the bones of this divine champion rest not far from the Pyrenean Grail Castle—and next to Port Vendres, Cap Cerbère recalls Cerberos, the guardian dog of hell. Hercules overcame him and leashed him, because he had no fear of death.

The myths of the Argonauts and Hercules also belonged to the national songs that the Cathars cherished. They are part of the remains of what once blossomed here.

The Argonauts, those Greek Vikings, are pointing my way to the north. If I follow midnight, I would arrive back in my homeland. The Germanic Chatten tribe payed honor to Hercules; an ancient Latin inscription confirms this. Even the Argonaut twins Castor and Pollux were known to all Germans. Tacitus called them Alcis.[46]

---

[46][In AD 43, Roman historian Publius Cornelius Tacitus (AD 55–115) wrote a treatise called *Germania* in which he praised the members of the Chatten tribe as equals to the Romans and renamed Castor and Pollux as Alcis. For the historian, the Chatten were primarily mountain folk. Rahn seems to use Chattenland as a coy reference to his home state of Hesse, where this tribe lived. —*Trans.*]

~ Marseille ~

Ships sail in and load up, others lie at anchor, and others sail out. Coal is trimmed, fruit is unloaded, cranes whir, and chains rattle; a siren blares, a dockworker gesticulates, a slightly drunk sailor howls, ugly hags shriek, popular tunes sound, newspaper hawkers shout to one another, trucks honk, streetcars ring, and in the distance, above everything and through everything, the nearby bells of the church of Notre-Dame-de-la-Garde boldly peal.

The Madonna of the Watch is beloved by every sailor, even those who have just been thrown out by a prostitute from one of the brothels near the port. The Immaculate Virgin Mary will accompany sailors over the sea and, it is hoped, will see that they return safely. Only a few of those who come home, however, express their thanks—and only a few offer their thanks upon departing. Most hurry elsewhere.

Some years after the death of Jesus of Nazareth on Golgotha, a ship made its way to the port of Marseille. It had on board Jewish refugees who were well known to us from the Bible: Joseph of Arimathea, Mary Magdalene, and Mary's sister Martha. As Church legend states, they apparently brought the Grail with them. It was, however, not a stone, but a bowl from which, on Maundy Thursday evening, Jesus ate the sacrifical lamb with his disciples before Judas Iscariot betrayed him to the henchmen. This bowl, so it is said, found a still holier use on the next day, Good Friday: On Golgotha, it captured the streaming blood of the crucified Jesus when he said, "It is finished!" just before his head bent forward and his life ended. His body was put into a prepared rock grave made available by Joseph of Arimathea. For this reason, the Jews threw Joseph into a dungeon and left him there without food. But, oh miracle, night after night an angel appeared to the prisoner and fed him from the Grail, the Blessed Virgin's bowl.

Finally, he was released by Jesus himself, who told him to take the bowl to other countries. With Mary Magdalene and Martha, he entrusted himself to God and the sea—and God willed that the waves and wind should take them to Marseille. Mary Magdalene is said to have kept the Grail in a cave near Tarascon on the Rhône until her death. Other Christian legends state that Pontius Pilate gave the Grail—a cup or a bowl—to Joseph of Arimathea for the services that he had carried out.

After he used it to catch Jesus' blood, Joseph took it to Great Britain. Upon Joseph's death, the Grail disappeared and then appeared again, when the highly respected Titurel was king. He was charged with keeping safe both the Grail and the lance of destiny, which was used by the Roman war slave Longinus to open the side of the Crucified. Titurel built a castle of incomparable splendor and beauty for these relics—particularly for the Grail. The Benedictine monastery of Montserrat near Barcelona in Catalonia should have been this castle, but it was not. The Church had changed its tactics and had reinterpreted the myth of the Grail in a Judeo-Christian context.[47]

Perhaps 2,270 years ago, an unattractive yet seaworthy ship arrived here in the port of the Hellenic colonial city Massilia. What name the ship bore we do not know. We do know, however, that her captain was called Pytheas, and he was a scholar, geographer, mathematician, and astronomer. Pytheas wanted to sail out onto the ocean to the country of the farthest midnight, far to the north.

When the little ship was provided with all it needed for the long and difficult journey, the captain sacrificed to his god before he went on deck and let the sails be hoisted. He rendered homage to the Pythian Apollo, the radiant one who had overcome the dragon Pythos and in whose honor he called himself Pytheas. In addition, the captain may have made a pilgrimage to a place located in today's Monaco, where a temple of Herakles (Hercules) Monoikos still stands. Hercules was the god who protected northern travelers at that time. As the old sagas say, this valiant hero had sailed over the sea on the ship *Argo* with the Argonauts to bring the golden fleece back from the sun island Aea, but he sailed too far to the north. As his adventures progressed, he arrived in the low countries, where he was a guest of King Bretannos. He therefore stayed in Britannia.

If Pytheas commended himself to Hercules in prayer, he did not slight the light-bearer Apollo in any way, for Hercules, Apollo's half brother, was Apollo-like. Before they boarded the *Argo,* Jason and the

---

[47][A stone is not a chalice; there are two grails—a pagan symbol, which was then "christianized." This new symbol, a cup that was used during the last supper and that later caught the blood of a dying Christ on the cross, has nothing to do with the former. —*Trans.*]

Argonauts—all sons of gods, all "saviors"—asked for Apollo's protection. Jason, speaking for all of the Argonauts, prayed thus: "Leave me, Oh Lord; in accordance with your wisdom, clear the ropes of wrongless fate! May a friendly wind blow us, by which we move along cheerfully over the tide!" Pytheas might have prayed similarly.

Many minds have since pondered Pytheas of Marseille and his travels to the northern lands and the legendary island of Thule, which is ranked among the most important acts of geographical research. The writings of Pytheas, which must have contained a careful description of his travels, are lost forever.[48] This loss is very unfortunate because Pytheas was the only Greek to undertake a journey that for that time was outrageous. (We know for certain that he visited the ancient main amber production area in the German Elbe delta.) He also struck out boldly from the northern point of Scotland into the unknown North Sea—the North Atlantic. What makes the Pytheas expedition particularly important is his daring courage "to travel without compass in the open northern seas, where clouds and fog so often cause the disappearance of all means of orientation by the sun and the stars." Finally, he advanced in the north to a far island that he called Thule. Since that time, Ultima Thule, "ultimate Thule," earned a mysterious renown as the border of the inhabited earth.

Even though the chronicle of Pytheas's travels never reached us, we can piece together scraps of his journey from the pros and cons in *Geographia* by the Greek geographer Strabo:

Thule lies six days' travel far north of Britain, on the curdling sea. There, the summer tropic is the same as the winter tropic. For those who live near the ice zone, the lack of edible fruits and animals is complete or very great, and they feed themselves from millet and other vegetables, fruits, and roots. Where grain, and honey prosper, a beverage is prepared from these. Because they do not have total sunshine, they thresh the grain in large houses [barns], into which they bring sheaves of grain, because threshing floors are useless due to the lack of sunshine and the downpours.

---

[48][Pytheas's account of his voyage, *On the Ocean*, is indeed lost and only fragments have survived, principally in the works of Strabo and Pliny the Elder. —*Trans.*]

In Pliny the Elder's *Natural History*, Thule is referred to as the outermost known place, where there are no nights in summertime, when the sun passes through the Tropic of Cancer. On the other hand, in wintertime, there are only a few days. In Geminos of Rhodos (who wrote the work *Astronomical Elements*), we find the following passage: "Pytheas seems to have arrived in this region from Massilia, as it says in the chronicle he wrote on the ocean: 'The barbarians showed us the place where the sun rises. It happened that the night was very short in these areas, in some places only two or three hours, so that the sun rises again only a short time after its sets . . .'" Still another remarkable commentary comes from the Roman Pomponius Mela, which perhaps likewise goes back to Pytheas: "At the time of the summer solstice there are no nights, because the sun appears there more clearly and does not show any reflection on the water . . ." This report must be the oldest mention of the midnight sun. How did they become aware of this natural miracle? Pomponius Mela was never in the north.

If his report is assumed to be based on the writings of Pytheas, then there can be no doubt that the Massilian sailor advanced to the Arctic Circle at the beginning of the astronomical summer. This was more than two thousand years ago at a latitude of 66 degrees, 15 minutes, and 22 seconds. Thanks to Geminos of Rhodos, we know that Pytheas arrived at a place where the sun came up again two or three hours after it set. We can calculate the latitude degrees for the year 354 BC by counting: 64 degrees and 39 minutes, or 63 degrees and 39 minutes. South Iceland and central Norway lie between these latitudes. This is where Thule must have been.

Pytheas probably began his travel to the northern lands 334 years before the birth of Jesus. After his ship had carried him to the land of the Hyperborea, Pytheas sailed home through the Pillars of Hercules and arrived again in Marseille Harbor. I suspect that he sailed to the north because he was driven by a thirst for knowledge. He already knew that the earth is a sphere; that the planets orbit the sun; and that in the north, a pole lies like the sun, which holds the planets in a spell of gravity.

Pytheas sailed toward midnight because a god had indicated the way. He believed that the pole, wise and Apollonian, as it remains in a calm. Like Apollo, both the pole and the sun (which is Apollo) have the same attraction, just as people who are never free from God; Apollo has his true homeland in the country, and the pole in the far north resides with the lucky people of Hyperborea.

I think that the god to whom Pytheas prayed before beginning his northern journey was none other than the hyperboreal Apollo! Pytheas prayed to this divine light once a year in Delphi, this god's favorite seat in the Hellenic area. It is said that Apollo went to the country of Hyperborea in a barque or a wagon pulled by swans. While Apollo stayed in the north, the Delphians composed their paean to the far-off god: They placed boy choirs around that holy tripod where Pythia spoke to the oracle and implored the god to return. He came back each time, but year in and year out he returned to the north, to the place of his origin.

~ *PUIGCERDA IN CATALONIA* ~

I drove up in the car with acquaintances who have some business here. I am waiting alone under an arcade on the picturesque marketplace of this small town. Cleaning ladies, serious-looking border guards, fat market women, simple farmers from Andorra, and overloaded donkeys animate the already colorful and lively picture. At a side table nearby, townsmen appear to be playing *belote*. There is controversy. One accuses another of cheating.

In Wolfram's *Parzival,* a character says: "Sir, I am not one who can lie!" He is a pure one, a Cathar pure one. The Cathars taught that there are two principal sins: hardness of the heart, which is the opposite of pity (not of compassion!), and the lie.

An express train thunders over the plateau of the Cerdagne. It's coming from Toulouse and is traveling down to Barcelona. After it crosses into Catalonia, it will pass the mountain monastery at Montserrat. Catalonia was once the country of the Goths and Alans.[49] It no longer warrants this reputation.

Countess P. was right: The Grail was never kept on Montserrat, and the Jesuits never maintained a Grail knighthood for a reason: because they are the masters of lies! St. Ignatius of Loyola, the founder of the Jesuit order, once recommended to his pupils that they gain the confidence of their superiors by adjusting their inner character, which means through the use of hypocrisy.[50] Later, Father Baltasar Gracián, Ignatius's faithful disciple who was rector of the Jesuit college of Tarragona, presented in his *Oraculo manual* his thoughts on how each companion of Jesus should act for *ad majorem Dei gloriam:*[51]

What gains favor, perform yourself; leave the unfavorable to others.

Appear to have deep concern, and in order to achieve this appearance,

---

[49][As their name suggests, the Alans were Indo-Aryans, etymologically. Alan is an Iranian dialectical form of the word Aryan. The Alans settled all over western Europe, and curiously, they are remembered for a massive hunting dog called the Alaount, which is now extinct. Another relative of this dog, the Alano, survives in the Basque country. —*Trans.*]

[50][Iñigo Lopez de Recalde—St. Ignatius of Loyola—(AD 1491–1556). —*Trans.*]

[51][For the greater glory of God. —*Trans.*]

use humane means (as if they are not divine) and the divine (as if it is not humane) to sweeten the refusal. Rely more on the crutch of time than the iron club of Hercules; keep the fortuitous outcome in mind, because the winner does not need to account for himself; refuse nothing flatly, so that the dependence of the petitioners continues; . . . do not say all the truth. . . .[52]

The Grail was never kept on Montserrat. Never.

As Spanish townsfolk play cards and drink absinthe, I can recall the antics of Don Quixote, who rode through Spain on his nag, Rocinante, and became the laughingstock of the people. He wanted to bring respect back to the lost knighthood of his native land. What a fool! He had read so many books about knights that they had destroyed his brain. He certainly never heard of or read, or so I believe, a particular poem by a troubadour and knight named Peire Cardinal, which was almost certainly forgotten at that time, because if he had he would never have retrieved his rusty armor from the junk pile, supplemented it with pasteboard, and ridden out on adventures in the garb of a former time:

> Let you be buried, knighthood,
> and that no more words tell of you!
> Mocked you are and without honor,
> no death has such little power,
> you are derided and ridiculed,
> the king revoked your legacy,
> and all your realm is deceit to be bought,
> and thus you are abolished!

We will stay a day longer as planned. I am not happy about it.

Spanish soil gave us another "knight," a Basque by birth, as I recall. He does not belong to Lucifer's court. As a young man he rode an ass. In later years he preferred a donkey because Jesus of Nazareth, the "king of the Jews," also rode a donkey into the City of David. The knight was

---

[52][Father Baltasar Gracian (AD 1601–1658) was a prolific writer and author of the classic work *El Criticon* (1651–1657), whose pessimistic message influenced Arthur Schopenhauer and Friedrich Nietzsche. —*Trans.*]

named Ignatius of Loyola. He established the Society of Jesus to find those survivors of Lucifer's court who had not yet been exterminated.

In the days when Don Quixote was said to ride through the Spanish countryside on the back of Rocinante, a page named Ignatius of Loyola waited at the table and held the cup of the Spanish queen Germana, the second wife of Ferdinand II, the Catholic.[53] Sometimes, when she departed, he carried the royal coat and held a candle. Germana, or Germaine, was Ferdinand's second wife and a French princess of Foix (the direct lineage of the House of Foix had died out, and the French king gave the title of Foix to a northern French feudal family).[54] The first wife, in accordance with her last wishes, was wrapped in a rough Franciscan habit and buried without ceremony. Hardly one year had passed when Germaine arrived in Valencia with a fleet of thirty ships loaded with dresses, shoes, hoods, pieces of clothing, perfumes, and cosmetics. For her pleasure, the rarest fish, birds, fruits, spices, and wines were brought from Sevilla. In the courtyards and houses of the grandees, one banquet followed another; enormous quantities of food were devoured and more than one participant died in the overindulgence in enjoyable meals and drink.

Only one figure remained above this wild ruckus at the court of the new queen, like a solitary reminder of the strict Spanish spirit: the gaunt monk Francisco Ximenez de Cisneros, archbishop of Spain, chief inquisitor, and royal chancellor.

Ignatius of Loyola was fourteen years old at the time. Coddled in an environment of limitless ambition, the adolescent boy's first passions were devoted to the queen. Thus for him, love became the equivalent of courtly attention. I think his fantasies for woman were related to his desire to be distinguished before the sovereign and to achieve her favor. When he finally became a knight and, according to custom, had to select a patroness or a lady dear to his heart, Ignatius (Iñigo) chose the queen. In festivals and tournaments he carried her colors, although the highest reward he could expect was a lace handkerchief thrown from her hand to the winner in the arena. When he met her, he was careful not to doff his hat, because

---

[53][Ferdinand II, known as the Catholic (1453–1516), was of the House of Trastamara and was king of Aragon and joint sovereign of Spain with his first wife, Isabella. —*Trans.*]

[54][Germaine de Foix (1490–1538) was the daughter of Leonor of Navarre. —*Trans.*]

that would have indicated crazed adoration—a violation of the rules the Minne laid down for court ceremony. Even if his love arose less from a genuine sensual passion than his vain striving for recognition by the most powerful woman in the land, Iñigo understood how to disconnect romantic adoration of an unattainable lady of the heart and the honor (however disregarded) of those women who became victims of his indulgence. After all, Iñigo was involved in precarious adventures and sought crude carnal pleasures, like the other young knights of his time. How little integrity he had as a young man comes out clearly in his own confessions.

Many decades later, when he was already head of the Jesuit order, he told one his fellow brethren remorsefully that as a young knight he was not ashamed to commit a theft and then watch as an innocent was punished in his place. By the time Iñigo lived at the Spanish royal court, knights had lost the virile bravery and proud dignity of their ancestors, only to substitue for these an idle life at the side of the sovereign. Among the young noblity, the fighting spirit of their courageous ancestors had changed into cheap amusement accompanied by all kinds of loutish villainy against defenseless men and women. These young knights were brusque and arrogant when they dealt with underlings and were humble with rulers and their favorites. Among themselves, however, their ceremonial politeness made them laughable. Iñigo's one-sided, superficial development and poor ideals grew from this vain way of life. Probably he had already learned to read, but his choice of material was limited to those chivalric romances and magical stories that generally aroused popular enthusiasm at that time. Not much time had passed since the invention of typography, and this great achievement at first served only to spread romances of chivalry through all strata and levels. It was in this epoch that there appeared the great work of Cervantes, *Don Quixote de la Mancha*.

Iñigo buried himself in the *Tirant lo Blanc* by Juan Martorell and in the *Knight Gotterbarm of Montalban*. The adventures of the Knight of the Green Sword (aka Amadis of Gaul) made the greatest impression on him. Spain at the time held its breath over the marvelous acts of this hero, and they also completely captured Iñigo's interest. The young knight spent his days on weapons exercises, hunts, gallant dalliances with ladies, wild carousing, and brutal quarrels. An official document from that time, the report of the corregidor of Guipuzcoa to the Episcopal court in Pamplona in the year 1515, has carefully preserved a picture of the knight Ignatius of Loyola. He is described as saucy and provocative in leather vests and suits of armor, armed with swords and pistol, long hair flowing out from under his small, velvet knight's cap. The judge then describes his character as "treacherous, violent, and vindictive . . ."

In part, I have recounted Ignatius of Loyola's career from the book *Power and Secrets of the Jesuits* by René Fülöp-Miller.[55] I do not need to report how Iñigo fell into disfavor due to court gossip and was forced to abandon the royal court. Years passed. "One night Iñigo got himself up from his bed, knelt down before the image of the Mother of God in the corner of room, and vowed to serve from now on as her faithful soldier under the royal flag of Christ (Jesus). When he had decided to do without the gloss of this world, both his reversal and every further attempt toward a life change stood in the spell of chivalrous ideas. Like a Crusader, he departed from his siblings, servants, and the rest of his household staff, mounted his mule, and took the road to the Montserrat mountains."

On the way he met a Morisco, a baptized Arab, and began a discussion with him about the Virgin Mary. The Moor acknowledged his faith in the virgin conception of the Mother of God, but denied believing that the virginity of Mary continued after the birth of Christ. Iñigo felt this opinion was an offense to his new Lady of the heart, and thus used vehement words to take to task the Morisco in a knightly manner. The Morisco suspected calamity and rode away immediately while Iñigo considered whether or not it was his obligation to hasten after the blasphemer and kill him. It was not his conscience and inner feelings that ended this doubt; deferring to an old country superstition, he left the decision to an outside sign—in this case, the will of his pack mule. When he released the reins, the animal stayed the course, and so the life of the baptized heathen was saved.

Thus Iñigo began his service as a fighter for the heavenly realm.

---

[55][René Fülöp-Miller (1891–1963) was an Austrian-Romanian author who fled the Nazis. —*Trans.*]

In the spirit of knightly deeds and in a similar way, he carried out his religious "knightly vows." He chose the mountain of Montserrat as the place of the legendary Grail Castle. After he had exchanged his clothes with a beggar, he carried to Montserrat the picture showing the night watch of the Mother of God exactly to the place where such a ceremony was described in the book *Amadis de Gaula* (that famous Iberian romance novel). The next morning, he strode down from that mountain, attired in the new knightly garb of a fighter for God—a poor beggar's skirt, a gourd, and a pilgrim's staff—in order to begin his conquest for the heavenly realm. He approached the site of Manresa and chose as a residence a damp cave at the foot of a cliff. There he underwent the strictest penitent exercises. Seven hours a day he prayed on his knees, and he spent his short sleeping hours on the damp ground with a stone or a piece of wood in place of a pillow. Often, he fasted for three or four days at a time, and if he ate something, it was only the hardest, blackest pieces of bread or some herbs that he had made even more unappetizing by sprinkling them with ash.

Nonetheless, he did not succeed in having the beggars treat him as one of them; they cursed him even more when he mingled among them with a bread bag over his shoulder and a large rosary around his neck. The street urchins pointed to him, laughed, and called him scornfully "father bag." Daily he lashed himself violently; he regularly beat himself in the chest with a stone until he was sore, and once he hurled a stone at himelf so hard that he became faint and seriously ill. A patroness had to be brought in to the house to care for him, and those looking after him summoned physicians who gave him up for dead. Indeed, some nuns had already asked the lady of the house if she might give them some articles of Iñigo's clothing as relics. Because he was presumed dead, in order to satisfy their desires, they opened Iñigo's closet in order to pick over his clothes. They were frightened immediately, however, because, neatly ordered next to one another, hung the most terrible tools: plaited wire penitent belts, heavy chains, nails strung together, and undergarments interwoven with iron thorns. Iñigo had worn all this on his body!

According to the well-known Jesuit priest Friedrich Muckermann, Fülöp-Miller's book, from which I have gathered all of the above reflections on Ignatius of Loyola's life and works, "is interwoven with the characteristic of greatest respect," so that the Jesuit order "must be content with this representation." Therefore, I may continue in peace with these reflections from Fülöp-Miller:

> On the stairs of the church of Manresa, Iñigo supposedly perceived a higher light, which showed him how God had created the world. Then he experienced Catholic dogma so clearly that he would have died for the teachings that he saw. But odd visions were not missing: There appeared to him daily "something white which looked like three keys of a clavichord or an organ," and he was immediately convinced that this was the Holy Trinity. In the appearance of a white body "neither very large nor very small," he believed he saw the human Christ. In a similar vision he saw the Virgin Mary. Quite frequently, he had a vision of a large bright ball, a little larger than the sun, which he himself interpreted as the presence of Jesus Christ . . .

Once he had a vision that, despite its radiating beauty, resembled a serpent and which soon became sinister. When he noticed that the cross of beauty lost shine in his vision, he concluded that this serpent was the devil, not God. He reached immediately for his pilgrim's staff in order to chase away the demon with violent blows. . . . Every action and every impulse had its prescribed time: The Mass was not allowed to last longer than about a half hour, and an hourglass ensured that this period was not exceeded. He permitted himself enlightenment only during the Mass, and even tears of emotion and shock were not simply irregular *gratia lacrimarum* (tears of gratitude), as they were at the beginning of his mental transformation. Rather, he cried only if it appeared appropriate to him for reasons of internal discipline. He noted such tearful outpourings in his own diary and, as if to measure their strength and their duration, whether it had been made up of only a few tears or a "tearful torrent with sobbing" . . .

The foundations of the Jesuit order, which would never have existed without Ignatius of Loyola, are found in Ignatius's Spiritual Exercises. As outlined in Fülöp-Miller's book, he who goes through them shall, with every sense, experience hell and heaven, from the burning pain to the beatified bliss. In this way, the soul remembers indelibly the difference between bad and good. Once prepared in such a manner, the student is then confronted with a great choice: Satan or Christ. The Spiritual Exercises present horrific scenery to depict evil. Hell is shown in its full horror, filled by the flocks of moaning condemned ones. The exercise begins with the pupil using his imagination to measure the length, width, and depth of hell. Then the other senses must participate. These strange instructions contain exact points.

The first point insists that the student see with the eyes of imagination those immeasurable burning embers and the souls as they are enclosed within blazing bodies.

The second point insists that the student hear with the ears of imagination the weeping, howling, shouting, and blasphemies against our Lord Christ and against his saints.

The third point insists that the student smell with imagination's sense of smell the smoke, sulfur, slop, and rotting things of hell.

The fourth point insists that the student taste with imagination's sense of taste all that is bitter: the tears, sadness, and pangs of conscience in hell.

The fifth point insists that the student make contact with imagination's sense of touch, that the student touches whatever the soul grasps and whatever scorches it.

If this point is reached, then the ideal, which shall be followed, is shown: Ignatius instructs the student to immerse himself completely in the life and suffering of Jesus Christ. As with the preceeding images of hell, all the senses contribute to this effort—and still Ignatius always demands an exact realization of the place: The student must see with the eyes of the imagination the synagogues, cities, and castles through which Christ passed when he preached. If a teaching is from the Holy Virgin, then the student must visualize the particular small house and apartments of our dear Lady in the city of Nazareth in the countryside of Galilee.

Reflecting on the birth of the Lord, Ignatius instructed his followers to follow with the eyes of imagination the route leading them from Nazareth to Bethlehem. To be considered are its length and width and whether the route is straight or goes by way of valleys and over heights.

A student should also imagine the cave of the birth: How wide was it? How confined or low-ceilinged or high-ceilinged was it, and how was it furnished?

By applying all our senses, Jesus can be introduced on the field before Jerusalem as the highest commander of his hosts, while opposite him, in the region of Babylon, Satan gathers his demons around him for the last Armageddon. We can see how Lucifer's innumerable spirits are appointed and sent out into the whole world, without ignoring country, place, tribe, or individual people. Similarly, on the opposite side, the highest and true commander—our Lord Christ—can be contemplated. How did he choose his apostles and disciples, who were sent out into the world and thus spread his holy teachings among all people?

When Don Quixote was said to have ridden through the countryside on his quest to resurrect errant chivalry—a quest that had been celebrated at the Spanish court in grotesquely distorted, triumphant minstrel songs since the time of the crusade against the heretics—a spiritual campaign was organized that reflected the religious delusion that Loyola suffered.

The symbol of Jesus was opposed to that of Lucifer, and Montserrat, in place of Montségur, which was long in rubble, became the Grail Castle. Even the Grail cave Fontane la Salvasche, the mount, and Parzival's cloak were not absent from this comparison—but the coat became a beggar's coat and the steed became a mule, for Jesus of Nazareth preferred to ride into Jerusalem on an ass instead of the Apollonian Pegasus.

Esclarmonde's spirit presided no more.

At this same time, the new world was discovered for the second time by Christopher Columbus. The name Christopher means "Christ bearer." So it was that Columbus carried over the ocean the teachings of Christ, who was Jesus of the House of David. In the footsteps of Columbus, Hernán Cortés sailed over the ocean and conquered the Aztec kingdom of Mexico for Spain. In a report to the emperor, he stated that Montezuma, king of the Aztecs, regarded him as the ruler of "those natural, higher lights" from where his own ancestors came. Montezuma even permitted Cortés to remove all images of gods. Not until the gold-crazed intruders took the king prisoner and seriously wounded him did he reject treatment of his wounds and spurn Christ. He wanted to die.

He had succumbed to a terrible mistake! Cortés was an agent of the pope and the Catholic emperor, not the messenger of the "white God," for which Montezuma and his people had waited in vain for such a long time. God should come from the north, from the ancient land of Tulla or Tullan—from Thule!—which had been a country of the sun and where now "the ice prevailed and the sun was no more." From there, Lucifer's courtiers had come. I quote from Gerhart Hauptmann's *White Savior:* "the spawn[56] that shamelessly defiles our Mother Earth's face with the dross of his atrocities . . ."

---

[56][Mankind is the spawn. —*Trans.*]

～ LOURDES ～

I am impressed by this place of pilgrimage, which is the largest in France. While I write these lines, I let a bonbon melt away on my tongue. A shop window advertisement announced that it is made from consecrated Lourdes water, *eau bénite de Lourdes*. It does not taste like anything. Where I find myself at this time, the air is filled with odors that settle in the chest and do not yield. Lourdes smells obtrusively of the most diverse perfumes, but it also stinks of carbolic acid and chloroform, which are better suited for hospitals. Only rarely does pure mountain air descend from the forest and the high mountains, which majestically encircle the place.

Since February of 1858, when a seventeen-year-old girl named Bernadette Soubirous saw the Virgin Mary here and received the command to build a church for pilgrims, this place has gradually become one of the most productive gold mines of the Roman Church. For anyone who wishes to know more, read Emile Zola's novel *Lourdes,* which nobody has been able to disprove until now. For those who wish to see this place's miraculous charms with their own eyes, taking a trip to Lourdes is like experiencing a great journey to a holy shrine.

Any pilgrim nowadays will probably embark at the Quai d'Orsay station in Paris or Montabiau in Toulouse. Access to Lourdes is clogged by those who are seriously ill, even those on stretchers. A pilgrim is obliged to travel in the same compartment with people who are actually carriers of disease or illness. With this overwhelming misery of mankind, the clink of prayer beads mixes with the sound of the rolling train, and in this way, a pilgrim commences his journey into the afterlife.

From the foothills of the Pyrenees there shines a cruciform neon sign, and a spotlight sends down its light from the castle high above the city. A pilgrim finds his way to the famous grotto before night finally arrives. The Mother of God stands on a rock there—white, rigid, and smiling. From there the holy waters always run and hundreds of candles flicker. Crutches and canes hang on the rock, silent testimony to those who were cured by the Mother of God. Other pilgrims—sometimes numbering less than one hundred, sometimes hundreds, sometimes thousands—kneel before her, praying. No pilgrim to Lourdes, whether Catholic or heretic, can forgo a visit to the baths, which are fed from the divine spring of the grotto. Here a visitor can witness the greatest "miracle" at Lourdes: The sick seeking a cure enter the ice-cold water, looking the whole time to the sky rather than in the bath, as pus-soaked wads of cotton or bandages and filthy plasters that can no longer stick to the wounds of the ill rise to the surface of the water. Yet in order to see this "miracle," the visitor must have connections.

Kevelaer in the Rhineland, Echternach in Luxembourg, even Rome cannot offer the spectacle that Lourdes has to offer. A splendid church towers over the grotto, and built above this there is a second, new church, which must have cost an enormous sum. At night, the mountains are black, but countless lights shine in the valley, on the slopes, and on the heights. Hundreds of thousands of people stream here. Many lead or carry patients. Prayers—the Our Father and the Rosary—are offered in all the languages of the world. Everyone who visits here searches for the healing of a mental defect or physical ill, for the actions of the Lord of Hosts. Mary will help . . .

When it is time, everyone lights a candle or a lantern and, with pious pictures or with holy sayings, joins the procession. The bells begin to ring; the multicolored holy pictures and heavy flags wave; the monstrance glistens; the priests and the laity pray; those who are seriously ill groan, and some of them are consoled by those who are healthy—and then everyone, and I mean everyone, pushes and shoves his or her way to the upper church. The gold and gems reflect even more; music blares; the tremendous multitude sings; and the loudspeakers roar a dance song, the song of Bernadette. Many consider it a chorale, yet it is indeed a dance song.

I stood aside, looked, and reflected: In ancient times, a temple of Venus stood here! During the Albigensian crusade in the twelfth century, Cathars were put to death here because they did not pray to Mary and revere the saints and the Lord of Hosts. Above all they did not want to be subjects of Rome and France. I recalled the cave of Betharam, which is not far from Lourdes. I visited it the day before. It is the most frequented Pyrenees cave. Visitors come in droves to see its beautiful stalactites [and stalagmites], which were carried off many years ago, just as they were taken from the cave of Lombrives near Sabarthès. These stalactites [and stalagmites] were created in eternal night by mountain water over the course of millions of years; they gave us the legendary graves of Hercules, the Pyrenean Venus, and King Bebryx, all of which grew too tall and powerful, necessitating their re-creation in another place. In the cave of Lombrives, the bones of the Albigensians also wait confidently for Judgment Day. I stood apart during the procession. Above me a cross radiated from the high mountain summit. From the north, Arktos (the large and small bear) greeted me. I must meet him, if I want to find my Germany.

A few days ago, I hiked into the mountains with a physician from Pau in Sierra Maledetta. My friend is also a *rimaire,* a rhymer, as Gascons call their poets. As we ascended the heights, he explained that his compatriots, especially the long established farmers, regard themselves as the descendants of Hercules and Pyrene. Even today, songs in Gascony recall how Apollo and Venus or the Graces and Nymphs rule their forests or wellsprings, and they proudly proclaim that the holy mountains of the Greeks—Olympus, Ossa, and Pelion—are less holy than their Pyrenees.

After a long hike through high forest and some difficult climbing, we found ourselves at a group of peasant huts made from rubble that leaned against the mountain wall for a better grip. They were stuck like birds' nests to the precipitous slope. We used all our provisions going up the slope, so, because we had another long trek in front of us, we decided to buy some bread and cheese. We saw people disappearing into the miserable small cottages as we approached, but although we pounded on the doors, nobody opened them. We called, but nobody answered. Dead silence. Only a cat began to mew. The doors remained locked. Because our journey was unfinished, we had to continue.

My companion was convinced that we had just been in a settlement of Cagots. There should still be some of them here, far from other people. Like most, he is of the opinion that they were originally designated Canis Gothi, presumably the "Gothic dog." The Cagots must be regarded as descendants of the Visigoths. They are uniformly tall people with expressive faces, blue eyes, and blond hair. I asked if the incredible scorn with which they are derided and that follows them even today has its origins in their faith. If not, they would have never petitioned Pope Leo X in mid-1517, imploring him to receive them in grace because the sins of their fathers had long been expiated. My companion offered that he did not know whether the pope heard them. To me, it is surely worth noting that in this country the Cagots are also called Salbatgés, which means both "savage" and "saved."

I thought of Wolfram von Eschenbach's Grail Castle called Munsalvat.

We hiked farther. We had left the forest far behind us. Tall rosemary bushes stood on both sides of the stony path. An eagle drew powerful circles above us. Suddenly, Sierra Maledetta sprang up. Such a strong light radiated from that glaciated, colossal mountain that our eyes began to hurt. Foolishly, we had forgotten to bring sunglasses with us. My companion noted that according to Pyrenean legend, the greatest troubadour of all, Bertran de Born, had soared up to Sierra Maladetta and there, on the glacier, had solidified into a block of ice because he was grief-stricken over the demise of his homeland and its freedom. I responded that I knew that Dante had this minstral singer transported to hell, where he carried his decapitated head before him to illuminate the way.

On my way to the rimaire's home, I reflected: Troubadour Bertran de Born and the Gothic dogs—the Cagots—belong to Lucifer's court. The rimaire had become just as thoughtful as I. When he asked about these courtiers, I said the following, perhaps too pedantically: In the Book of Isaiah, in the name of the Lord of Hosts, the thunderous God of the Jews brings woe unto all the questioners and the righteous. They will be treated in the same way as Lucifer, who fell from the sky to the deepest depth because he wanted to set himself on the "mount of the congregation, in the sides of the north." This mountain must lie in the far north, because there can be found the country of the midnight sun. Ice and snow are the masters there, as they also preside over the glacier of Sierra Maledetta. Further, who first called this mountain the cursed Sierra, the highest and the most beautiful mountain in the Pyrenees? Perhaps the tragedy of the Cagots has its origins here. I understood why the pope of the Albigensian crusade in the Languedoc wanted to prepare Provence for a new race: He proposed that Teutonic blood should finally be exterminated in southern France because those northern peoples were holy, unlike those from Jerusalem or Rome. The Teutons were made into the barbarians, the Vandals were made into destroyers, the Burgundians into the Bougres—which is a derogatory term used in France by only the most uncouth—and the Cathars into heretics. How much must Rome have hated German culture! They could not have chosen means that were more ignoble and more contrary to God. This is how Western religious history appears: Rome degraded by force those who arose from unknown depths. It acted on the assumption that those who sought to unravel the secrets of the world and of life should be driven to hell or overwhelmed or destroyed with curses and defamation. Yet is it a crime that people chose the highest possible goal of all? Rome put to death those who did not want to pray to Yahweh, a God who once regretted that he had produced the world and people. Rome's pope burned or tortured those who did not want to recognize him as the supreme representative of God. As history sufficiently shows, popes were often ranked among the scum of humanity.

Lucifer's court is composed of those northern bloodlines that chose a "mount of the congregation, in the sides of the north," and not Mount Sinai or Mount Zion, in the Middle East, as the goal of their search for spirituality. The members of Lucifer's court understood that an intermediary is not required to feel the presence of God or to converse with him; rather, they searched for their God through their own actions, and it is my belief that their prayers were answered. The members of Lucifer's court had no need for rough medieval flagellates or the Arab dervishes who lost themselves in ecstasy and imagined they saw God. Instead, they looked to those who viewed life with its common misdeeds and contradictions and burdens as one of the obligations imposed by God. Thus, they patiently untangled the misdeeds they committed in order to bring the contradictions into agreement. Lucifer's courtiers did not whine and whimper to heaven, but instead beseeched admittance heartily, because they did their very best as humans and were therefore worthy of deification.

My hiking companion could agree with me only to a limited extent. Because I spoke more than once of the troubadours, however, he mentioned troubadour Peire Cardinal's disregard of heaven's doorman: St. Peter begged God impetuously for admittance into Paradise. On the way back from Sierra Maledetta—whose icy glacier, as rival to Dante's fiery hell made stiff from grief, had harbored troubadour Bertran de Born, and which was perhaps therefore cursed—my companion recited to me, in the Provençal language, a heretical poem of Peire Cardinal:

> *I versify now a newly censured song*
> *That shall be heard on the Day of Reckoning.*
> *He, the One who had created us from nothin,*
> *To us, His gate should never be locked,*
> *And that the holy St. Peter guards it*
> *Serves Him the greatest dishonor. No:*
> *From qualifying strength*
> *Cheerful and laughing*
> *We gather within there! It seems to us an imperfect court,*
> *In it the courtiers laugh, whereas the others cry*
> *And He is also admired as a high lord.*
> *We quarrel if He resists our admittance.*
> *It would liken us to Him, an exclusive comparison of*
> * only piety:*
> *He created us, from where He has us taken!*

My thoughts speak all of love
And in so many different musical manners.

DANTE

PART TWO

~ Night Journey ~

Just now, two French naval officers left the train that connects the Spanish border with the Italian, in the port town of Sète. Like me, they boarded in Narbonne. Because I told them that I was going to spend the whole night on the train, they gave me some books to read before they left. These are horribly illustrated inexpensive novels, but they are not unwelcome diversion for the long night. The train is filled with noisy people in its humid stuffiness. There cannot be any thought of sleep tonight: A thunderstorm is hanging over the Mediterranean, and torrential rain is beating against the windowpanes in buckets.

A Jesuit priest prays silently with his rosary. His lipless mouth, just a line, moves only now and then. Sometimes his small, hard eyes examine the other travelers. One of these is fat. As beads of sweat rise on his forehead, he wipes them off with a balled-up handkerchief. He wears rings, including a gold wedding band, on each of his fingers. Although the man is probably Jewish, a Christian medallion hangs on his heavy gold watch chain. Sitting opposite the Jesuit, in the corner by the other window, is a plain housewife. Her hair is parted and she wears glasses. Her hands (I can notice the housework on them) are knitting a boy's sweater, which will soon be finished. She does not look up, yet it seems to me that she is quietly smiling. Perhaps she is traveling back to her baby. As I mentioned, one of my fellow travelers may be Jewish, although he could be a Christian convert. Ignatius of Loyola, the founder of the Jesuit order, would have gladly belonged to the "chosen people." He once stated that he would have regarded it as a very special favor from God if he were of Jewish heritage and thus "a blood relative of our Lord Jesus and our beloved Lady, the most Blessed Virgin Mary."

I am watching how the plain woman performs her work eagerly and cheerfully with her hands. Perhaps she is thinking of her baby to whom she is returning, and does not know the Jesuit moral: "As habit and conditions permit, children may steal so much from their parents, when these do not involve questions and ideas." I think of my own mother and father: Although my brother and I caused them a great deal of worry, I do not believe that we stole from them. Had I wanted to become a Jesuit, I would have been obliged "to cast off all familial ties with blood relatives," and I would not have been permitted to say that I *have* parents or brothers, and sisters, but that in fact that I *had* them. Thank God I still have them.

I am German, but for Jesuits, "there cannot be a separation of peoples into nations and races; for them there are only people who struggle under the flag of Lucifer and people who fight under the flag of Christ." Concerning my own faith, I am fighting under the flag of Lucifer. I am a heretic and a child of this world, for I like to visit the theater and attend concerts. "The pupils of the Society of Jesus may go neither to public plays or comedies nor to other performances except for the execution of criminals, and only when it concerns the execution of heretics." In other times, the Jesuits would have burned me.

⁓ GENOA ⁓

Now I am on Italian soil, and it is glowing hot. I spent yesterday in Monaco, which derives its name from Hercules Monoikos. Tonight I continue on to Milan. A sentimental song assaults my ears: A tenor laments his *nostalgia di baci* and *nostalgia d'amore*—his longing for kisses and love. A remarkable wordplay occurs to me: The reverse of *amor* is Roma.

The Genoese were once very proud of the Sacro Catino, the holy chalice that Joseph of Arimathea used in the Passion of Jesus Christ. Archbishop William of Tyre, a medieval chronicler, reported that the Genoese Grail was kept in the temple of Hercules in Tyre, where it apparently fell into the hands of the Saracens when they overran that city.[1] Later, the Genoese recaptured it during the Crusades and returned with it to their city-state. It was long believed to be a gigantic emerald until Napoleon had it examined in 1806. The results revealed it to be olive-green glass. This is said to have greatly annoyed the citizens of Genoa.

I should also mention that the Genoese speak ill of the true discoverer of the Americas. Only reluctantly will they admit that a heathen and barbarian Viking from Iceland discovered the new world more than a half millennium before a Genoese Christian named Christopher Columbus set out on behalf of Spain. The New World does not attract me, but I would like to see Iceland, which many believe to have once been the mythical island called Thule, whose existence was first confirmed by that brave Massilian sailor Pytheas. I still need the clouds and storm and snow and ice . . .

Rome, Milan, and Verona are the only Italian cities I can visit. I would have also gladly visited Naples and its surrounding area, where the last Ostrogoths under King Teja were annihilated in 555 at Mons Lactarius. I would also have visited Florence, a city once completely devoted to Catharism and the place where Dante Alighieri "married" Beatrice in Minne poetry; and Ravenna, where the Ostrogoth king

---

[1][William, archbishop of Tyre (ca. 1130–ca.1190), was a historian of the Crusades who published *Historia rerum in partibus transmarinis gestarum* (The History of Deeds Done beyond the Sea). —*Trans.*]

Theodoric resided in times of peace and personally cultivated his garden. If we trust our old poets, when war clouds gathered, the king moved his court over to Verona. Alas, Rome, Milan, and Verona are the only cities that I will see. I would also have traveled happily to Loreto, on the Adriatic Sea, to see the holy house of Nazareth, the Catholic shrine where you can visit the cottage of Mary, the Mother of God, which an angel is said to have transported there from its place in Palestine.

King Theodoric (Dietrich von Bern) had the famous treasure of the Jerusalem Temple taken from Carcassonne—where Alaric, the Visigoth king, kept it—to Ravenna before the Romans captured it. The Grâl is said to have been part of these riches. I ask myself if Dietrich of Ravenna (the much heralded City of Ravens) is the Grâl king. *Der Wartburgkrieg* prompts a second question: According to the poem, "living in Rome was a rich caste who landed in poverty" but who rose "through their noble mild courage."[2] Were the members of this caste once the masters of Solomon's gold?

Exactly one hundred years before that fateful encounter at Mons Lactarius, near Naples, Theodoric, king of the Ostrogoths, was born. In direct lineage, he was the fourteenth of the royal dynasty of the Amal "who triumphed as if by fate, and who would go by the Gothic name of their deities: Ansis or Asen." The first Amal monarch was reputed to be Gaut, who was their ancestral god of war and the founder of both their dynasties.[3] Others "whom the Goths admired as gods of their people" were Taunasis or Thanauses and Ermanaric, who proclaimed himself king of Scythia and ruled over the largest portion of Germania. According to the sixth-century Gothic historian Jordanis, he was "the most noble Amal."[4] This writer left behind a compendium of twelve books comprising the lost history of Cassiodorus, who was Theodoric's chancellor and most trusted associate. Jordanis also informs us that the origins of the Goths were celebrated in sonnets that commemorated the time when they left the island of Scandia, and he

---

[2][*Der Wartburgkrieg* was composed by an anonymous hand. —*Trans.*]

[3][Gaut is considered the founder of both the Visigoth and Ostrogoth dynasties. —*Trans.*]

[4][Ermanaric was a warlike king of the Gothic Greuthungi who committed suicide after his defeat by the Huns in AD 376. His kingdom was called Oium or Scythia. At his death, it fell under Hunnish domination for seventy-five years. —*Trans.*]

tells us how Gothic customs were preserved in "old, nearly historical songs." The chorales and songs have long since disappeared.

Theodoric first saw the light of the world two years after the death of Attila the Hun in the vicinity of Vienna. Attila, who entered heroic legend as King Etzel, was buried by the Ostrogoth nobility. On their chargers they rode past the corpse, which was magnificently laid in state in the open air. At the same time, the dead warrior was praised in hymns chanted in his honor.

Theodoric eventually ruled over the Italian peninsula from the Alps to the southern tip of Calabria—and thanks to him, the Vandals peacefully relinquished Sicily. Envoys from the outermost areas of Germania journeyed to Ravenna to pay homage to him. One day, the king of the Heruli, a northern Germanic tribe, arrived to seek Theodoric's friendship.[5] By Gothic rite, Theodoric raised him to the status of a son. Even the Ästhen sent messengers from the shores of the Baltic Sea and placed amber at the feet of the great king. Gothic royalty maintained preferential exchanges with the Scandinavian court, and a Swedish prince was always in attendance at the Gothic court, which was fashioned on the English model. This prince:

> . . . ruled over one of the thirteen tribes which at that time populated a part of the Scandinavian peninsula. This Norse country to which is attached the vague name Thule was explored up to the 68th parallel of latitude, where the inhabitants of the polar circle either enjoy or lose the sun for forty days at each summer and winter solstice. The long night of the sun's absence, or "sun death," was a tragic time of misery and angst. As a consequence, messengers were dispatched to the pinnacles of the highest mountains to witness the first rays of the returning light, who would then announce to the lowlands the celebration of its rebirth . . .[6]

The island of Scandia, where the Goths originated, and the penin-

---

[5][Theodoric had the chieftain slain after he learned of the Heruli's ritualistic homosexuality. —*Trans.*]

[6][The Gothic Jordanis, the chronicler. —*Trans.*]

sula of Scandinavia are really one and the same. If the Massilian sailor Pytheas landed in Scandia, then Scandinavia must be Thule.

When Theodoric died in AD 526, the Ostrogoth kingdom seemed firmly established. Yet a mere thirty years later, his realm was no more and his people were devastated. No monument recalls his rule apart from a wonderful tomb erected by his daughter Amalasuntha, over-looking the city of Ravenna. He has lived on in the heroic legends of Dietrich von Bern and Thidrek, but Catholic poets of the Middle Ages had Theodoric abducted by the devil and, as a result, according to them, he met his end in scorching embers and eternal damnation.

⁓ Milan ⁓

Milan's patron saint is Ambrose. Between AD 374 and 397, when Theodosius I reigned over eastern Rome and Valentinian I ruled over the western part of the city as rival emperors, he was Milan's archbishop. His body rests here in the church of Sant' Ambrogio, which was the coronation site of the kings of Lombardy and German emperors from the ninth to the fifteenth century. In the year 387, in this church, he baptized St. Augustine, the man who caused such problems for the Manichaeans.

Augustine belongs to Lucifer's court no more than Ambrose does, but I should describe him. Augustine was born to a Christian mother of Punic-African descent in Numidia (today's Algeria). His father was a heathen and Semite.[7] Augustine went to school in a town not far from the steppes of the Berber nomads. At sixteen years of age, "he was, as he related, a handsome fellow, so his father gratified himself with the boy in the bath, and in genuine Syrian-Punic fashion, he already thought of grandchildren." Two years later, his father probably regretted his wish, because an illegitimate grandson came into the world and was named Adeodatus (God-given). For thirteen years Augustine lived in sin with the mother of his son.

In his early life, Augustine became preoccupied with Manichaeanism. He hated the Manichaeaists' dreary pessimism, and he brazenly compiled his discussions with Faustus, a scholar who was one of the most famous and gifted Manichaeans of that time, into an essay called *Contra Faustum*.[8] One day, Augustine decided to move to Rome. Yet he did not remain in the Eternal City for very long. Having decided on a career as a teacher of rhetoric in Milan, he repudiated the woman who had

---

[7][Like many other common mistakes, the term Semite has been adopted without denoting real ethnicity. Today, the term can mean several groups of people who inhabited the Levant and spoke similar languages, but who were not of the same ethnic origin: Arabs, Jews, Phoenicians, Arameans, Syrians, and so forth. The expression is derived from the mythical biblical "table" of nations and the descendants of Noah and his sons, Shem, Ham, and Japheth. Yet the term does not have any historical significance. It came into use at the end of the eighteenth century in Germany and thereafter became a standard term for a group of languages, including Hebrew, Arabic, and Aramaic. The same applies to Hamites and Japhethites, since they are Semites as well. —*Trans.*]

[8][Against Faustus. —*Trans.*]

borne him a son and lived with him for so long. He believed that he should have a marriage in keeping with his station. The mother of his son returned, depressed, to North Africa, where she spent the rest of her life unmarried in a Christian community. Soon, however, he found a suitable woman who would satisfy his sensual needs and ambitious goals. The marriage took place two years later. Meanwhile, Augustine had taken a mistress. When the day of the marriage approached, he chased from the house the woman he was to marry and called off the wedding. In the intervening time, he had converted to Catholicism and embraced God and the celibacy of the Church. Of course, as he said in later years, whores are just as indispensable an element of human society as are hangmen, yet the words of the Apostle Paul that had converted him became his guiding principle: Only by shunning voracious eating and drinking, fornication in bedchambers, and strife and envy is it possible to get closer to the Lord Jesus Christ." Tend to the body, but avoid becoming licentious! Augustine reported: "I read, but no longer was it necessary to continue, because immediately at the end of these words the light of peace pierced my heart and the night of doubt escaped!" Because his child, Adeodatus, was produced in sin, though he was baptized by Ambrose, he died one year later.

As the great Vandal king Geiseric laid siege in 430 to Hippo Regius in North Africa, the city where he had at long last become bishop, Augustine departed this world.[9] In the end, however, it was the dying bishop and later beatified Father of the Church who triumphed over the Teutonic warrior, for from then on, all popes, priests, and emperors of the Holy Roman Empire, the German nation, and, above all, Charlemagne used his most significant work, *Civitas Dei* (City of God), as a powerful hammer (in addition to the Bible) to forge a new Europe. They nearly succeeded. Despite everything, it is my hope that one day Europe will be free from all Jewish mythology.[10]

---

[9][Geiseric (AD 389–487) was king of the Vandals and Alans from 428 to 477. —*Trans.*]

[10][The concluding sentence of the paragraph is very curious, because in his previous book, *Crusade Against the Grail,* Rahn cites the famous passage by Ernest Renan: "We do not owe our politics, our art, our poetry, our philosophy, nor our science to the Semites. What do we owe to them? Our religion." (*Mélanges d'histoire et de voyages* [Paris: n.p., 1878], 16). —*Trans.*]

When Augustine arrived in Rome, he found the city occupied by the Goths. The citizenry complained to him that the Gothic domination had become possible only because Rome had accepted the new Eastern religion: Christianity. Augustine asked the Romans if the Goths went into the Christian churches. The answer: No, they avoid them, because the Goths are a people different from Augustine or the Romans.

So Augustine taught in his *City of God:*[11] Of the two first parents of the human race, Cain was the firstborn, and he belonged to the city of men. After him was born Abel, who belonged to the city of God. The quarrel between Romulus and Remus thus shows how the earthly city is divided against itself: That which fell out between Cain and Abel illustrated the hatred that exists between the two cities—the city of God and that of men. . . . Fallen angels of God created the Assyrians, Persians, and Athenians. Only in Shem did Abel's line continue. Because Adam fell from grace, he certainly had a fatal flaw. In the history of the people of Israel, sin always showed itself anew, but Jesus Christ appeared in Israel in order to save mankind. . . . Out of Israel comes the Christian Church. The Christians can obtain the certain release of salvation from the weakness of the flesh. Without the Church there is no true community; there is only violence and war and a world cumbersomely subdued by laws! Now, however, there is great unity: The *civitas Romana,* Roman civilization, has been overcome and converted and now their emperors are Christian. They and all their servants now belong to the Church. The worldly state must serve them. Church and state are the two organs of the great oneness of Christianity: Both build the City of God within mankind. That is a

---

[11][Rahn is wrong to situate Augustine in Rome under Gothic domination. Augustine visited the Holy City before the Gothic conquest. Throughout these passages, the author often replaces Augustine's name with the German term Semit. In fact, the African-born Augustine was of Berber stock on his mother's side. In Johann Gottfried Eichhorn's *Repertorium*, Ludwig Schlözer was the first to propose the term Semite for Hebrew-related languages (see vol. 8 [Leipzig: n.p., 1781], 161). Only then did the word come into general use (cf. his *Einleitung in das alte Testament*, vol. 1 [Leipzig: n.p., 1787], 45). By the time of the publication of his *Gesch. der neuen Sprachenkunde*, part 1 (Göttingen: n.p., 1807), it had already become a common expression. (Taken from *The Catholic Encyclopedia*, vol. 13; for readers of French, see also Guy Rachet, *La Bible, mythes et réalités* [Paris: Le Rôcher, 2004]). —*Trans.*]

goal and purpose of history. On Judgment Day, Jesus Christ takes for himself all dominion, separating the chosen ones from those who are eternally condemned.

Opening the first book of Moses to the fourth and fifth chapters, I read this:

And Adam knew Eve his wife; and she conceived, and bare Cain, and said, I have gotten a man from the LORD. And she again bare his brother Abel. And it came to pass, when they were in the field, that Cain rose up against Abel his brother, and slew him. And Adam knew his wife again; and she bare a son, and called his name Seth: For God, said she, hath appointed me another seed instead of Abel, whom Cain slew. And to Seth, to him also there was born a son; and he called his name Enos. And Enos lived ninety years, and begat Cainan.

And Cainan lived seventy years and begat Mahalaleel. And Mahalaleel lived sixty and five years, and begat Jared. And Jared lived a hundred sixty and two years, and he begat Enoch.

And Enoch lived sixty and five years, and begat Methuselah.

And Methuselah lived a hundred eighty and seven years, and begat Lamech.

And Lamech lived a hundred eighty and two years, and begat a son:

And he called his name Noah . . .

And Noah was five hundred years old: and Noah begat Shem, Ham, and Japheth.

Augustine was somehow mistaken: He should have continued Abel's lineage to Shem, who was the offspring of Seth and Yahweh's replacement for the murdered Abel! In the Bible, Shem was a grandchild of Lamech, who was a grandchild of Enoch, who in turn was a grandchild of Mahalaleel, who was a great-grandchild of Seth. The same chapters of the first book of Moses remain open, and I continue:

And Adam knew Eve, his wife; and she conceived, and bare Cain
    And Cain knew his wife; and she conceived, and bare Enoch;

> And unto Enoch was born Irad; And Irad begat Mehajael; and
> Mehajael begat Methusael; And Methusael begat Lamech;
> And Lamech . . . begat a son: And he called his name Noah.
> And Noah . . . begat Shem, Ham, and Japheth . . .

The Bible clearly contradicts itself: Shem is a grandchild of Lamech in both cases, and then the confusion begins. Lamech is both a grandson and great-grandson of Enoch, and Enoch is both a great-great-great-great-grandson and grandson of Adam! And what about Shem? In the Bible, Shem is either the offspring of Seth or Cain—not, however, as Augustine states, the offspring of Abel, whom Cain slew and for whom Yahweh produced a replacement: Seth!

Saint and Father of the Church, Augustine must have known the Bible in general and specifically the first book of Moses. Why did he stray from the Word of God? I think I can answer the question. Augustine was very concerned over the ancestry of Jesus of Nazareth. He was careful to avoid stating that Jesus descended from Cain, who was a murderer. Yet on the other hand, he was quite happy to assert that the B'nai Israel were descended from Shem, and Christianity, which had originated in Israel, was descended from Abel. Concerned over his religion's Semitic origins, Augustine was eager to win over the city of Rome—which mistrusted the "new Eastern religion"—for the conquest of the world by the church of Verus Israel, which was bent on proselytizing and dominating the world.

For this reason Augustine grabbed the statement out of thin air. Rome belonged to Cain's descendants: Abel-Remus had been murdered by Cain-Romulus. This was the real reason why Rome fell into sin and degradation. Only Jesus could free the Eternal City from the tyranny of the Gothic conquerors—but the Goths were not descended from Shem or Cain or Seth. By the same token, they couldn't have descended from Abel, because the Bible says nothing about Abel's descendants. Then who were the ancestors of the Goths? In answer: The Goths were descended from the "fallen angels of God," as Augustine refers to them. The God of the Bible condemned these angels, along with Lucifer, to the deepest pit in hell. Augustine's fallen angel of God and his offspring—the Goths—were in one form or another members of Lucifer's court.

Augustine's racial theories should be studied closely. We should also take into account the little-known suggestion of the British statesman Benjamin Disraeli, a Jew who believed that history can be understood only if racial questions are properly understood.

Remember Hercules and the Argonauts? One of them, Perseus, was the "creator" of Persia. Yet Hercules and the Argonauts all belonged to the fallen angels, even though they remain constellations in the sky—despite Yahweh! The similarity of the words Abel and Abellio (which recall the word the Cretans used for "the sun") forces us to reflect—and as I muse over all this, I think that perhaps I will write about it in another book.

As an anonymous hand told in *Der Wartburgkrieg,* there was a rich family in Rome that "became poor through its noble and mild courage." Quite probably, this family descended from Aeneas and his father, Anchises, both of whom arrived in Rome as refugees from Troy. Aeneas carried his father, Anchises, on his back, as if he were carrying a tall pillar, which was referred to as Alcis or Ansis or Asen in the north. Northern men honored all their forefathers or ancestors in front of such pillars.

In the end, the crumbling Roman Empire was overcome and converted by a Near East religion. Since then, Rome has become synonymous with the Catholic Church, whose origins are in ancient Israel. *Catholic* refers to an "all-encompassing" grip on the world.

The Ostrogoths reigned for a relatively short time. Were they "the rich family" mentioned in *Der Wartburgkrieg?* The name of the royal Gothic dynasty was Amaler, and their ancestors were said to be "deities" known as Ansis or Asen, the lords of the Gothic treasure, which included the Grâl. When the Ostrogoths approached Rome's walls, the citizens of the Eternal City trembled. They had been warned of the Ostrogoths' strength and of the ghastliness of their short swords. Rome fell, but it would soon triumph: At Mons Lactarius the northern men were struck a mortal blow by Byzantine forces led by the eunuch Narses.[12] The mountain known as Mons Lactarius lies at Puteoli, near Naples. I would gladly have visited Puteoli (today's Pozzuoli): Near there are the

---

[12][Narses (AD 478–572) is sometimes spelled Nerses. —*Trans.*]

Phlegraean Fields, where the Gigantomacchia—the struggle between the gods and the Titans for the domination of Olympus—was to have taken place. This conflict is probably the same that occurred between the Asen and the Wanen in the *Edda*. Puteoli also attracts me because the ruins of ancient Cumae, a Hellenic settlement, are there. Although the cult of Apollo spread from Cumae across Italy, it is probably best remembered as the place where ancient Sibyl or wise Sibilla, an Italian *pythia*, spoke her words of wisdom. Troubadours such as Wolfram von Eschenbach proclaimed her a prophetess of the Grâl and told that Sibilla dwelled inside a magical mountain.[13]

I would have looked for a hollow mountain if I had visited Pozzuoli. It is probably near Lake Avem, where the ancients believed the entrance to the underworld was located. According to Dietrich von Nieheim, a bishop at Verden at the end of the fourteenth century, many people lived in the mountain and amused themselves with diabolical desires. Perhaps among them was the veneration of the Grail?

Those who led me here, we must not forget, are the Cathars. In Lombardy, they were as numerous as the sand in the sea, and they made "heretical Lombardy glow." They were condemned by some as Manichaeans and by others as Arians. Like German heretics, they probably greeted one another with the salutation "Hail Lucifer, who was wronged! Greetings to you!"

---

[13][A *pythia* was the high priestess of the cult of Apollo at Delphi. The name derives from Pythos, "snake." This legend seems to have merged with the Italian tale of the Lady of the Lake, known as ancient Sibyl or wise Sibilla, who lived inside a hollow mountain with snakes. The grotto was accessed from the town of Norcia, in the Umbrian mountains—a place believed to be inhabited by witches. See the works by the Sicilian university professor and Capuchin missionary Giuseppe Bonomo (1923–2006) that deal with traditional legends, witchcraft, magic, and, in particular, the medieval story of Guerin Meschino. See also Antoine de la Salle, *Le Paradis de la Reine Sibylle,* a book from the 1400s. —*Trans.*]

～ ROME ～

Tannhäuser, as the people of the Middle Ages called this German knight, knelt before the pope. He had committed a great sin: Upon entering the forest to appreciate its marvels, he discovered the Venusberg. Lady Minne, who was also called Lady Saelde or Frau Holde, presided over this mountain.[14] Residing within the mountain were many heroes and singers, such as Tannhäuser, who dwelled with the goddess Lady Minne for seven years. Then doubts overcame his sense of salvation. He bade Lady Minne farewell, and began his pilgrimage to Rome. In vain she beseeched him to remain with her, because she was his salvation. When Tannhäuser tore himself loose, he did not hear the goddess call to him that he should not forget "to say good-bye to the old men."

Scores of pilgrims had trekked to Rome on bleeding feet. As the bells tolled and choirs chanted, as candles flickered and monks sang, the pope celebrated Mass in St. Peter's massive cathedral. Both the repentant and near-dead stopped and stood humbly behind a column near the entrance. Though tears ran down the pontiff's pale cheeks and his heart ached in his troubled breast, he was jubilant, because it was Christmas and thousands sang: Glory be unto God in heaven and peace on earth to those with whom he is well pleased! The pope then murmured a biblical text in Latin: Come unto me, those of you who are weary and heavy-laden, and I will give you rest.

As Tannhäuser knelt before the pope, he stammered sobbingly: "I come to you, because I am weary, and heavy-laden. Refresh me!" Holding a dry branch in his hand, the pope then spoke a ghastly curse upon the pilgrim in the dust at his feet: "You dwelled in the mountain of Venus—in hell. Be accursed! Just as the dry branch in my hand will never bloom again, in no way can you expect pardon and grace. Leave!"[15]

---

[14][Most accounts refer to the goddess as Venus. Frau or Lady Holda or Holle is a well-known figure in German folklore. Curiously, Otto Rahn doesn't mention that "the original name of Frau Holle was *perahta Holle,* which means "luminous spirit" or "luminous form." See Alain de Benoist, *Les traditions d'Europe* (Paris: Le Labyrinthe, 1982). —*Trans.*]

[15][There is an obvious allegory between the sterile dry branch and the pope's staff. —*Trans.*]

Then Tannhäuser stood up abruptly. He regretted having cried on his knees before this man, a mortal like himself. Yes, so I see Tannhäuser! Upright and strong, he stands in silence, because he feels the spirit of the German forest. Snow covers the meadows, ravens caw gently among falling snowflakes, the reddish sunset is obscured through a cloudy haze, and icicles hang on dark firs that are nearly buried by the snow. He trudges through the snow. He is not weighed down, but is instead happy because he is at home. He will never speak another word to the pope. He looks at the pope from a distance and then leaves to go north. For a long time, the pope shivers from the gaze until the Roman sun puts him at ease once again.

When Tannhäuser reentered into marriage in Frau Holde's mountain, like an old song, he blessed for eternity the sun, the moon, and his dear friends, which may have been the stars. Then he sat down with the old men whom he had foolishly left without offering any parting words. They were not angry with him, for they were wise and they had erred no less when they were young. Mistakes temper those who are of good and strong will—those who are pure. And the German fir, blessed by Tannhäuser's homecoming, wrapped itself still more deeply in Lady Minne's blanket of snow and hummed itself a lullaby. Then Tannhäuser fell asleep and dreamed about spring and the god of spring who was already on the way.

Saint and pope Gregory the Great once had a vision.[16] Although Ignatius of Loyola would introduce his Spiritual Exercises nearly a thousand years later, the pontiff described in Latin all the blessed delights of the Christian heavenly kingdom just as the Jesuits would later portray them:

When the righteous watch the unrighteous in their agonies, their joy grows. The sight of the punishment of the condemned does not tarnish the light of great purity in the spirit of the righteous; because compassion is not greater with the wretched, the joy of the blessed cannot be reduced. What wonder, then, if the sight of the agonies of

---

[16][Pope Gregory I (AD 540–604), who was later canonized, was also known as Gregorius Dialogus. —*Trans.*]

the unrighteous becomes nourishment for the joy of the righteous. As previously said, the joys of the blessed grow all the more as the misfortune of the condemned, which they escaped, increases under their very eyes![17]

The Austrian poet Lenau depicted Pope Innocent III on a quiet night in the Vatican, as he knelt before a portrait of Christ and prayed aloud after he had permitted the extermination of the Albigenses.[18] After he silenced an entire world in such a way, did silence horrify him?

> *He raised his gaze to the image of God,*
> *Whose love and tenderness frightened him.*
> *While he thinks of what he did, of the bloodthirsty way*
> *   in which he led the world,*
> *He looks intensely into the face in the image.*
> *A moth blocks the light*
> *And everything around him turns dark*
> *And silent because he poses no more questions to the*
> *   image . . .*

Suddenly flames dart around him: the flames of Provence, which he had prepared for a new caste. Those flames illuminate the cross upon the chest of his loyal followers, who swiftly carried out his orders when he declared the Albigensian crusade and who were promised eternal salvation because they were "soldiers of Christ."

> *The ruins collapse, the swords rattle,*
> *And the wild fire crackles savagely.*
> *He listens to how his name is cursed.*
> *When this horrible vision assaults him,*
> *He presses his conscience in his fist*
> *And mumbles impassively: Amen! Amen!*

---

[17][Gregory the Great. —*Trans.*]

[18][Nikolaus Lenau was the *nom de plume* of Nikolaus Franz Niembsch Edler von Strehlenau (1802–1850), Austria's chief lyrical poet. —*Trans.*]

The name of Pope Innocent III can be read as "the innocent one." No pope belongs to Lucifer's court.

As the dramatist Christian Dietrich Grabbe once wrote,[19]

Faust sat in his study on the Aventine Hill. It was night, and he searched for light. He looked toward Golgotha. Disappointed, he turned away because there was no light there. Around him there slept people who awaited their supposed salvation. "Well and good," said Faust, "they were blessed, those drowsy souls who were weak enough to be dazzled by the illumination—an illumination that took the place of light and was blindly believed, because they hoped blindly. I, however, would rather bleed than suffer such agonies! I fled to you, Rome, to accept all mankind in me, because you are the broken mirror of our most comprehensive past. Gallant depictions of heroes sparkle in the gleam of the blood of nations and in the faces of simple people—faces that appear more often in the broken pieces of this mirror the more deeply one looks into it. You are the city where thousands of years merge into a single moment—popes in the capitol and the ivy pantheon from yesterday! All realms sank before you into dust. Why? Nobody knows, because you were not better than they. By your sword you achieved everything, and by your sword you fell in night and barbarism."

How right you are, Faust. Perhaps you are more than merely a namesake of that Manichaean Faustus whom Augustine so ignobly fought. Would you rather bleed than suffer such agonies? Do so, because that is the destiny of all Germans, if we wish to achieve salvation.

Faust, I wonder what you would have said if you had been in Rome in 1536. What happened at that time could happen again today: In that year, a comet began to illuminate the Roman night sky. Out of fear, people ducked under Rome's roofs. The Holy Father consoled his worried sheep and banished the star as a demon. Yet nothing he did could make it go away, because a million cubits separated it from the

---

[19][Christian Dietrich Grabbe (1801–1836), an influential German dramatist, was strongly influenced by Shakespeare. These passages are from *Don Juan und Faust,* a drama from 1828. —*Trans.*]

Eternal City. He failed; amusedly the comet wagged its tail of light and confidently continued on its cosmic way. No doubt it was completely unaware of all the men, candles, bells, and choirs as well as the cursed displeasure of the pope. If the comet should return one day, the pope's Jesuit astronomers at the Vatican observatory will be there to observe it in a thousandfold magnification *Ad majorem Dei gloriam.*[20] They recognize now that the earth's orbit around the sun is in harmony with God. The orbit of the globe cannot be stopped—despite Rome!

Faust, you most German of Germans, let us follow Tannhäuser's example and visit those old men. We will learn more from them than from Rome, that broken mirror of a more comprehensive past. More than two thousand years ago "old men" like Heraclitus and Pytheas from Marseille knew that the earth circles around the sun. They taught that we revolve around the sun in its service! A thousand years later, another astronomer, the celebrated Claudius Ptolemy, said: "No, everything revolves around us!" Ptolemy's doctrine pleased papal Rome, which required that if each Christian did not want to fall into perdition, he or she must believe that "we are the center, and everything revolves around us!" In time, though, some wise and courageous men appeared: Galileo and Copernicus. They said: "We revolve after all!" Because of his heretical teachings, Galileo had to answer before a tribunal of the Inquisition. In 1613, as Christians in Germany were preparing the ghastly Thirty Years' War in Christ's name, a shoemaker named Jakob Böhme confided to his fellow man the secret of a crown that lies in midnight—the secret of Lucifer's crown . . .

Come, Faust, let us leave Rome. Together we will search for the the "mount of the congregation, in the sides of the north." They may be proud there, but they are not vain as those in Rome are vain. And it is better to wait for a light bringer than for a light caller or a broken mirror dripping with blood. We must traverse hell to reach the light! As Faust spoke:

It is!
I look for divinity

---

[20][To the greater glory of God. —*Trans.*]

And stand at the gates of hell. But still I can
Walk farther, plummet farther, be it also by flames. I must
    have a goal,
A final goal! There is a path to heaven,
Yet it leads through hell, at least
For me!
So mote it be, I dare it!

— Verona —

After a night on an overcrowded train, I dozed in the sun at the walls of Verona's old fortress until the early afternoon. Then, in a fresh breeze from the north, I took a refreshing dip in the waters of the Adige, a river that descends from the Tyrolean mountains, and washed off Rome's dust. Finally, I visited the beautiful city with its impressive amphitheater and several remarkable churches.

So I am in Bern, the place from which King Theodoric once ruled and attempted, in vain, to unify all Germanic peoples under his scepter. He died in Raven, which later became Ravenna. Also buried with him were the Goths. Soon after his death, Catholics saw to it that the ashes of this cursed heretic were thrown out of his tomb and scattered to the wind. Where has Dietrich von Bern's soul gone?

In the age of the Crusades, when Crusaders returned to their homelands from afar, they brought back all kinds of tales. Many had not returned directly from Palestine. From there they chose to visit other lands and seas where fire-breathing mountains made a strong impression on them. Mount Etna seems to have been the most extraordinary of these regions—even more than the volcanic area around Naples—where a Grail mountain can be found. According to Gervase of Tilbury, the chancellor of the kingdom of Arles, at Mount Etna King Arthur cured his painful wounds, which opened year after year.[21] The thirteenth-century German pilgrim Ludolf von Suchen, who also wrote a *Life of Jesus,* called Mount Etna by the name Bel Mountain and believed it was the entrance to hell. And Caesarius von Heisterbach reported that those who travel past Mount Etna in Sicily can clearly hear "how the arrival of the condemned is announced by ghostly voices commanded to fuel the fires. It is horrific to approach the area."

Arthur was not alone: An illustrious cadre surrounded him, and, as many chroniclers have claimed, among them was Theodoric the Great,

---

[21][Gervase of Tilbury (AD 1150–1228) was a lawyer, statesman, and writer. His major work, *Otia imperialia,* which is also known as *Liber de mirabilibus mundi* or *Solatia imperatoris* or *Descriptio totius orbi,* was a much read compilation of history, physics, and geography in the Middle Ages. Leibniz was not impressed, calling it "a bagful of foolish old woman's tales." —*Trans.*]

that lifelong Arian heretic also known as Dietrich von Bern. Pilgrims to Palestine and zealous monks have consigned him to a realm of volcanic fire, but courageous heroes such as Dietrich must be laughing with gusto, for they did not have the slightest fear of hell! Instead of being damned to that flaming realm, they went to it of their own free will. Newly emboldened, they must have realized that eternal damnation to hell, a place of simmering heat and icy cold, sulfurous fumes, and Beelzebub and demons armed with the cruelest instruments of torture, does not exist at all! These heroes were special men, and their legacy was not lost in the late Middle Ages, which we are told were dark. As one of them frequently said: "I would rather be on Bel Mountain with kings and princes than in heaven, where there are only evil men and pious women, the blind, and the lame!" This medieval proverb impressed me.

In the Bible, the Prophet Isaiah gladly pronounced the following curse on Lucifer and his children in the name of his ghastly Lord of Hosts: "The Bel is afflicted!" One day, I will unravel the secret of the Old Testament's Bel, the medieval Bel Mountain, and Lucibel (as the Albigenses called Lucifer), though I do not know if it will be sooner or later.

With King Arthur and Dietrich we return to *Der Wartburgkrieg*, written anonymously around the turn of the thirteenth century. It recounts a contest of Minnesingers at Wartburg, the castle of Landgrave Hermann I of Thuringia. In 1207, the year of the birth of St. Elizabeth, seven poets, including Heinrich von Ofterdingen, Walther von der Vogelweide, and Wolfram von Eschenbach, struggled with the subject of life and death in a poetic contest. In the thirteenth and fourteenth centuries, there was a constant risk of being accused of heresy, being hauled before a judge, and then being burned. As the Wartburg Minnesingers contended, the "wood chopper of Eisenach" awaited those who were defeated in order to hack off their heads. He must have been a magister of heretics. Each time one of the competing Minnesingers—especially Wolfram von Eschenbach—referred to delicate questions of faith, that Minnesinger stopped abruptly, as if frightened by his own courage. He probably had no desire to be killed by the axman.

Regarding the course of that famous lyrical clash, Wolfram von Eschenbach created such difficulties for Heinrich von Ofterdingen that

Heinrich was obliged to summon Master Clingsor from Hungary, homeland of St. Elizabeth. (Master Clingsor was said to be in league with the devil, referred to in one of the handwritten originals as Nazarus, or Nazarene.) Wolfram ultimately overcame Clingsor. In one passage, Wolfram referred to a conversation between Dietrich von Bern and Laurin, the king of the elves in bygone times. Said Laurin to Dietrich: "You have fifty years yet to live, Dietrich. While you are a strong hero, death will nevertheless overcome you. But know, my brother, that the German lands where you are at home are able to give a life of one thousand years. You need to choose a mountain which is ablaze inside. Then the people would reckon that you are similar to an earthly god!"

Answered Dietrich, "King Laurin, this I want to do and I am glad to do it. Never will my mouth proclaim it to other people." For his part, Wolfram von Eschenbach adds: "I will not betray how the Romans passed by such mountains in open hostility!"

Then Wolfram assails Clingsor in a harsh sonnet:

Master Clingsor, there was a king who is called Arthur. Can you name another king who resembles him? Continue to listen to me: Arthur lived in a mountain. His court was inhabited by noble knights who amused themselves with manly meals and pure drink. They lacked neither armor, garb, nor steed. Play actors also tarried there. From this mountain, Arthur sent champions with a glad message to Christian lands. The same message announced a bell, and as this bell began to toll, Arthur's courtiers, even the most artful, fell silent abruptly. The courtier's joy came to an end. Do you finally understand me, Master Clingsor? No? Then you cannot also know whom Arthur dispatched as a warrior to Christian lands and who rings the bell so loudly. You must guess for yourself. I can name the warrior for you, his name is . . . Lohengrin!

Lohengrin belonged to the family of the Grail King: Parzival was his father and Anfortas, who carried the crown of the Grail before them, was his great-uncle. In *Parzival*, Wolfram declares that Anfortas suffers from an incurable wound because he had courted "illicit love" and in so doing had offended the highest law of the Grâl knighthood. As ardently as he might have wished death at this point, he could not die. There was only one way to heal the ailing king: Without any knowledge of the nature of the Grâl and its secrets, a noble knight must find on his own the castle of Muntsalvaetsche and there ask the redeeming question. Parzival, Lohengrin's father, became this redeemer. The suffering of King Arthur and the suffering of Anfortas are the same! Likewise, the mountain where Arthur reigned over his circle of illustrious courtiers and the Grail Mountain are one and the same. Lohengrin sailed from this mountain to the people on his swan boat. From which direction did he come? From the west, where Montségur lies? From Bel Mountain in Sicily or the Grail mountain near Naples? From the East? Or from the "mount of the congregation, in the sides of the north"?

In the year 1183, a church council took place in Verona. Debated were the means necessary to fight the neo-Arian and neo-Manichaean heresies, and conclusions were adopted: A half millennium after his death, in the city of Dietrich von Bern, an Arian, it was decided to exterminate the Cathars to the last man or woman. Before the Goths arrived, the Lombards had already found a home on the south slopes of the Alps and on the plains of the Po. They were also Arians, who were considered heretics.

⁓ MERAN ⁓

Ahead of schedule, for only a few hours I am in Merano, as this town is now called. Nothing holds me here. The Tyrol is overrun with tourists and patients at health spas from all nations. I have seen Trauttmansdorff Castle and also the Tappeinerweg and the botanical gardens—yet these can be seen in other southern Tyrolean cities, but those parks are more beautiful and cozier. On the piazza, where some Jews were reading Hebrew newspapers, I spotted someone who was a well-known member of the German Zentrum Party and who fled when it became too hot for him to remain on German soil.[22]

In the Middle Ages, the people of Meran were once praised in a fable called *Duke of Merania*.[23] The legend recounts how Berchther, the duke of Meran who later raised the young Frankish hero Wolfdietrich, advised the lonely king Rother to marry and proposed as a suitable wife the Byzantine emperor's daughter, Princess Oda. Berchther's seven sons volunteered to journey to Constantinople to ask for Oda's hand, but the emperor cast them into a dungeon suddenly when he learned the true nature of their errand. They were rescued by the harp and sonnet of King Rother, who passed himself off as Dietrich von Bern. I will come back to this story a little later. It is clear that I will certainly not find the Claugestiân stone in Meran.[24] Legend says that old Duke Berchther, King Rother's white-haired tutor, wore it as a luminous crest on his helmet, and that "even at midnight, the stone shone bright as day." Alexander the Great had found it in a country that, he told, "never has seen a Christian person." Indeed, like Claugestiân, I will have to search for the stone elsewhere!

Among the descendants of the legendary dukes of Merania was

---

[22][Zentrum was a Catholic party that formed the nucleus of the Christian Democrats after World War II. It played a key role in helping the Nazis assume dictatorial power in the final years of the Weimar Republic: Former Zentrum member Franz von Papen arranged for Hitler to become Reichskanzler in 1933. Shortly thereafter, when the Zentrum demanded and received assurances from Hitler that he would respect Roman Catholicism, they voted with the Nazis in the Reichstag to give Adolf Hitler dictatorial power for four years in the so-called Ermächtigungsgesetz, the Enabling Act. —*Trans.*]

[23][Restored from H. A. Guerber's 1895 work *Myths and Legends of the Middle Ages*. —*Trans.*]

[24][Claugestiân stone, or *lapsis exillis*, is yet another name for the Grâl. —*Trans.*]

Gertrude von Andechs-Merania, wife of the king Andrew II of Hungary and mother of St. Elizabeth.[25] As I recently read in an essay published in a south Tyrol newspaper, "Gertrude has left a wicked legacy in Hungarian history: Because of her pride and preference for her foreign-born relatives who abused her confidence and despoiled Hungary in every way, the queen was assassinated at the age of twenty-eight. When her mother was murdered, little six-year-old Elizabeth was no longer in Hungary." Elizabeth was born in 1207, when the famous *Der Wartburgkrieg* contest took place. One of the contending Minnesingers was Master Clingsor, who was summoned from Hungary to compete in the contest. As other legends say, and as I also found in my good Catholic Tyrolean newspaper, it was Clingsor who "focused the attention of the indebted and splendor-loving Thuringian landgrave upon the recently born Hungarian king's daughter, Elizabeth."

As a consequence, a delegation from Thüringia visited the Hungarian royal court when the little princess was no more than four years old to win her hand for the landgrave's firstborn son, Hermann. In this way, at the age of four, Elizabeth became engaged to be married to the heir to the Thüringian throne. According to the customs of the period, the child arrived at the court of her future father-in-law with a fabulous treasure. A solid silver cradle and bathtub—whose weight was no less than two hundred pounds of fine silver—formed part of this fabulous dowry. Destiny soon intervened when the bridegroom, Landgrave Hermann, died. Those family members of the Thüringian court who were still hostile to the Hungarian alliance wanted to send little Elizabeth back to Hungary. If this were the case, they would also have been obliged to return the dowry, which had been squandered. As a consequence, without giving her any time to reconsider, Elizabeth was reengaged to the landgrave's second son, Ludwig. To highlight the distinguished origins of the eleven-year-old Hungarian king's daughter and because the princess was being treated like a Cinderella at the Thüringian court, Clingsor, who was still in attendance, composed the Hunnish Hungarian royal legend—the earliest lyrical poem of Hungarian prehistory.

---

[25][Gertrude of Merania (AD 1185–1213) was murdered by Hungarian noblemen who were jealous of her favoritism. Her sister Agnes of Merania, a famous beauty, married King Philippe-Auguste of France. —*Trans.*]

At fourteen, the princess was married to a bridegroom who was seven years her senior. Landgrave Ludwig led an affectionate and pious life with his little sister, as he called his wife. In fact, Ludwig was admired as a saint, although he was never canonized. The marriage of Ludwig and the princess was blessed with four children. In her nineteenth year, a unique figure entered the life of the landgravine: Grand Inquisitor Konrad von Marburg, a Dominican monk, was called the scourge of Germany by his contemporaries because of his irreproachable religiosity and severity—and he always pushed Elizabeth toward asceticism. As her personal confessor, Konrad demanded from Elizabeth absolute obedience, which included financial matters. To this end, he placed the landgravine under such strict discipline that to her relatives she soon came across as an utterly foolish woman, and her reputation soon fell into disrepute. Oddly, she insisted upon providing charity that bordered on fervid profligacy—she turned her entire paternal inheritance into money and she even gave away the proceeds from selling the silver cradle and offered her own clothes to beggars.

It is surprising that Elizabeth could somehow turn her entire inheritance, even the famous silver cradle, into money. I thought that all her dowry had been squandered by the Thuringians. No matter. Let us continue reading to the bitter end the newspaper article, which, as I noted, is not heretical. Because it is written in an incomprehensible manner, I have made some stylistic changes:

After six years of marriage, Elizabeth's husband died suddenly while en route to a Crusade. From then on, her life at the Wartburg court became pure martyrdom. Her mother and brothers-in-law persecuted her and her children. The proud Arpad [the Arpad dynasty of King Andreas, Elizabeth's father, was a branch of the first ruling family of Hungary] found accommodations in the stable of a kind-hearted farmer. When news filtered through to the Hungarian royal court that her father-in-law wanted to place her under even tighter discipline, her father decided to bring her home. Yet because she wanted to protect her firstborn son's rights to the Thuringian throne, she could not leave the country. The hard lot of the refugee princess became embarrassing to her family. It was thus agreed that a hospital should be built for Elizabeth in Marburg-am-Lahn. As its prioress, she dedicated herself from then on to the care of lepers. At the same time, she entered into the recently created Franciscan order as a tertiary and lived only for a few years, though this time was dedicated to public welfare. She was barely twenty-four years old when she exchanged this earthly vale of tears for the heavenly kingdom. During her life there were already miracles that were attributed to her. In particular, those who experienced her three rose miracles did the most to burnish her legend.

As a small child still in her father's court, she was seized by the passion of charity. In her apron she always carried the table scraps out to the beggars. Her father forbade her to come into contact with these beggars, probably in view of the contagious nature of leprosy. Despite this prohibition, however, she could not master her passion, and one day, she brought bread to the beggars. When her father noticed that she was saving something in her apron, he took her to task, whereupon the small girl invented a white lie: She said that she had roses in her apron. What's more, when she undid her apron at her father's command, through God's special grace, it was filled to the brim with roses.

The second rose miracle occurred shortly after the death of her first bridegroom. She decided at that time to dedicate the rest of her life exclusively to the memory of her divine bridegroom, and as a token of this covenant, from then on, she wore a rose garland in her hair. [The author of the newspaper article apparently did not dare to say the word *rosary*.] When her father's envoys arrived at Wartburg and told her that it was her father's wish that she should become the bride of Landgrave Ludwig, she took the rose garland from her head and threw it into the river in her distress. The roses suddenly multiplied, and soon the whole surface of the water glowed in the rosy sheen of a sea of blooms.

The third rose miracle occurred during her married life. Unselfishly, she cared for lepers, and because she could not find a sickbed for one of the ailing, she put him in her own bed. When her husband returned home, he took her to task for harboring a strange man in her bedchamber. Despite the holiest feelings of loyalty to her marriage, she was not able to utter a word. Her husband tore the cover off the bed and saw the Savior himself on the cushions in the midst of flowering roses, whereupon Ludwig knelt down before her and begged her forgiveness.

Although we know well the traditional sworn statements from the landgravine's four handmaidens (among them a Jutta or a Judith who had been with Elizabeth since the princess was five years old) confirming the veracity of these miracles, in reality they meant nothing and confirm only that the deceased had visions. It is important to repeat these famous rose miracles for any religiously inclined people, who should take them for what they are worth. Let us continue, however, with the newspaper article:

Immediately after Elizabeth's death, at her grave there occurred several healing miracles which prompted her former father-in-law—who, shortly thereafter, was slain by some members of the nobility—to urge the Roman pope to canonize his daughter-in-law. The canonization, which took place in 1235, when Elizabeth's father was still alive, helped him greatly in his constant quarrel with the Roman curia: It could not proceed with severity against the father of a saint of the Roman Church. Within that same year, there began the building of a church in her honor—the first high-Gothic cathedral in Germany. In Budapest, the Rudasbad was established in her honor and a hospital was named after her. Soon after her death, the story of her life was compiled by Konrad von Marburg, Caesarius von Heisterbach, and Dietrich von Thüringen.

Of the earthly inheritance of the Arpad princess, the only remains are a staff carved from the simple wooden bed of the saint and fashioned in gold. It is preserved in Hungary in the safe deposit of the archbishop's high church at Esztergom.

Two other staves were taken from Elizabeth's bedstead as relics, but I will tell that part of the story as soon as I am in my homeland again. St. Elizabeth is "a comfort and a treasure of the often poor Hessian land" and also is alleged to have been Tannhäuser's beloved lady.

— BOLZANO ROSE GARDEN —

I have now lived for weeks on a mountain meadow lying high up in the Dolomites. We must be at the beginning of autumn; snowflakes are gliding down, and a white blanket now covers the fragrant gentian, arnica (whose extract can bring relief to some illnesses), and alpine roses. Poised between what is below and all that is above and bounded by rising granite walls, this alpine pasture exists in its own magical world.

Hidden by the magnificent heights, my meadow may be far from the world, but it is not by any means unworldly. Although it is not bound to what is generally accepted as the world, the pasture is now very much attached to me: Reaching it requires taking a steep footpath past bold, cantilevered mountains. Foaming torrents often drench the trail, as if to hinder the union between the abysmal depths and the towering peaks. The path climbs relentlessly past precipitous walls and the torrents of a waterfall. Finally, only moss-draped silver firs obscure the view of alpine pasture. When I followed the trail for the first time, I could only guess at the altitude to which it rose because the fog, seething and cold, enveloped everything. Then I arrived up here, and I stayed.

Three times I have been as far as Bolzano, where I bought crude shoes and even cruder clothes. It takes about four hours to get there. Time and again I climbed into the ravine below the meadow, over uprooted trunks and mossy boulders and past bright red agaric mushrooms as the unbelievably steep path, made for hunters, leads from this spot. Tree trunks rise up in the middle of the lane because no storm could break them. Sunlight finds it hard to penetrate the darkness of the ravine. On days when the light does not reach the bottom, I like to climb into the dark. Quite often, I strike out on the path that leads from the meadow toward the peak. Red cranberries hide themselves in the vast stretches of heather along the way, as the path winds through a forest of dark, Swiss stone pines. Now and then, it is possible to spot the gleam of the distant snowfields of the Adamell Mountains between their tattered branches. In one place, the path curves around a water trough for livestock and thirsty forest birds. At long last, I arrive, looking toward heaven past the elongated towers of Rose Garden Peak as it stands alone, with that intangible nobility that is revealed only on the lonely summits of great mountains—a nobility of which I always wish to be part.

I will never forget this evening. I stood in front of my hut and watched the sun set. The bells of a forest chapel on another slope tolled, announcing the passing of the day. All of it was part of a dreamy life near that wonderful Rose Garden Peak, whose rock glowed red like the costliest roses. Sometimes it flamed, as if a fire burned within it and as if the fog that enveloped the peak was a smoke trail. As I watched, I thought about the old songs, which recall a miraculous event on the mountain: The dwarf king Laurin is said to have once cultivated an exquisite rose garden here, during a time when mankind was better. Wonderful aromas floated on the breeze from myriad flower cups, and thousands of birds were jubilant for the Creator's reward by day and by night. It happened, however, that wicked people kidnapped the dwarf king and took him to their city, where they forced him to perform as their juggler and jester. Soon thereafter, Laurin was able to free himself from his chains and secretly return home to his paradisal realm. To stop an unworthy intruder from again gaining entrance to his garden, Laurin spanned the path leading to it with a silk thread. A man who has strong arms may not have the strength to tear apart a spiderweb-thin thread. A man may be rich, yet he never can buy the view of Rose Garden Peak. And a man may be well read, but there is no book that can describe Laurin's wonderland. I reflected on this in front of my meadow hut.

Overhead, the night had finally come and the moon had followed, leaving its rays on the rock. The day had gone, and in my mind a beautiful song composed by Brahms presided over the cool night that had set in like death. The mountain was no longer before me. For me, the greatest of Laurin's wonders is the knowledge of day and night, which is also the understanding of life and death. Oh, how we should learn from him! People sigh and say they do not need to learn. It is still possible to gain admission to Laurin's magical kingdom despite the silk thread—but only for those who are knights or children or poets!

On the ancient Tyrolean Troj de Réses, the Rose Path, which leads from the Karer Pass through the Tierser Valley to the north, a warrior from the retinue of Dietrich von Bern is said to have once ridden. He tried in vain to find an entrance to Laurin's realm. Whenever he believed he had reached the goal, insurmountable cliffs rose up before him. Then he saw a ravine, and he descended into it. In the vicinity of a brook he heard the breathtaking songs of countless birds. He stopped and listened.

He saw a woman, who was tending lambs in a sunny meadow. Would the small birds always sing, he asked her? The woman answered that she had not heard them for a long time, but now the mill could finally be found and people could now be brought back to health. The knight asked what the mill was for, and the woman responded: It was enchanted and had stood still for many years. In former times it belonged to King Laurin and was operated by dwarfs who milled flour there and gave it to the poor. They had become possessive, however, and one of them had thrown a dwarf into the water because he didn't produce enough flour. Since then, the mill had stood still and would not move until the birds begin to sing again. The mill, deep in the ravine, was called Rose Mill because it was overgrown with rose hedges.

The knight hurried into the forest to search for the mill, and he found it. Moss ran riot on the roof, the timbered walls were blackened with age, and the wheel did not turn. The roses were so thick that anyone who did not know about it would have passed by without a glance. The knight tried in vain to open the door. The lock would not give way. Then he spotted a small window.

From the back of his horse he looked though the panes. In the miller's room seven dwarfs lay asleep. The knight called out and pounded on the door in vain. From there he rode back to the meadow and lay down to rest. The next morning, he clambered above the forest ravine, and there stood three rosebushes. The knight broke a rose from the first bush. An elf then called from the bush: "Bring me a rose from the good old time!"

"I would do it gladly," said the knight, "but how do I find it?" Grumbling, the elf disappeared. The knight walked to the second bush. He broke off a flower. Again an elf appeared, asked the same question, complained, and disappeared. When the knight broke a rose from the third bush, a third elf asked: "Why do you pound on our door?"

The knight answered, "I want to enter King Laurin's rose garden because I am searching for the May Bride!"

"Only a child or a singer may enter the rose garden. If you can recite a beautiful song, the way is open to you."

The knight responded: "That I can do!"

"So come with me," the elf said, before picking hedge roses and descending into the ravine. The knight followed him. When they reached the mill, the door sprang open by itself. The dwarfs were still sleeping. The elf stroked them with the roses and called: "Wake up, you sleepy-heads; the young roses bloom!"

The dwarfs rose and rubbed their eyes and the mill began to grind.

Then the elf directed the knight into the cellar of the mill. From there a passageway led into the mountain, ending in the brightest light. With delighted eyes, the knight looked at King Laurin's garden of Paradise with multicolored flower beds, laughing groves, and parading roses. He also saw the silk thread, which spanned everything.

"Now begin your song," said the elf.

The knight sang of love and May, and the rose Paradise opened itself unto him forever. The knight had entered eternity.

There is another, no less wondrous Tyrolean legend: A princess brought the rose of memory to her bridegroom's homeland. Questioning the essence of the rose, the bride answered that it typified the memory of a time when there was no hate and no murder and everything was beautiful and good. Centuries passed. In that time, a large garden had developed from that single rose, covering the mountain until crimson shone all over the land. In the rose garden, Laurin ruled as king. He was the bridegroom to whom the May Bride had brought the rose of memory. Finally, he locked the rose realm, but children once found a mysterious key while playing and so went into the garden. Was that key a *Dietrich?*[26]

Memory is love.

The pinnacles of Rose Garden Peak glow. The night fills the "chimneys" of the Schlern, as it does the other beautiful mountains. Snow fills the Runsen. A golden sunbeam, the last for today, shines on the slope of the Vogelweiderhof. There, Minnesinger Walther von der Vogelweide, who so gladly sang a merry Tandaradei, beheld the light of the world. As a son of the Tyrol, he surely knew the fairy tale of the rose garden, the rose mill, and the singing birds. He also knew of the importance of searching for blessed and divinely inspired love, for he sang:

> *Love is neither man nor wife,*
> *It has no soul or body;*

---

[26][*Dietrich* in German means "skeleton key."—*Ed.*]

Your essence remains to be invented.
It cannot be compared
And yet you can never reach
God's grace without it.
Into false hearts she never goes,
It only belongs to noble ones.

For Walther von der Vogelweide, love was spirit and the key to the realm of God!

Bolzano mountain climbers came to arrange a climbing tour with me. They accepted me as one of their own and remained until late into the night. I read to them from my diary and taught them some new songs of my homeland. I, however, received the greatest benefit: I have heard a popular song in Tyrol; therefore I count this dear fraternity of mountain climbers among Lucifer's courtiers:

And I once had,
So God wills it,
The last fall:
I would begin as always,
Leaving and climbing
The last mountain.
Whether ice or stone
Or some falls pain us,
We are the princes of this world
And just want to be up there!

Woe unto you mountaineers, your striving for God was cursed in Isaiah. You are rebels! You shall no longer climb the cliffs to see the glory of the world, which is far more wonderful than seeing it in musty rooms and dark churches! If you do, the Lord of Hosts will let you fall from the ice and stone, and you will plummet from the mountains into the depths. You will fall from heaven as did Lucifer, the prince of this world, who also wanted to be up high. Do you believe that Jehovah, in whose service the bells of your Tyrolean cathedrals and churches and chapels toll from the early morning to the late evening, and his gatekeeper

St. Peter, who lived on the Palestinian Sea of Galilee but never in the land of Tyrol, will allow you into heaven to be received into Abraham's fold? They abandoned you to hell! Go confidently there at any time, whether or not you have found death in the mountains, in the rose garden, where people of your kind have so gladly gone! Lucifer's courtiers, to whom you belong, are to be found there. To enter this Luciferian realm, which is not heaven, you do not need that key that represents Jehovah and Jesus Christ's governor in Rome, who sits on the holy throne occupied by Peter. To unlock the gates to Lucifer's realm, you need a Dietrich, a "skeleton key." To partake in rose magic, we must secretly unlock the gates to this wonderland. Otherwise, even the thief's key could be stolen. In lower Germany, a Dietrich is also called a Peterschen.[27] Before St. Peter and his servants, nothing is safe.

---

[27][Little Peter. —*Trans.*]

~ ON THE FREIENBÜHL ABOVE BRIXEN[28] ~

A hike for several days led me here from the Seiler mountain meadow across the Peitlerkofel by the Gabler and the Plose. I walked on the high path from the Brixen ski hut to Palmschoss, which faces the extremely wild towers of the Geisler peaks—Rigais, Furchetta, and the rest of them—and I walked on the narrow forest track along the flanks of the Plose, which drops steeply to the Aferer Valley. Now I can rest in radiant sunshine on a bank by a forest chapel whose dank interior, tasteless and cold, made me flee quickly. In older times, a sanctuary to the goddess Freyja stood in its place. Freyja means "lady" in old Norse.[29] It is a quiet day. Not a breath of wind moves the branches of the firs. A few small, milky-white cloudlets are in the sky. Dazzling white ones rise above the Ziller Valley, Stubaier, Ötz Valley, and Ortler Alps. The less high Sarn Valley Alps, close enough to grab, are sprinkled with new-fallen snow. The descendants of the Goths still live in those valleys and in their mountain meadows. In the valley under me, the sea of clouds obscures the track of the ice field wherever I look. Only now and then, a small tattering of cloud detaches itself, billowing, and passes. The silence and light are overwhelming. Here, above, there is nothing to do other than meditate and look onto the world, which is so sublime and beautiful! Also, here above I am alone with that direct dialogue that is to be had on high mountains.

---

[28]["Freienbühl" means "peak" and Brixen is also called Bressanone. —*Trans.*]

[29][Freyja was the Norse goddess of fertility, the first of the Valkyries. She rode a chariot pulled by two lion-sized cats. —*Trans.*]

— BRIXEN —

Only today, some three days after my arrival in this beautiful city, could I visit the gravestone of the Minnesinger Oswald von Wolkenstein at the cathedral with its colorfully painted cloister and old gardens. I saw also many young men in long, black frocks who will never experience the happiness of being a father. Prospective priests, they have betrayed life and its natural law. Soon they will resemble those old priests that I have just now seen going through Brixen's lanes to the Augustine cloister's new monastery. Their feet shuffled and their withered bodies gazed heavenward. One day, they all will die and someone will bury them hastily. Nobody on earth will remember them as a son remembers his father or as a grandson recalls his grandfather. The blood dies and the rose of memory withers.

Recently, I became acquainted with Count Consolati. He told me that his ancestors, who were landed gentry and Tyrolean, once bore the name Tanhausen and, in times long ago, had their ancestral seat in the fortified farmstead called Tanhausen in Cembratal.

Count Consolati is of Gothic stock and was always well aware of this: An often occurring first name in his family is Gaut. (The first Amaler, a Teutonic deity of war, was also called Gaut.) This first name was retained, but in the fourteenth century, for some nontraditional reason, the Tanhausen renamed themselves Consulati—to and from—Heiligenbronn.[30] In Italian, Heiligenbronn is translated as Fontana Santa.

That causes me to recall the Font Sant in the Sabarthès. Near these sacred springs lies a cave where the Provençal heretics solemnly celebrated their Consolamentum! All the participants in a search for solace were comforters: *consolati!*

The coat of arms of the House of Consolati contains the Norse *man* rune.[31] Until sometime around 1790, as Count Consolati explained, his ancestors, along with the counts Kunigel, Thun, Toggenburg, and Wolkenstein (the Minnesinger Oswald von Wolkenstein, born on the

---

[30][In German nobility, sometimes you are count or baron "von und zu," or from and to. —*Trans.*]

[31][A symbol of a man with outstretched arms. —*Trans.*]

Tyrolean Trostburg belonged to their clan), met twice a year, for the solstice, in the Bolzano rose garden. It was called also Laurin's garden. There they reaffirmed their blood brotherhood, which probably means that these descendants of the Goths toasted to love. To keep alive their common Gothic heritage, they conjured up thoughts and recollections— which is love—of their Gothic ancestors. To this end, they searched for the same mountain Paradise that Dietrich von Bern had once attained: Laurin's rose garden!

Along with Arianism, Manichaeanism, and Catharism, these toasts to love were a thorn in the papal eye. In a decree dated 852, Rome cursed the ancient custom as diabolical. A large piece of amber was still held in great esteem in the Consolati family. It was once an orb, though later it was reworked into a cross. All this gives me much to think about.

Early tomorrow, I leave Brixen. I am planning to wander on foot on the path over Sterzing, today to Vipiteno, then on to the Gestensitz,[32] and finally to the Colle Isarco, where anyone can see the Wolfenburg,[33] an old blacksmith's shop. Wieland once worked there. Then I will ascend the Brenner Pass.

The mountain trail I will travel is one of the ancient amber routes that lead from Venice to the Adige Valley and from there to the Brenner, over the Rosenjoch,[34] and into the Inn Valley. At Rosenheim it passes Passau and traverses up to the Friesian coast and the shores of the Eridanos. There the Elbe or the Eider, which divides Holstein from Schleswig, was a major river earlier, but today it is just a stream. The Eridanos was, as Herodotus reports around the year 450 BC, "a river which flows into the North Sea," where amber is found. Already, in the eighth century BC, Hesiod knew of this precious substance.

A second amber route led from Marseille through the Rhône Valley. At Châlons it forked. The western arm passed by Metz and Trier, skirted the Hohe Acht, crossed the Eifel Mountains, and reached the ancient city of Asciburgium (today's Asberg, near Mörs on the Rhine). Before the emergence of Cologne, this was the most important place on the

---

[32][Also known as Gossensass. —*Trans.*]
[33][Wolf Castle. —*Trans.*]
[34][Rose Yoke. —*Trans.*]

river. Beyond Westphalia, the route passed the Lüneburger heath and the land of Stedinger, ending at the Eridanos. The eastern arm of the road coming from Marseille connected Châlons with Basel and this with Frankfurt and Göttingen. Again the Eridanos was the goal. Travelers on this road saw the Black Forest; the Odenwald (where Siegfried was killed); the Feldberg in the Taunus, where you can see the rocky bed of the Valkyrie Brunhilde; the Wetterau and the Upper Hessian Vogelsberg; the Westerwald; and the Siegerland and the Rothaarebirge. All these roads crossed the Herkynischen Forest and merged at Helwegen in north Germany. Then they reached the Friesian Sea at the North Sea, in view of the island of Helgoland, which in former times was called Abalus and Balcia. Baldr was laid to rest on this island, as the old songs relate. A third great road was celebrated by those who brought the amber of the Samland Baltic Sea coast over Thorn past Aquileia, a commercial town on the Isonzo, which was the predecessor to Venice and one time was razed to the ground by King Attila the Hun. This road is the newest of the three, because in early times what is today's east Friesian and west Jutland coast, and not the Samland Baltic Sea coast, was actual amber country. On this third and newest road, the Ästhen brought "the gold of the north" to the Ostrogoth king Theodoric of Ravenna.

Tomorrow, I will travel on an amber route that leads over the Brenner and through Germany up to the North Sea, whose waves wash ashore on Helgoland, the "holy country." Greek historian Diodorus knew that Helgoland was "a day's journey removed from the mainland coast of the ocean" and reported that "[o]n this island, the waves of the sea wash up *elektron* [as the ancient Greeks called amber], which does not occur anywhere else on earth. The elektron is collected on the island and worked by its inhabitants on the mainland; from where it is brought to us." Pliny, a first-century Roman historian, states in his *Natural History* that the inhabitants of the island Abalus used amber in place of wood for the fire boat and sold it to the Teutons, their immediate neighbors. To him, amber was an "ejection of the concentrated sea" (which most likely should be understood as the muddy tidewater flats). Finally, Pytheas of Marseille visited the island of Abalus. Abalus is our holy country—Helgoland!

Amber was brought over the ancient amber routes from the North

Sea to the south: to Egypt, which knew of it in the third millennium BC, and to Greece. In the Dodonian oak grove, the highest sanctuary of Greece, it was accepted along with other gifts from the north—bear skins and honey—and was sent on to the other Hellenic sanctuaries.

The Argonauts, those Greek Vikings, inserted into the prow of their ship, the *Argo,* a plank made from the wood of a Dodonian oak in order to prevent them from dying when they heard the voice of their god. In the course of their travels, they were in close proximity to Helgoland. In his *Argonautica,* Apollonius of Rhodes, a Greek poet of the third century BC, tells how Jason and his companions reached the northern "amber" river—Eridanos—on their return from the land of the golden fleece.

Amber is very special indeed.

～ GOSSENSASS ～

Although the winter is fast approaching, the weather is so sunny and mild that I have decided to stay here a few extra days. I want to reflect back and look forward, so I have chosen a spot in the Alps to rest: a spot that separates the north from the south. The Brenner Pass, the main gate between Germany and Rome, swings on age-old hinges. Sometimes it would have been better if the gate had remained locked.

My journey has taken me from Germany to southern France, Italy, and the Tyrol. Now I am crossing the Brenner, and I will shut the gate behind me. After a few months in Geneva, I will make my way north on an amber route—the same path the last Goths took after the terrible battle near Naples, and the route taken by the Provençal troubadours after the Catholic Church destroyed their humanity and their laws of love. All are pulled toward midnight not in the east but in the north, where the light becomes truly bright.

Tannhäuser also went down this path.

As Walther von der Vogelweide, Wolfram von Eschenbach, and other Minnesingers composed their sonnets venerating love and May, the Grâl, the rose garden and the Venusberg—compositions that the people of the Middle Ages loved far more than the Latin chants and holy legends of the Church—a unique lyrical contest was organized at Wartburg Castle. While a certain Tannhäuser also took part in the competition at Wartburg, it cannot be said for certain if this Tannhäuser was the knight who honored St. Elizabeth and ultimately returned to Lady Venus in her underground realm of desire.

A Minnesinger named Tannhäuser (or Tanhuser) lived and wrote poetry between 1240 and 1270 in Vienna at the court of Frederick II, the duke of Babenberger. After the death of his patron, he frittered away everything that had been given him and led an adventurous, nomadic life. Eventually, he took up the cross, traveling as far as Palestine. His poetry belongs to the mature age of minstrel sonnets: Tannhäuser felt most comfortable with dance; he often led the round dance by playing the violin until the strings split or the fiddle bow broke.

The second Tannhäuser was that unholy knight who, tortured by doubts over the welfare of his soul, implored the goddess Venus to allow him to seek salvation. With a heavy heart, she bade him farewell. As we already know, the penitent then trekked on bleeding feet to Rome, where he threw himself before the pope (allegedly Urban IV) and pleaded for the absolution of his sins. The pope held a dry branch in his hand and declared: "Just as this dead branch will never bear roses, so you can never expect forgiveness. Be cursed!" Immediately thereafter, Tannhäuser returned to the charms of Lady Venus. Before he was received in the wondrous interior of the mountain, he again blessed the sun, moon, and his beloved friends, who were probably the stars. Only then did he enter the mountain. On the third day, however, the dry branch that the pope had held in his hands bore exquisite roses. Messengers were immediately sent throughout the land to announce the grace of heaven for the unholy knight—but to no avail. Tannhäuser remained with Frau Holde. He was blessed without Rome.

The frequent questions became louder: Could the Tannhäuser of legend be connected in some way to the Minnesinger? It has already been established beyond any doubt that there existed a poet of the thirteenth century, as his poetry denoted, with the allegorical name of Tannhäuser. Although names are more often noise and smoke, it is quite possible that a third Tannhäuser was a god!

The Bavarian chronicler Johannes Turnmair from Abenberg, better known as Johannes Aventinus, left a strange account.[35] More than half a millennium old, it reads:

> I found that the Teutons and the Goths overran Middle Eastern Asia under a king called Danheuser, or Thananses in Greek, who was venerated as a god. Wolfram von Eschenbach and several others like him appropriated the old Teutonic lords and princes, placing them in the annals of bawdy bluster, and composed poetry of bloodshed, but not caused by war, for the pleasures of women are almost never heard of, but love . . . has come to pass. In this way Danheuser came to pass. He was a great hero and warrior . . . he was venerated by the ancient Greeks, our forefathers, as a god for whom the keys of heaven were ordered and special help invoked.

---

[35][Johannes Turnmair (AD 1477–1534) was also known simply as Aventin. —*Trans.*]

I can append a second, third, and fourth alternative to Turnmair's account. The second story, which originated around 1580, argues that Tannhäuser was more in the service of Mars than Venus, and confessed to the pope his villainy in war, not his sojourn in Venusberg. The third account, which is somewhat older than the second, sees in Tannhäuser a direct successor of the twelve masters who founded the song of the Minne. The fourth asserts that a fifteenth-century master singer, who was part of "the twelve old master singers in the rose garden," contended that Tannhäuser presented himself to the twelve old masters as the fourteenth member.[36]

We tend to dismiss these reports as utter nonsense. It seems to me, however, that there is essential knowledge to be gained from them: We know nothing of a Greek or Germanic god Thananses. On the other hand, as I wrote earlier, Jordanis reported in his *History of the Goths* that a Gothic king and Amaler called Taunasis or Thanauses was venerated by the Goths as a god of his people. After his death, he departed to join those heroes "who, as if fate had triumphed, were called the Asen by the Goths." It is generally accepted that the Asen were twelve in number—they must have been the twelve masters of the rose garden— and, if we further spin the thread, the rose garden was called Asgard, the paradisal Asen garden. Tannhäuser, who wanted to become the fourteenth of the twelve masters, recalls the Amaler and Ostrogoth king Theodoric, who was the fourteenth descendant in a direct line from the Amalers. Further, perhaps the ancestors of the Tyrolean count Consolati originally bore the old name Tanhausen in memory of the king and god Thanauses. Perhaps.

If the Tannhäuser of Aventinus, who reached the rose garden, had been a king, he was later considered a god. His divine status was confirmed when he was received into the rose garden and the keys of heaven were given to him. The god of the rose garden could not have been the God of the Bible, and the keys of heaven—to the rose garden—can only be that Dietrich which, in Lower Saxony, is called Peterken, little Peter!

The information reported by Aventinus seems no less significant and

---

[36][The number 13 was not used because it was commonly regarded as bad luck. —*Trans.*]

by no means unreasonable as far as the words of the Minnesingers are concerned. Aventinus asserts that they "appropriated the old Teutonic lords and princes, placing them in the annals of bawdy bluster . . ." I agree with him: Originally, the Minne did not have anything to do with love and constant courting. *Minne* means "memories." And if the true sonnets were like those composed in praise of Germanic nobles, they could render the last honors to a deceased king, prince, or freeman by singing as they rode around the burial mound, just like those Gothic knights who buried and then praised Attila, the deceased king of the Huns.

In *Der Wartburgkrieg*, Clingsor from Ungerlant, or Hungary, the homeland of St. Elizabeth, competed with Wolfram von Eschenbach. (It is undecided whether Aventinus rightfully slandered him.) At Wartburg, Wolfram, who was described as a wise amateur, did not summon the swan knight Lohengrin from the Grail Mountain known as Montsalvat. Instead, Lohengrin came from those mountains where King Arthur lived with his courtiers. Located there is an Aget stone that once fell from Lucifer's crown.[37] This stone (the Middle German word for "amber" or "magnet") and the Grail stone must be one and the same, just as the figures of Arthur and Anfortas are the same: a suffering king and the guardian of a holy stone. As the fifteenth-century *Halberstädt Saxonia* chronicle relates, Lohengrin came from the mountain where Lady Venus resided in the Grail, and as a chronicler from the same period related, this was false. Further told was that there was once a king who gave his people happiness. The Grail was once Paradise, but became an unrighteous place. Yes! The mountain of the Holy Grail was degraded to the hellish Venusberg.

What the Teutons revered as the dwelling place of Asgard and the realm of the dead goddess Hel in the pagan era became, for heretics and Minnesingers in the Middle Ages, the Grail Mountain, the rose garden, Arthur's Round Table, Venus Mountain, and Dietrich's fiery Bel Mount—and this place, to use Wolfram von Eschenbach's language, was "the highest prize of earth's desire." In addition, what the ancient Greeks

---

[37][This crown is referred to as the Crown of Righteousness in *Der Wartburgkrieg*. —Trans.]

understood to be the sunny island of Aea that was long sought by the Argonauts and Hercules was nothing other than the Hellenistic image of the northern Asgard. Later, this became the model for the medieval Grail Paradise, Arthur's Round Table, the rose garden, and Venus Mountain. Their prototype was the "mount of the congregation, in the sides of the north," as Isaiah calls it. To reach this mountain, Lucifer, that Apollyon of the New Testament, wished to pass over the highest clouds. Instead, Jehovah cast him to the bottom of the deepest pit; for this Jewish God of intolerance, the paradisal Asgard had become a place for the damned: hell. In late medieval Germany, when someone was hanged, care was taken to see that the face of the hanged looked to the north—to hell.

I am crossing the Brenner Pass on an amber route and heading north. As Laurin, the king of the rose garden, entrusted Dietrich von Bern with the secret of Fire Mountain, he had also indicated the path to reach it: a "well cleared road." By that he could have meant one of the age-old amber routes:

> . . . So said all the people, we traveled
> In great heat. I will warn you:
> There we become relished earthly gods
> The Bernese spoke: "is now your affair also,
> It may happen.
> I am happy with it,
> My mountain that men never shall lose."

~ GENEVA ~

From here, Calvinism went out into the world with a messianic goal: the conquest of the world for Christ. It did not and will never achieve this. This Christianization of the world did not stop at anything—even murder. John Calvin, the fanatical and somber founder of Calvinism, had Michel Servet, the man who discovered the principles of our circulatory system, burned alive because he did not accept Christian Trinity teachings.

Today in Geneva, delegations from all over the world gather at the League of Nations, or the Société des Nations. The Genevans have found another name for it: the Société des Passions (the League of Passions). There, many nations and nearly all races from Europe and the world are represented—to create even more disorder. For the assemblies there was built an imposing palace where the Jewish representatives of Soviet Russia speak loudly or smile quietly.[38] A few previously unemployed Germans were allowed to earn a few francs when they built it. The wages were handed over to them directly so they could eat. The fifty *centimes* a day failed to pay for a bed in the dormitories of the Salvation Army, so only the homeless shelter remained open to them. Today, all these Germans have plentiful bread and a good bed—at home.

The palace of the League of Nations, with its garish whiteness and enormous dimensions that so brutally invade the graceful Geneva landscape between Jura, Salève, and the Voirons, stands in the middle of a large park of which the Genevans were at one time rightly proud, and whose loss of tranquillity they regret. The park is called the Ariana. The name Ariana has within it a power that intertwines fate with the history of the world: Ariana is the ancient name of Iran. Ariana was born in the land of the Parsi in memory of an ancient Aryan land created by a god of light. The sacred writings of the Iranian Aryans state that one day, the light god arose as the "serpent of winter," and out of the light of Paradise, where humans were prosperous and where they always

---

[38][Prominent among the representatives of Soviet Russia at the League of Nations was Maxim Litvinov (1876–1951), who was born Jewish as Meir Wallach Finkelstein. As the ambassador to the league in Geneva (1934–1938), Litvinov was closely identified with Stalin's anti-German policies prior to the Molotov-Ribbentrop Pact in 1939. —*Trans.*]

looked upon the godhead, a land had become "cold for the water, cold for the earth, cold for the plant world." In that place there were now "ten months of winter and two months of summer." (Thus this god rules the arctic climate.) The Aryan people came from Ariana. In spirit, we must always think of this country because its memory confers Aryan strength. The Aryan Indians also knew of this light surrounding their ancient homeland of Uttarakuru: the island of radiances on the White Sea or Milk Sea; the "godly Aryan land." They taught: "Be your own light, work acts, become wise, become louder, and you will arrive in the godly Aryan land!" Oh, Geneva park called Ariana! Oh, League of Nations!

Palm Sunday. The ringing of Calvinist and papist bells assaulted the morning. I thought of that treasure which was guarded by serpents at Montségur in the Pyrenean Tabor Forest. Only on this day, during Mass, could it be raised.

The landlady of my room, a native of Vienna, means well. Not only is she incessantly anxious about my love life, but she is also concerned for my salvation. She gave me a frightened look when, on the first day, I asked her to remove from my room all the plaster saints and nauseating prints depicting Christ with a bleeding heart. Since then my landlady prays all morning in church for the welfare of my soul—or so she told me after she brewed a splendid coffee and had thoughtfully kept it warm for me. Therefore, I was hardly surprised when she brought into the room one of her priest-blessed palm fronds. It will certainly keep away misfortune and pain for all of the coming year. I was not able to reject the gift. Now the magic branch lies on my desk beside two paperweights: a piece of the frieze from the temple at Delphi and a stone from Montségur Castle. That castle was condemned to death on Palm Sunday eve. On Palm Sunday morning, the flames blazed and the bodies of more than two hundred heretics were incinerated. Instead of bells, the executioner in a monk's cassock sang a chant: *Veni Creator Spiritus* . . .

It is shortly before noon. Under my window, people are getting ready for lunch on the promenade, rolling up in elegant cars, laughing and joking. A nearby coffeehouse orchestra plays Handel's *O Daughter Zion, Rejoice!* On the lake a paddle steamer sails off to the Savoy coast and sailboats propel out to Grand Lac. I also observe Mont Blanc. It rises up proudly, as if conscious of being Europe's roof. The coffeehouse music still has Jerusalem cheering loudly the arrival of its king. Better to shut the window and put on a record that I have loved since the first time I heard it. Only a few know the song that I myself cannot hear often enough because it is truly beautiful. The words are in French:

> *Land where I was born,*
> *poor and naked land,*
> *Your ground is stony*
> *and your fields ungrateful.*
> *When I lead*
> *my old plow through it,*
> *I feel your soft heart beating in my arms.*
> *With you: It is my country!*
> *Land where I was born,*
> *poor and naked land,*
> *Your dark forests*
> *cry in the wind.*

In a foreign country, and curiously through a French-Italian song, my fatherland has suddenly become so close, closer than it has been ever before. I can hear those dark forests crying in the wind. Those who have never experienced a misty forest in November do not know that the forest can cry. When the damp cold pervades it, the forest is like an old grandparent whose grandchildren, the leaves, are blown away and whose sons, the trees, are uprooted by the gusty winds. They do not know that the forest air, which is praised in song, contains a disturbing tragedy. They also cannot know that ancestral forests are at their most endearing and most communicative when they emit a loud groan from pain.

What I am now feeling is called homesickness; in view of Mont Blanc, I am thinking of Germany, Faust, and the poet Christian Dietrich Grabbe—his devilish character Mephistopheles built a magic castle on Mont Blanc. Faust, that most German of Germans, had a "tear on his eyelash, when he thought of Germany." Through them, the memory of Germany came back to haunt me—and the most beautiful feeling a homeland can offer in foreign lands is that of homesickness that arises as soon as a traveler thinks of her. When abroad someplace, I once heard a radio play a song a German soldier wrote for young Germans. A soldier says to his captain upon returning to the trenches from furlough: "The farther one travels from Germany, the more near it is." This apparent contradiction contains a deep wisdom, perhaps essential knowledge about Germany and the German spirit.

Germany's autumn is evoked on Palm Sunday in my small room in Geneva. The dark forests cry. The November wind hums in the wires and poles that cross the country along prominent highways. I see and also hear a late apple from the tree falling to the side of the road. Perhaps the apple would also like to cry because a worm is eating away at it—but it doesn't do so. It falls quietly, and so, with its fate nearly fulfilled, it needs only to decay to live again, provided its seed revives. If this fails, the apple will help life by revitalizing the earth nearby and aiding healthy, natural germination in other plants. My little Empire pendulum desk clock, which I brought along, strikes twelve times with its ting-ting. The witching hour has come, for the spirit spoke to our ancestors and Tiubel the devil appeared to people only around noontime, or so they believed in the late Middle Ages. A knight named Heinrich von Falkenstein saw the devil once around noon, because a warlock had advised him that he would appear at this time. Tiubel came out from the forest "in a howling wind and cracking of the trees," as the chronicler Caesarius von Heisterbach reported. Tiubel is Lucibel: our Lucifer, to whom injustice occurred. Midday magic . . .

Lucifer came from the German forest into my room. I cannot see him, but I can feel his presence. It can be only Lucifer who lifts the piece of temple frieze from my desk. Columns grow under it and the other rubble conforms to it as a roof. Apollo's Delphi stands suddenly in virginal beauty before me, and, through the sacred darkness of the olive trees and laurel bushes, I gaze at the sentence: "Know yourself!" It can be only Lucifer who picked out that inconspicuous stone from the rubble of Montségur Castle. It was a piece left from a stone bench railing. I see the bench clearly. Laurel bushes cast shade upon it. A man sits there, blond and noble. He wears a black tunic. A cap, like a beret, covers his head. The man, a Cathar, looks at me and speaks: "Greetings to you, Lucibel, to whom injustice occurred!"

It can be only Lucifer who relegated the palm frond to the tree of its origin in an Eastern city. The frond stands for Jerusalem, where Jewish scholars argue among themselves whether or not they should take literally King David's adulterous and murderous ways, of which their sacred writings tell. There is noise and people pass by. They call loudly: "Hosannah to the son of David!" Now I see a man riding on a donkey. He is the one whom the crowd acclaims. His face cannot be seen because, as if bent over by weakness, he keeps his head lowered. He does not ride into the City of David for a coronation. He is approaching a violent death at a place of execution. Doesn't he secretly harbor the desire that this bitter destiny awaiting him will pass him by? He is not a hero and did not wish to become one upon the fulfillment of the scriptures. He storms about like a passionate Middle Easterner who can be found in every play. Therefore, this is actually a play, with various cries and many gestures. Someone from the crowd tears my palm branch from me and throws it to the king of the Jews, who sits on the back of a donkey and looks at the ground. A man leading the donkey by the halter waves the branch and hands it to the sorrowful king. The king takes it and does not look up. Midday magic . . .

A dazzling white highway lies before me. I know it. It connects the cities of Toulouse and Castelnaudary in the Languedoc. Isn't somebody speaking to me? I recognize him now because I saw him once in a miniature figurine. It is the troubadour Peire Vidal. He speaks ardently and with sacred fire in his bright eyes: "I believe that I just saw God on this road! He came riding like a knight, beautiful and strong. His blond hair fell around his bronzed face and his bright eyes shone. One shoe was decorated with sapphires and emeralds, though the other foot was naked. His coat was studded with violets and roses, and on his head he wore a wreath of marigolds. He rode a wonderful horse, like no horse I had seen before: One half of the beast was as black as the night and the other half was as white as ivory. A gemstone on the reins shone like the sun. Yet I did not know that this knight was God. I also did not know his escort: the lady, the damsel, and the paladin were unlike any I had seen. Then I listened, entranced, as the knight and the lady sang a new song and the birds joined them with chirping. When the song had ended, the lady told the knight that she wanted to rest, but in a spring meadow because she does not like the castle! The knight then showed her a lush place under a laurel tree, beside which a spring gushed over stones. Then the knight spoke to me: 'Friend Vidal, know this: I am Amor, the lady is called Grace, the damsel is Modesty, and the paladin is named Loyalty.' So it was: I saw God, and the god Amor is the Minne." I answered, "Peire Vidal, you have met Lucifer, whom you call Lucibel!"

I am alone. Despite the closed window, there enters a new song for today. Actually, it is a song to be sung under African palms. Between the stone from Athens and the stone from Montségur lies the palm branch. If it was an oak branch or a bundle of laurel, I would leave it. I close it away to end its spell.

Today I received the bitter message from Carcassonne that my dear friend Countess P. has died. She passed away in her sleep. Is there something similar between the homeland and the people we truly love? The farther away people are, the closer they are to our spirit. And when these people begin the passage to eternity, they come nearer to us than ever before: Suddenly, we carry them within. In memory we grow only more aware of the dearly departed.

With great intimacy I recall the aged woman. As she recently wrote, she had a workroom furnished for me in a side wing of her house, where I often stayed as a guest. In it she had placed her most valuable books and even a grand piano, so I could play for her as in the Sabarthès. Yes, they were unforgettable evenings we spent together a year ago in Ornolac. During the day, I was in the caves. Well advanced in years and handicapped, she could no longer accompany me. When I returned in the evening, she waited for me at the guesthouse. In my converted darkroom in the cellar she helped me with the process of developing the photographs I had taken during the day. Then I told her what I had seen and found, and then I began to play the piano. Once, I improvised Handel's suite *Gods Go Begging*. It was night outside. The wild waters of the Ariège sang their constant song and a nightingale flapped. I played on. When I ended, the cicadas had awakened the valley to a bewitched night as only the Sabarthès can conjure it. Thousands of owls had flown out of hundreds of caves and grottoes on their ghostly flight, their haunting sounds filling the sparse area between the cliffs and gorges. My elderly friend spoke:

"Do you hear it, *mon ami*, how the souls of my ancestors sound? Rome and its heaven should hear them! First, Caesar murdered them. Later, the Franks invaded our country and tried to exterminate them on behalf of Rome, which hated the Goths, whose Nordic blood had united with the Nordic blood of my Celtic and Hellenic ancestors. One day, the pilgrims of the Albigensian crusade slaughtered those who were in their way. They did it for Rome. Then came the Inquisition. It tortured and burned those who were not of its faith, because it was in the service of Rome. Finally, the Huguenots were persecuted and annihilated, because Rome could not tolerate them. Now we are Roman Catholic and a part of France, which claims to be Rome's eldest daughter. My ancestors cry aloud. Listen to them! I am an old woman and my days are numbered. I did what I could to help rationalize and recognize my ancestors and their divinity of light. Will you promise me to continue the work when I no longer exist? You, a German, can do it, because we are of similar blood! Will you promise me that?"

I promised that, and I will hold to my promise.

Another time, we were staying at Montségur. We had left the car where the highway descends to the hamlet and had gone to the Camp des Cremats, the Field of Flames. Chard was growing there. In silence we looked up to the castle, which had been recently abandoned by the bathhouse-works engineer and the treasure seeker. The funds of that "secret society" had run out quickly. Finally, I had to tell the countess of my German fatherland. I did it with fervency. I spoke of Hölderlin, the German poet who, poor and hounded, once stayed in southern France. While writing to his beloved Diotima, he was struck out of the blue by Apollo! I felt consoled as I thought of Hölderlin. Shall the spirits of the dead Cathars, who were burned on this field of fire by Roman priests and monks, confidently await their judgment day? In particular, I repeated the verses Hölderlin's Empedocles hurled in the face of a wicked priest before, in order to die, he scaled Aetna, called Mount Bel in the Middle Ages. Empedocles took as a model Dietrich von Bern's path to the afterlife. He loathed the despicable priests:

> *. . . For a long time it was a puzzle to me,*
> *how nature abides with you in your turn.*

And when I was yet a boy, my pious heart could avoid the
complete corruption, while incorruptible intimate love
*   hung on sun*
and ethers as messengers of all great, long-avenged nature;
because I probably have felt in my fear that the heart's
*   free*
love of God would like to talk it over to common service
*   and that I*
should force it so as it. Away!I cannot see the man before
*   me,*
the divine impelled like an industry, his face is false and
*   cold and*
as dead as his Gods. What stand for it affected
Pray now!

With intimacy I think of the deceased. And the little Empire pendulum desk clock, which she gave me, ticks away quietly, marking the time.

⁓ On a Southern German Roadside ⁓

It is summer and I am again on German soil, wandering on German roads and sleeping under German roofs. My soul echoes with *Tandaradei* by Walther von der Vogelweide. I will spend tonight in Tübingen, where Hölderlin lived, suffered, and wrote poetry. The people there honored him with a gate. But he struck Apollo. . . !

Sitting in the shade of an apple tree, I have to squint through its branches and twigs at the sky. Bees, wasps, and mosquitoes buzz and crickets chirp. A lark rises jubilantly in the light. Now I take pen and paper from my backpack. Who chides my writing? I must do it, because only I can speak my language. Who thinks ill of me because I compose? I must do it, because the urge to write poetry wells up within me.

One after another, the spirits of those of the twelfth and thirteenth centuries file past me on the road. "What is your name?" I ask a man. He is no longer young. His hair is gray and his cheeks are pale. He wears a long, black tunic, dusty and frayed at the seams, but his step is springy.

"I am Bertrand from the land of Foix," he says.

"Where are you going?"

"To the Rhine and beyond," he answers simply.

"Are you a heretic?"

"I am one," he says.

The man then looks at me. I ask him, "Are you fleeing from someone?"

"I am a faydit and must flee the Roman Catholics."

I offer, "I know your homeland."

He says, "Perhaps, but you don't know it as I do."

The man continues to speak to me in my language: "I was a knight! You once drove past the ruins of my castle without looking up because you were reading a book. You should read less and look and listen more! My castle stood near Foix on a hill in view of Montségur. While I was afar, my brother and his wife and children were burned in the Inquisition. I celebrated the winter solstice on the heights of Ornolac, near that underground church that you saw in the Pyrenees, at Mount Lujat on the Pathway of the Cathars. We call this celebration Nadal, Christmas."

I stop him and ask: "Have you commemorated in devotion and celebration the birth of the Jesus of Nazareth?"

"No! The birth of the redeeming sun! Some of us called him Christ, as the pre-Christian Greeks already referred to him. Jesus is not Christ; he was a Jewish sectarian whose disciples proclaimed him the sunlike savior only after his death. The early Christian bishop Melito could rightfully say that the teachings of Christ are not a revealed religion, but rather a philosophy that was at first avowed only by the barbarians. Only under the Roman emperor did it begin to spread in a modified form, developing in lockstep with the growth of the Roman Empire."

I then asked, "In other words, both Jerusalem and Rome acquired the teachings of Christ and changed them for their own purposes?"

"Yes, but the teachings of the earthly life and death upon the cross of Jesus Christ are contrary to God."

"Why are they contrary to God?"

"It is contrary to God to visualize divinity as a man."

"What is God?"

"God is spirit and light and strength."

"Is there also an Antigod?"

"Yes. It is weakness, which shows in humans as falsehood and doubt. It is also the spirit of lawlessness and destruction."

"If that is so, isn't Lucifer, whom you call Lucibel, the devil?"

"Lucifer is nature as you see it in you, around you, and above you. He has a dual appearance: He is the earth of darkness and the vitalizing light of heaven."

"Is Lucifer your God?"

"Why do you speak of the divinity as masculine? Your designation of God betrays your conception of the personification of God. My German contemporaries designate divinity with a neutral gender. Biblical ideas have taken root within you, whether you want to admit it or not!"

"So, is Lucifer your divinity or not?"

"No, he is an intermediary."

"Do strong people require an intermediary?"

"Yes!—but not as an intermediary who redeems. Instead, those who are strong need one that precedes them, giving an example and model. Lucifer is also the sun, which you need in order to live. You also need it when your time comes to die."

"Why?" I asked, although I suspected the answer.

"In the winter, the sun dies and in spring, it arises anew. It brings the light of life and certainty, which are the opposite of doubt."

"The certainty of rebirth?"

"Yes, if you want to call it that. Perhaps it is better to speak of victory over life, of immortality."

"Are humans immortal?"

"You have to find the answer for yourself. Look around you!"

The trunk of the apple tree where I sit is old and rotten. One day it will decay; however, it can still sprout blooms. These are then fertilized and grow into fruit. Then the fruit drops to the ground and subsequently arises into new trees. I see the man before me. He is no longer young. I ask: "Are you a father?"

"I was. My four children were burned at Toulouse in an auto-da-fé. Disguised, I stood in the midst of those people who justified and excused their own atrocities with passages from the Old Testament and stressed the right faith while my children died."

"How will you live on after your death?"

"By example, for despite everything, I remained strong and proud up to the last breath, and thus I fulfilled the law . . ."

"Of which law do you speak?"

"You have to find the answer for yourself. Look above you!"

I look up and am dazzled by the sun. Nonetheless, I recognize what he means: Every evening, the sun must leave so that each morning it can rise again above the horizon. Annually, it sinks only to rise again on its prescribed daily course. The sun gives life to the earth and light to other stars. Magnanimously and chivalrously, it allows larger and brighter suns, which only appear smaller, the right to work in their own way. It is strong because it triumphs over the dark clouds, the black night, and the dead of winter. It is proud because it gives the light of the day and of the year.

"Look within you!" the man says. I can hear within myself two voices arguing with one another. "Be silent and still," says the first to the second. "You are the affirmation of life and trust, the puzzle of life, the world, things! What is life? Strife and work, illness and death. What is this world? A cornucopia of misery, a valley of tears, a struggle of passions. What are things? From the beginning, they are imperfect, fleeting, and mutable material. Even the star where you are living and feasting will one day no longer be. It also awaits its end. Nothing that you can grasp with your senses is changeless or godly, because God is eternal. There is only one certainty: death. On this rock you shall build your temple!"

The second voice answers: "Yes, I am! Yes, I will remain strong, proud, and courageous! It did not create the world, all visible things, and myself. Of this I am certain—and this certainty makes everything sacred for me: the stars, the earth, the elements, and above all, where the divinity of the world has allowed me to behold the light, my land, and my kin. As life has given me divinity, on that life I build. I am who I am. But I would be not be so without kin if it were not for my homeland, and there would not be a homeland if it were not divine."

The first voice counters, "Divinity does not have any more to do with your home than with the land of every other person, because before divinity all individuals and all peoples are alike!" The second voice is silent. The gray man speaks to me.

"My homeland is no more. It was transformed into a heap of rubble at the pope's behest to make way for a new caste. We were exterminated because we did not recognize Yahweh, Moses, and the Prophets. We did not pray to Jehovah because this divinity was a God for the Jews and hasn't any relevance for us. Only the Jews have the arrogance to proclaim themselves divine as God's chosen people. Who is Jehovah other than a reflection of the soul of the B'nai Israel, presumptuous, intolerant, disturbed, greedy for power, and ignoble? The soul of my people was different. Our God was light and brightness and nobility. It was we as people who were imperfect."

"Why do you refer to as *perfect* those heretics who received the Consolamentum? Why do you call them *pure ones?* Is it not also presumptuous to call yourself perfect or pure?"

"We called ourselves thus in opposition to Rome, which considers all people, even those of the same blood, spoiled and impure. As grandchildren of our ancestors, the Greeks and the Goths, we felt noble but not transient or separated from God, not spoiled and godless! We didn't need Rome's God, because we had our own. We had no need for the commandments of Moses, because we carried in our breasts the legacy of our ancestors. It is Moses who was imperfect and impure, otherwise he would never have taken a Moor for his wife,[39] reprimanded his siblings, and let his God strike them with leprosy. It was Moses and his tribe who imposed upon us their faith, writings, and laws; it is they who are imperfect and impure, the souls of slaves and bastards. We are a people of Nordic blood who call ourselves Cathars, just as an Oriental people of Nordic blood called themselves Farsi: 'pure ones.' You can understand me, or is your blood also impure?"

"Farsi . . . ?"

"Yes! The Farsi, the ancient Aryans, and we, the Cathars, have not betrayed our blood. This is the secret link for which you are searching and searching. If you reflect upon Parzival, then you should know from now on that this name represents an Iranian word. That word means 'pure flower.' And if you look for the Grail, then you are looking for the holy stone—the *ghral* of the Farsi. The Grail only summons, which those in heaven know and so you read in Wolfram von Eschenbach's works. Our heaven is not Jerusalem's or Rome's Paradise. Our heaven speaks only to the pure ones, not to base or mixed-raced creatures—but to Aryans, the noble and lordly!"

I look up. I am alone.

I can hear singing growing nearer and nearer. It is the singing of young men's voices. A scout patrol of German youth hikes nearby on the highway. We call out glad tidings to one another, then we camp together under the flowering tree and sing a new German song:

> *If one of us becomes tired,*
> *The others are awake for him.*
> *If one of us wants to doubt,*
> *The others who believe laugh.*
> *If one of us is to fall,*
> *The others stand for two,*
> *Because each fighter is a God,*
> *The comrades together.*

---

[39][In the scheme of things in 1930s Nazi Germany, race mixing was frowned upon, to say the least. It is part of the Zeitgeist of that time. —*Trans.*]

― WORMS ―

I stood on the bridge over the Rhine. The old angular towers of the cathedral rose through the haze above the city. In the west lay the Donnersberg,[40] once holy to the Nordic god Donar-Thor, and in the east, under hanging clouds, the beautiful Odenwald, where once Odin's forest could be seen. I could even recognize the vineyards along the mountain route and the castles of Auerbach, Heppenheim, and Weinheim. Somewhere there must have been the village where Hagen killed Siegfried:

> *When you look for the wells where Siegfried was killed,*
> *You shall be the right patron as well to still hear me say:*
> *There before the Odenwalde lies a village Odenhain;*
> *The well still flows there—there can be no doubt.*

Between the Odenwald and the Rhine, I saw the spire of a church tower rising up over the treetops of a large forest. It belongs to the village of Lorsch, famous for its monastery ruins. Today, these include a memorial site for the dead of the world war. There may be more magnificent and more impressive cemeteries commemorating Germany's heroes, but only with difficulty can I imagine one more worthy:

> *Here Lady Krimhilde was buried—she wanted thus to have it—*
> *The dead Lord Siegfried for the second time:*
> *At Lärse near Muenster with great splendor and honor:*
> *There in a long casket lies the hero, so bold and sublime.*

A rose garden may have been planted at Lorsch, whose old name was Laurisham, to recall that great rose garden from the thirteenth century: King Gibich of Worms wanted a fairy-tale Paradise on earth, a rose garden a mile long and a half mile wide. Just like Laurin's Tyrolean garden, this one was also enclosed with a fine silk thread. It was guarded by twelve heroes of the Rhine, one of whom was Siegfried. Krimhilde, Gibich's daughter and Siegfried's betrothed, had heard many wonders from Dietrich von Bern. She invited him along with the other twelve

---

[40][Thunder Mountain. —*Trans.*]

to come to the Rhine so that he and his fellow compatriots could compete in contests with her warriors. The victor would receive a wreath of roses and a kiss from her. Dietrich accepted the invitation. Eleven Bernese triumphed. In the end, Dietrich fought Siegfried, and Dietrich's sword glanced off Siegfried's calloused skin. Then, Dietrich bristled with anger and flames shot out from his mouth, as if he were the devil. Siegfried sank defeated in the lap of Krimhilde, who quickly threw a protective veil over him. Dietrich and his heroes received their wreath of roses and a kiss.

This wreath of roses could not have been the Church's rosary, that chain of beads that aids in meditation during prayer. In pre-Christian times, the wreath was hung merrily on the May tree and from houses for the prize of songs. A clergyman from the village of Elysacia (today Elz) in the diocese of Trier did just this in the thirteenth century, when the Cistercian monk Caesarius von Heisterbach lived and wrote his chronicles: The clergyman had won a wreath of roses in Reigen as a victory prize and hung it from his house. "Thereby the people amused themselves and performed dances there." Then one day, he sat in the tavern, drinking some wine, when a terrible riot abruptly arose there. With his sacristan, who had also drunk a jigger, he hurried into the church in order to ring the bell. Both of the men arrived in the church, and both were struck down by a terrible impact—so strong that the sacristan found himself beneath the clergyman. Although the sacristan was unharmed, the priest was dead. He was punished with death by heaven because he had hung a wreath of roses and danced in a round dance—or so the chronicler believed.

Instead of the wreath of roses, a ram or a buck was often the prize. As Caesarius tells it, in Hertene (today, Kirchherten in Niederrhein) a ram festooned with silk bands was solemnly issued, and a barker requested the people of the land to dance around him. The ram was to go to the best dancer. The round dance began to musical accompaniment. At the same time there was a violent thunderstorm over Hertene, which disrupted the festivity. Another chronicler of the thirteenth century, the bishop Oliver von Paderborn, reported that such dancers would have bowed humbly before the ram. That must be regarded as heresy. As it was stated, a leading sin of the Cathars had been the "diabolical admiration of the buck."

The buck and rose were sacred to the god Donar-Thor. I must ask, is Thor the brother of King Laurin, who spanned his Tyrolean rose garden with a silk thread to stop all unworthy intruders? If Thor is Laurin's brother, who was at home in those German lands, which gave a life that lasted a thousand years, did he travel a clear road to a fiery mountain? According to Wolfram von Eschenbach, Laurin said to King Dietrich von Bern: "You still have fifty years to live, and you would also like to be a strong hero. Nevertheless, death will overcome you. Yet know that my brother at home in German lands is able to give a thousand-year life. You need only choose a mountain that is ablaze inside. Then you will be akin to earthly gods!" Lorsch's old name is Laurisham. Perhaps Laurin also maintained a rose garden here. The monastery of Lorsch lies on a sand hill. As Wolfram von Eschenbach said, it very well could be that the Romans (read the papists) were "driven against this mountain" to be able to cultivate a rose garden with a cloister annex. Question after question, mystery after mystery.

~ MICHELSTADT IN THE ODENWALD ~

My mother brought me into the world in this small town. Her ancestors are all buried here. As a child, I felt a deep love for this beautiful piece of ground. When my parents, who were at that time living in Bingen on the Rhine, began to prepare for our summer stay in Michelstadt, my questions started: Was it really true that the spring where the hags of Tronje killed Siegfried is surrounded by linden trees like the one shown me the previous year? As reported to me in Hessen by a much read children's book, should I believe that the last priest of Odin lived in the Odenwald, near the house in the grove where a megalithic stone seat can still be seen today? Was the ancient basilica at Michelstadt's gates built out of defiance for this priest by Emperor Karl's daughter Emma and the priest's historical writer, Eginhard? During the holidays, there were new and mysterious things to see again and again: a dreamy forest lake reflecting Mespelbrunn Castle; the wooded forest that hides Roman castellets;[41] the hunting lodge Eulbach, with its splendid animal park full of red deer and wild boars; and the suit of armor of the Swedish king Gustavus Adolphus in the collection at Erbach.

One time, we drove over the mountains that separate Hesse from Bavaria to the Engelberg cloister on the Main. It was a day for pilgrims: On their knees they shuffled up the many hundred stairs to the mountain church and prayed together. Already by that time, I couldn't understand the sense of such an exercise. We returned to Upper Amorbach from Michelstadt. I sat next to the coachman. I will make the same journey the day after tomorrow, for near Amorbach, which I did not see when I was a boy, lies the castle of Wildenberg,[42] also known as the Grail Castle in the Odenwald. Here Wolfram von Eschenbach, as the guest of a knight from Durne, wrote parts of his *Parzival*. Some even suggest that this castle was the model for Munsalvat, Wolfram's Grail Castle.

Thus I was under the spell of the Grail when I came into this world. Parzival and Siegfried and Odin and Wotan were my godfathers. It is late at night. I hear trees murmuring and wells speaking. Somewhere, a dog bays. Before me lies the Bible. In the fifth book of Moses,[43] whom

---

[41][Castellet is a small fortification in Occitan or Catalan. —*Trans.*]

[42][Wild Mountain. —*Trans.*]

[43][Deut. 7:16. —*Trans.*]

the Cathars called a liar, I read a terrible sentence that makes me shudder: "And thou shalt consume all the people which the Lord thy God shall deliver thee, thine eye shall have no pity upon them!"

Today, on Sunday, I was in the church where I was baptized. The minister gave a long sermon highlighted with biblical expressions. At the center of his unctuous examination of the words of the apostle Paul were these words: "For that which I do I allow not; for what I would, that do I not, but what I hate, that do I. I find then a law, that, when I would do good, evil is present with me. Therefore hath he mercy on whom he will have mercy, and whom he will hardeneth. O wretched man that I am! Who shall deliver me from the body of this death?"[44]

After the church service, which was like a dreadful nightmare, I went out alone into the city, and I preached a sermon for myself. I began with Schiller's words: "Be, as you will, nameless afterlife—only this for mine own self remains true: Be, as you will, when I take only myself over there. Emissions are only one layer of man. I am my heaven and my hell! The noblest privilege of human nature is to determine for oneself that which is good and of the good that will be done. Noble people pay with that which they are!" I continue my sermon with words of Meister Eckhart:

The righteous person serves neither God nor his creatures. He stands so firmly in righteousness that he in contrast respects neither the agonies of hell nor the joys of heaven. It is the righteous people also serious about righteousness that, were God not righteous, they would not care about Him. The person shall not be afraid of God! God is a God of the present. One shall not frantically seek or wrongly believe in him, rather take him, as he is my own and within me. Truth is also noble that, if God would like to turn from the truth, I will attach myself to the truth and leave God!

True words of philosophers spoken in our own time, which act on me as a cure:

That is the knowledge of the courageous: Who wishes to escape guilt, escapes life. Yet one who atones for and lives through it and

---

[44][Romans 7:15, 21; 9:19; 7:24. —*Trans.*]

finds eternity in it, becomes new in it. No savior of the world does anything for us, nothing. Savior of the world! Alone life triumphs over death. Only by a strengthening of the good, the noble within us, by our own act, by a gorgeous example our own self can become help to free oneself and to appoint oneself. All salvation, all justification is anticipated by the fact that we grow only through will. Punishment is the consequence; there is only one genuine punishment of sin, and this punishment is actually carried out by the evildoer inevitably and at the same time with its resolution: the downward spiral. Atonement is also a consequence; there is only one atonement, and it is also a reward, involuntarily, but unobtainable and carried out by the evildoer himself: the upward spiral! From its works and products, a person that results from one's own accord finally escapes—either upward or downward, to the better or to the worse level. We have only one reality: works! We have only one reality: the deed.[45]

I conclude my sermon with words from Nietzsche's *Zarathustra:* "What is great in man is that he is a bridge and not an end; what can be loved in man is that he is a transition and not a demise. I swear to you, my brothers, remain true to the earth!" Earth is a part of the starry heaven.

---

[45][Eckhart's sermon. —*Trans.*]

~ AMORSBRÜNN ~

Near the small town of Amorbach, whose baroque church towers, monastery buildings, and castle ramparts overwhelm the handful of simple or humble houses, is the tree-shrouded, graceful site of Amorsbrünn,[46] with its small church. Even in pagan times, so unjustly called dark and merciless, a sanctuary stood here. "As the first heralds of Christianity came into the valley, they too were fond of it. As explicitly reported by messengers of other faiths, they chose the same place that the pagan population selected for preaching. And so the tradition will continue when the first Christians are baptized here with the holy water, at this place revered from time immemorial." It is alleged that the first Christians here came from Ireland: St. Pirmin and his disciple, St. Amor, the two who "still stroll in the shadow of death, brought the light of the gospel." St. Amor is said to have stayed here as abbot for another thirty-three years, after Boniface had consecrated the first church in Amorbach in the year AD 734, and is said to have "requested and received a calling and the health-restoring strength of God" in Amorsbrünn.

An archivist from the Würzburg bishopric proved about twenty years ago that the story of the founding of the Amorbach abbey before the tenth century was true. Pirmin was indeed involved in the founding of Amorbach; St. Amor (there was also a Roman amatory god called Amor) was a fantastical creation from a much later time. The Amorbach monastery was not founded until toward the end of the tenth century by monks from the Burgundian Cluny monastery. Amorsbrünn owes its name to St. Amor, a "fantastical creation from a much later date." In the inside of the little church stands a wooden figure of the saint donated three hundred years earlier by a Würzburg city councilman who was thankful for the blessings of children. In 1889, when a local poet—forgotten today—contended in his narration *St. Amor* that the wife of that Würzburg city councilman was not blessed by the intercession of the saint, but "by the strengthening and refreshing stay in the healthy air of the beautiful Odenwald mountains," people screamed bloody murder regarding this heretic, proving that the same persecution could still happen today.

---

[46][Amor's Fountain. —*Trans.*]

From a local Amorbach guidebook I gathered that "the wax figures, child dolls, and pictures, which, until thirty year ago, had still covered the altars and walls, have disappeared" from the Amorsbrünn chapel. As a result of the affected religiosity of this place, I also viewed the carved late-Gothic altar, which depicts the family tree of the Virgin Mary in predella.[47] An ancestor named Jesse is depicted sleeping, because the family tree originates from him; the center panel depicts the Virgin Mary with the boy Jesus. Both baroque altars, the wooden figure of St. Amor, the rococo praying chairs, the Marian pillar, and the crucifixion group combine, as the local guide book infers, to form a harmonious general impression that is completed with a copy of the Lourdes grotto. St. Christopher "does not quite fit in with the original wellspring cult." Except for the trees, springwater, and the heavenly canopy, nothing of this—all of which can be seen in Amorsbrünn today—reminds me in the least of the original wellspring cult . . . least of all St. Amor himself and, as the guidebook also suggests, the tasteless reproduction of the grotto of Lourdes.

Amor told the Provençal heretics about the Minne. *Minne* refers to "commemoration" and "remembrance," but, as the endearing poet Jean Richter said, "remembrance . . . is called the only Paradise from which one cannot be driven out." And this is the way in which I remember: All Germanic tribes solemnly admired their wells and springs. When they approached a fountain, they remembered the divine keeper of water, Freya-Holda (who was also called Venus), and the other invisible well maidens and water damsels who populated the holy water. Our ancestors did not foster their admiration and piety or lend visible expression to their belief by means of plaster figures or wax dolls, praying chairs, or fake grottoes. Neither did their divinities require a family tree. Their Father was the Lord in his own right, many-named and yet nameless, multifaceted and yet one, manifestly potent and yet unfathomable. The line did not descend from Jesse, but from heaven, of which the earth is a part.

---

[47][*Predella* refers to a series of small painted panels at the bottom of an altarpiece. —*Trans.*]

～ *AMORBACH*[48] ～

With two literary historians, I drove to Wildenberg Castle near the village of Preunschen, in the midst of a wonderful hardwood forest. It was referred to as the Grail Castle in the Odenwald. My companions agreed that Wildenberg is one of the most beautiful castle ruins in Germany. They debated, however, whether the Minnesinger Wolfram von Eschenbach had actually resided in this wonderfully romantic building, which has been in ruins since the Bauernkriege.[49] First and foremost, I asserted that we should try to determine whether Wolfram's *Parzival,* shaped by the greatest heretical movement of that time, may have been written at Wildenberg Castle with the knowledge of, or on behalf of, that knight from Durne. My consideration would have investigations lead to the goal in the following way: In 1233, a relative of Lord von Durne, the countess Looz (her house poet was the Minnesinger Heinrich Veldeke), was accused of Luciferian heresy by the inquisitorial magister Konrad von Marburg in the Mainz Diet. Hardly had I spoken when the previously divided scholars were confederates against me.

Amorbach, a delightful town, may owe its name to the fantastic legend of St. Amor or, as I would like to suggest but would not dare state, the word *amor* (which, in heretical Provence, meant Minne). The venerable walls of Wildenberg Castle may or may not have witnessed Wolfram produce his greatest poetic masterpiece seven hundred years ago. I maintain, which I noted at that time in southern France, that as Wolfram himself indicated, the true story of the Grail and of Parzival had come from Provence to Germany; Wolfram had used a Provençal poem as a model for his epic. His authority, Kyot, was in fact the troubadour Guiot de Provins, who performed his sonnets for knightly heretics and heretical noblewomen. Munsalvat, the Grail Castle, had as its model the Pyrenean castle Montségur. The Terre de Salvat was the area of the Pyrenean Tabor. And perhaps the treasure of the church, which four chivalrous pure ones had taken from the threatened castle of Montségur to the caves of the Sabarthès, was the Grâl—not the Church's distortion known

---

[48][Amor brook. —*Trans.*]

[49][Farmer Wars, ca. 1525. —*Trans.*]

as the chalice of Jesus of Nazareth, but a stone fallen from Lucifer's crown that bestows food and drink and immortality to those who are worthy of his display.

Only once before did I ascend Wildenberg Castle—and I was alone. For a long time, I contemplated the stone works and various marks made by the stonecutters. Then I looked out to the country. My thoughts went off into the distance. To the east, according to Pyrenean legend, Countess Esclarmonde de Foix, the mistress of the Grail Castle of Montségur, transformed herself into a white pigeon and flew off to Asia's mountains. Esclarmonde did not die, a shepherd told me. To this day she lives there in the earthly paradise. I also recalled the lonely Paradise of the Iranian Parsi and the Indian Aryans—a Paradise from which they could not be driven. The far north, as is generally known in its holy tradition, had been the Aryan people's ancient home—that prosperous land of Ariana, where the sun was at home and people were thankful. There a person could live a long life and could hold a trusted dialogue with the gods, who seemed to sojourn in the midst of people. There, a drink flowing from marvelous trees bestowed heavenly immortality and intimacy with God: Haoma, or, as the Aryan Indians called it, Soma. With one gulp, a person could assume Aryan strength.

One day, however, the serpent of winter rose there. It became cold for people, animals, and plants; the sea froze; the sun departed; an arctic climate prevailed year in and year out; and the winter was ten months long. The people had to emigrate to the south. The far north, however, remained cherished in their memory. Once in their new land, to remember their lost home in prayer, the Aryans went to a mountain, a Paradise mountain: *paradêsha*. (This word means "high-altitude area.")

Thus the Aryan Paradise was originally a hallowed mountain, and on its summit, people could go in spirit to the north, the land of God and their ancestors. For their sign of devotion, the Iranian and Indian Aryans used the word *man*.

The divinity was benevolent to the Aryans who emigrated to the south; as age-old legends tell, it had sent an eagle or a dove with the assignment to bring them to the Soma tree from which could be prepared the drink Soma so that people would not lose Aryan strength. From that time forward, the Soma drink could be enjoyed in the south—

to remember, to Minne. (This word is, as is certain, the Sanskrit *man* and the gothic *munni*—"memory" or "cognition.")

Just such a paradêsha, as the more-than-four-thousand-year-old Rig-Veda reports, was called Mûjavat and lay west of India. Hundreds and thousands of years passed. Jesus of Nazareth was born; Jews and Romans exalted him as the God become flesh; Christianity spread across the world; a new calculation of time began. From the third century of the Christian calendar, next to Germanic Aryanism, Iranian Manichaeism was the greatest enemy of Christianity. Meanwhile, the Iranian mountain Mûjavat had become the supreme sanctuary of the Manichaeans. Today it is called Kôh-i-Chwadschä (Mountain of the Kings or Mountain of God) and it is abandoned and deserted at the swampy Lake Hamun, on the border between Iran and Afghanistan. The Greeks had referred to this lake as the Aria Palus, the Aryan Lake. Alexander the Great was there.

A present-day Austrian researcher, Friedrich von Suhtscheck, sees the mountain sanctuary of Kôh-i-Chwadschä—which can be easily compared to Jerusalem, Mecca, and Rome—as the archetype of Wolfram's Grail Mountain, Munsalvat, and in Lake Hamun he sees Lake Brumbane, where Parzival arrives on his quest before finding the Castle of Salvation. Suhtscheck concludes that even the names Wolfram gave to his characters could reveal their Iranian origin: Parzival, properly Parsiwal, is called Parsenblume, or "pure flower," because *parsi* means pure. His father, Gamuret, must be the ancient Iranian king Gamurt. Parzival's son Lohengrin (in Wolfram's *Der Wartburgkrieg* he is Loherangrin) is the Persian god Lohrangerin, which means "red courier." To a great extent, Wolfram's work *Parzival* might be the rhymed treatment of an original Iranian text. The Manichaean Song of the Pearl, which should be regarded as the oldest literary model and one of the most profound expressions of a people's spirit, came from the third century imbued with the noblest Iranian spirit. Some refer to the fact that the *Song of Mani*, referring to the founder of Manichaeism, was written by Mani himself. The Song of the Pearl praised the achievements of the highest symbol of the Manichaean faith: the mystical pearl (*ghr-al*). There is no contradiction when Wolfram calls the Grail a stone, for the Persian word *ghr-al* also means "jewel."

I ask myself: Could that book found in the rubble of Montségur and written in an unknown alphabet be filled with Manichaean writing, perhaps even a copy of the original Iranian version of *Parzival?* Further cause for thinking: Clay doves were found in the rubble of Montségur, and annually, on Good Friday, the day of the supreme Minne, according to Wolfram von Eschenbach, a dove brought down from heaven to earth a communion wafer, white and small, to be laid upon the Grail:

> *Then she lifts her bright plumage*
> *Homeward again to the high heaven.*
> *When Good Friday returns,*
> *The gift of the stone is admired anew . . .*

Wolfram's day of the supreme Minne need not have been Good Friday, the day when Joseph of Arimathea is said to have caught the blood of Jesus of Nazareth in a chalice on Golgotha, the Place of the Skull, near Jerusalem. He may just as well have meant the Manichaean Naurozfest,[50] the celebration of the vernal equinox. In the Naurozfest, the dove, as it is called it in the old Manichaean songs, carries the holy Soma seeds of the holy stone *ghral.*

When I am alone on Wildenberg, my thoughts go to the west and the north and the south. It was from the north, the land of Tulla or Tullan, that the ancestors of the ancient Mexican people, the Toltecs, are said to have come. They regarded Tulla, where the ice began to prevail and the sun was no more, as their ancestral land. Though changed, it was still the "Paradise" of their heroes. This Toltec Tulla corresponds perfectly to the mysterious island Thule, that *Thule ultima a sole nomen habens,* Ultimate Thule, which owes its name to the sun. I recall Pytheas of Marseille, who departed more than two thousand years ago to look for this land. He tried to reach it, the land "which is next to heaven and is holiest" and where he hoped "to look upon the father of the gods and enjoy a day nearly without night."

An Ultima Thule was also the land of the Hyperboreans, who dwelled beyond the north wind in the eternal light and over whom the

---

[50][The Persian new-year festival. —*Trans.*]

Delphic Apollo presided as a divinity. The Greeks regarded the land of the Hyperboreans as the ancient seat of their kind and the homeland of their divinity. It is none other than that sun island Aea that the Argonauts sought. Like the Iranians, the Greeks also had their Paradise: The divine mountains of Olympus or Parnass or Oeta were each a paradêsha where the Nordic land of light, that sun island, and immortality and blessedness were enjoyed as nectar and ambrosia were commemorated through prayers on their peaks. Greeks designated this devotional recollection by the word *mimneskein,* cognate with the Sanskrit *man,* the Latin *memini,* the Gothic *munni*—and the German *Minne.*

The wonderful Montségur was also a paradêsha, situated in the mountain wilderness of the Pyrenean Tabor.

The Provençal Cathars kept national writings and songs, including Wolfram's *Parzival.* The bibliography of the heretics was as varied as their history, shaped by the Greeks, Celts, and Teutons. In Wolfram's lyrical work, we can find, apart from Oriental nomenclature, an abundance of Occidental references. Some examples: Wolfram sang of Persia, Babylon, Euphrates, Tigris, and India. In addition, he praised Alexandria, the Trojans, and the country Hiperbortikon—the country of the Hyperboreans. He amalgamated Provençal, Spanish, French, and British place-names (Aragon, Catalonia, Gascony, Paris, Normandy, Burgundy, Brittany, Ireland, and London) and German and Scandinavian names (Worms, Rhine, Spessart, Thüringia, Denmark, Norway, and Greenland). Further, Wolfram works imaginative play with Zarathustra; Aeneas; Plato; Hercules; Alexander; Virgil; Siegfried and the Nibelungen; Sibich, an opponent of Dietrich von Bern; and Wolfhart, Dietrich's follower. Each true troubadour had to know by heart history and myths and had to possess an encyclopedic knowledge. Wolfram or his alter ego Kyot-Guiot meets these conditions to such an extent that even today, *Parzival* fills us with awestruck admiration. Indeed, it is among the greatest achievements of the human spirit.

Until the thirteenth century, Catharism in Europe remained powerfully independent from the Vatican in Rome, which did not need to be cleansed of Jewish mythology because it had not, or only superficially, accepted its teachings, which had been felt in an enormous area—from India to the pillars of Hercules, from Greenland to Sicily—and which, however, still knew its center at only one pole: the north pole, the *polus arcticus,* as Wolfram called it during the contest at Wartburg. This power unified all humans from the most diverse regions and nations, but of the same race and the same origin. Following the age-old Aryan myths, we call this strength Aryan power.

This Aryan power was at the origin of the lineage of those from the far north. They formed a society that was oblivious to political borders and spatial distance. This Minne society, as it was already identified in those times, kept and maintained the holy scriptures of the Occidental Aryans, the myths of the Celts, the poetry of the Greeks, and, not least, the lore of the Teutons. The Minne was a unified band whose people were overcome with the remembrance of their fathers of Nordic origin, of the "Nordic divinity in the Nordic Paradise." Their common opponent was the Augustinian *Civitas Dei,* invented by people from the seed of Shem and practiced by priests so that the law of Zion became the law of the world. The small shadow of Mûjavat, the mountain of the gods, is reflected in the gloomy and shallow waters of Aryan Lake, near the Grail Mountain known as Montségur. Under Montségur's spell, the Cagots, the Gotenhunde,[51] endured a cursed existence, as they did on the Neapolitan Grail Mountains where martyrs, guardians of Aryan thoughts, lay buried. A Pyrenean farmer said to me that as men become more unworthy of it, the Grail moves farther from mankind. The legend is incomplete: The Grail moves closer to people as they become worthy of it.

---

[51][Gothic dogs. —*Trans.*]

"Hell, you call it?" asked Don Quixote.
"Call it by no such name, for it does not deserve it,
as you shall soon see."

MIGUEL DE CERVANTES

PART THREE

― WITH RELATIVES IN HESSE ―

Because I wanted to present a gift to my youngest cousin, I took him to a bookshop to select something for himself. The choice was not hard for him: He reached for a volume called *German Heroic Legends* and began to leaf through it. Soon to be fourteen, he probably thought it too daunting for him, considering its length of 470 pages. Although the price was most likely affordable, vacillating, he put the book aside. I remained quiet as he looked through other books, took up *Heroic Legends* again—and looked at me as his eyes went to and from the page. I finally had to laugh, and I cheerfully knocked the boy on the shoulder. The book belonged to him. He radiated with happiness; now he can enjoy the wonderful legends of the Nibelungen, King Rother, Gudrun, King Ortnit, Wolfdietrich, Wieland the blacksmith, Dietrich von Bern, Parzival, Lohengrin, and Tannhäuser—all of the legends of Lucifer's courtiers—and it is certain he will remember their adventures his whole life. The bookseller had a second copy of the same edition in stock. I purchased it for myself.

"When the emperors of the House of Hohenstauffen reigned over Germany," wrote the author, "the tree of German poetry sprouted an abundance of new buds and blooms. Walther von der Vogelweide, Wolfram von Eschenbach, and many other Minnesingers let their sonnets ring out. The people gladly listened to them and honored them as the darlings of heaven."

I continued reading: "You are in Paradise, Tannhäuser, in the paradisal realm of the goddess Freya, who is now called Venus. Freya, the goddess of the Minne and the golden-haired and gracefully smiling mistress of the Valkyries, resides in this wooded mountain. Inside is the Folkwang of the gods of the Asgard: the Venusberg!"[1]

Finally, I read how Dietrich von Bern may have met his end:

Once, as Lord Dietrich bathed in a stream, a magnificent stag came from the forest to satisfy its thirst. The old king ran to the bank,

---

[1][The Asgard, or Asagardr, is the northern Germanic celestial Paradise of the Asen, who were a caste of divinities that included Thor, Odin, and Freya. It is also a castle with two major halls, the Folkwang and Walhall, and two courtyards, the Idafeld and the Wingolf. —*Trans.*]

threw on his robe, and called after his steed. And lo, a raven-black stallion approached, and Lord Dietrich swung himself on the animal's back. With the force of a heavy gale, he galloped behind the stag. The yeomen were not able to follow and no human eye ever saw him again; but singers vaunt and praise him to this very day, and people say that he hunts with Wodan's wild host on dreadful nights, his spear swinging through the air.

My cousin slammed shut his book with a loud thud. His mother had reminded him that he had to learn songbook verses by heart for his confirmation hour. Propping his head in both hands, he began to murmur some incomprehensible phrases:

> How beautiful shines the morning star,
> full of grace and truth of the Lord,
> arisen from Judah!

On the table where my cousin and I are sitting stands a vase of primroses, which are also called "heaven's key," and an inkwell, like the one Martin Luther threw at the devil. Beside it lies the Bible translated into German by Luther. I open it to the Prophet Isaiah:

And it shall come to pass in the last days, that the mountain of the Lord's house shall be established in the top of the mountains, and shall be exalted above the hills; and all nations shall flow unto it. And many people shall go and say, Come ye, and let us go up to the mountain of the Lord, to the house of the God of Jacob; and he will teach us of his ways, and we will walk in his paths: for out of Zion shall go forth the law, and the word of the Lord from Jerusalem. And with the false gods it will be entirely out. And it shall come to pass in that day, that the Lord shall punish the host of the high ones that are on high, and the kings of the earth upon the earth. And they shall be gathered together, as prisoners are gathered in the pit, and shall be shut up in the prison, and after many days shall they be visited. Then the moon shall be confounded, and the sun ashamed, when the Lord of hosts shall reign in mount Zion, and in Jerusalem.

... But ye ... that forget my holy mountain, that prepare a table for that troop [Gad, god of good fortune], and that furnish the drink offering unto that number [Meni, god of destiny], therefore will I number you to the sword, and ye shall all bow down to the slaughter: because when I called, ye did not answer; ... Therefore thus saith the Lord God, Behold, my servants shall eat, but ye shall be hungry: behold, my servants shall drink, but ye shall be thirsty: behold, my servants shall rejoice, but ye shall be ashamed: Behold, my servants shall sing for joy of heart, but ye shall cry for sorrow of heart, and shall howl for vexation of spirit. And ye shall leave your name for a curse unto my chosen: for the Lord God shall slay thee, and call his servants by another name: For, behold, I create new heavens and a new earth: and the former shall not be remembered, nor come into mind. ... Ye shall be comforted in Jerusalem.[2]

My cousin and those who will be confirmed along with him were caught laughing when, in the church service, the minister spoke of Moses, Abraham, Sarah, and Isaac. The boy had interrupted the silence. The minister became bitter. I asked the boy, "Do you prefer the legends of German heroes to the biblical history?"

"Yes."

"Then never forget to whom we owe these tales: the wandering folk of the Middle Ages."

As the boy listened, I recounted the story of the Cathars and troubadours who escaped along the highways into the forests, because there wasn't any place for them—those "servants of the devil"—in the Holy Roman Empire. I also told him the mystical story of Parzival, who searched for his father and God. Ultimately, he found understanding of both through an anti-Christian pledge to the God of Minne which was revealed in the stone that fell from Lucifer's crown. I recounted to him the tale of the legendary knights of King Arthur and the guardians of the Grail: how they had arranged a magnificent table to their God and drank to the Minne. When the Romans assaulted Arthur's mountain, his courtiers' merriment stopped.

---

[2][Isaiah 2:2–3; 24:21–23; 65:11–15, 17; 66:13. —*Trans.*]

No account exists that supports the contention that the German troubadours, those engaging singers of the Minne and May, were in collusion with Cathar heretics. Indeed, it has never been confirmed that German Cathars kept national songs. This makes my journey in search of Lucifer's German courtiers a hard undertaking, but it will be even harder to find Isaiah's "mount of the congregation, in the sides of the north." I prefer to walk confidently into the shadows, knowing that the light shining in the gloom will be bright. When we are seeking God, we can walk on seas or move mountains. I am not traveling blindly, however; should my eyes fail, I will grope.

I will zigzag, but I have a final goal: to find the stone that fell from Lucifer's crown, if not the crown itself. I have searched for years for the philosopher's stone. How many more years will I need?

The sense of touch is one of our five senses. As the sense of sight weakens, a person becomes more discerning and sensitive. Why not grope through the darkness until the light becomes bright? The Sabarthès caves were good teachers. If my sense of touch also fails, I know a final means to keep me from losing the way: I will let my soul stretch its wings. Surely, he who believes in himself after a disappointment ultimately succeeds.

~ Mellnau in the Burgwald ~

An acquaintance took me on his motorcycle to his little hometown. Nestled in the Burgwald Forest, Mellnau is located in one of the most beautiful landscapes of Hesse. The fruit trees along the highways and fields are laden with the first foliage, and some still flaunt their blooms. The whitewashed farmhouses and the slender castle tower, constructed from light-colored sandstone, make the coniferous forest seem black, and everything seems enchanted in the May sun, which plays with light and shade. In the village lanes, boys and girls dressed in the decorative traditional garments of the Marburg region offered us a cordial welcome. They half expected us. We went on our own through the border. The fruit was already on the trees and the sun burned as it does in summer.

The aim of our morning hike was a pasture called the Lord's Pigsty. This name can be found only on topographical maps. Farmers call the place by its old name: the Rose Garden! If the Tyrolean rose garden belongs to Laurin, the garden in Mellnau belongs to the Lurer, the place on the other side of the pathway that separates the fields. It was named after a tribe that inhabited the area; numerous prehistoric weapons, including hatchets of stone and bronze, were turned up when the field was plowed. In the rose garden, as in the Lurer, we are forced to remember our ancestors.

I now know of three rose gardens. The second was near Worms, somewhere near the remains of the monastery of Laurisham-Lorsch, near where we find a memorial for the victims of the world war. Siegfried is also said to rest there, if this godlike warrior was a man of flesh and blood. In fact, the designation *rose garden* was commonly used in earlier times for a cemetery. As I only recently became aware, such a rose garden and cuttings from a rose hedge were "essential to a ritual consecrated to the thunder god Donar-Thor for the cremation of the dead by firethorn." In this way, the bodies of our dead pagan ancestors were turned to ash in a blazing fire of rose thorn, and Donar-Thor was the rose garden's divine lord.

We arrived at last on the Sonnenwendskopf, falsely plotted on maps as Sonnabendskopf, a dome-shaped mountain that towers above the rose garden. On the summit stands a stone monument, placed there by some Huguenots, those Calvinists who were forced to flee France. The stone carries the inscription *Résistez!* More properly, it should read *Resist Rome!*

From the Sonnenwendskopf I could see the district of Hesse and Nassau, an area that abounded with Cathars in the twelfth century. Their followers, who were mostly aristocrats and free farmers, called themselves God's Friends or the Good Men.[3] I didn't need to remind myself that Wolfram von Eschenbach's Grail King was also called good man Anfortas.

---

[3][A pre–World War II group of *Völkisch,* neo-pagans in Germany, was known as the Bund der Guoten. —*Trans.*]

‒ MARBURG AM LAHN ‒

Seven hundred years ago, Konrad von Marburg, Germany's all-powerful grand inquisitor and papal visitator,[4] lived and worked here. In 1231, Pope Gregory IX wrote him a letter in which the Holy Father expressed to his visitator his sincere appreciation for his efforts to eradicate the heretics and provided his "dear son" with the following authority: Master Konrad was allowed to make use of any suitable help from whomever he wished. He could halt the interdiction and cast spells at his discretion. The judge and his henchmen (one of them, name unknown, boasted that he could see heretics through the walls of a house) then began a reign of terror without parallel in Germany. Giving credence to virtually any denunciation, they dragged in anyone rumored to have had contact with heresy. Those who denied the accusation were burned, "on the same day that they were condemned, without recourse to defense or possible appeal." There was only one chance for anyone innocently accused to escape the flames: He had to declare himself a repentant heretic. Only then could he remain alive. With his hair cut above his ears and a cross sewn on his clothes, the victim was obliged to appear every Sunday in church, between the Epistle and Gospel, half undressed in order to be flogged.

Around the year 1212, when a group of heretics were seized in Strassburg,

> . . . [a] deep and wide pit was dug, which today is called "heretics grave." The execution of the heretics was conducted with great expression of grief. Their children and friends asked them if they would like to convert, but they persisted, and sang and prayed by calling to God. They said they could not abandon their God. Even in going willingly into the fire, they were surrounded with wood and burned to ashes at once with great grief. There may have been hundreds of them, and among them were many aristocrats.

---

[4][A *visitator* is a special investigator who is directly responsible to the pope. —*Trans.*]

Many assume that Konrad von Marburg was involved in this mass execution. Everywhere in Germany

> . . . innumerable heretics were cross-examined by Konrad's apostolic authority as visitator, and were condemned and burned after the pronouncement of the sentence by the secular authorities. On one occasion, Konrad seized a number of knights, priests, and other outstanding burghers in his hometown of Marburg. Although several converted, several others were burned alive behind the castle in Marburg, at a place that is still called the Ketzerbach.[5]

Today, the Marburg Ketzerbach is a road like any other. Only the name commemorates the atrocities that were committed here by Rome's special representative. A modern-day visitor to the Gothic church of St. Elizabeth, which was built to house Elizabeth's remains, or to the Ketzerbach will not find any reference to the fact that Konrad—Landgravine Elizabeth's confessor—was a mass murderer. Yet without Konrad's scheming, there would never have been a St. Elizabeth! Because she was the daughter of King Andreas of Hungary, Elizabeth was betrothed as a child to Landgrave Ludwig VI of Thüringia and Hesse, who was Konrad's sovereign prince. Consequently, Elizabeth became Ludwig's wife at the tender age of fourteen, and bore their first child at fifteen.

We do not know the circumstances that induced the landgrave to grant some very strange privileges to Konrad, whom the pope appointed as his wife's confessor. These were some very bizarre privileges indeed! Isentrud von Hörselgau, who was chambermaid to the landgravine, related the following incidents: Konrad once requested his penitent to listen to a sermon. Elizabeth stayed away because a relative, Countess von Meissen, had unexpectedly arrived on a visit. The monk let the young landgravine know that because of her disobedience, from now on he would no longer attend to her. Only if she were to fall at his feet and beseech him to reconsider his resolution would he rescind his decision. What's more, only if Elizabeth's maids stripped her, except for her nightgown,

---

[5][*Ketzerbach* means "heretic ditch." —*Trans.*]

so that Konrad could strongly whip her—*usque ad camisiam bene sunt verberatae*—could she be forgiven. When Rudolf Schenk von Vargila felt himself obliged to warn the landgravine of the gossip circulating at court concerning her relationship to her confessor, Elizabeth showed him her back, which was scarred from Master Konrad's whippings, and said that the confessor's lashes were the expression of his love for her and her own love for God.[6]

Elizabeth became a widow at twenty-one years of age, when her husband died in southern Italy. She left Wartburg and moved to Marburg, where Konrad lived. A special papal dispensation still had her placed—unconditionally—under the visitor's supervision. I shall ignore the life that the woman had to endure in Marburg and state only what one chronicler wrote: "She praised the Lord to have been released at last from the love for her children, as if her prayers were heard." She betrayed her maternity to become a saint.

When Elizabeth died at the age of twenty-four, orthodox Catholics took possession of the corpse and promptly cut off her breasts as relics. Then she was buried at the chapel of St. Francis in Marburg. Four years later, she was declared a saint and her bones were taken from the crypt, laid in a sarcophagus, and displayed on the altar of the chapel. Because this exhumation directly affected the state, Emperor Frederick II was present. The emperor, better known as Stupor Mundi,[7] crowned the skull with a golden coronet and presented a golden chalice to the church so that his name would be forever attached to the bones of the saint.

The dead saint rested in peace until 1249, when Pope Innocent IV gave instructions for a second burial of the corpse. From the wording of the bull, it appears that the Marburg chapel had become too small for the large numbers of pilgrims who visited. We do not know where the bones were taken. When the remains of the landgravine and saint resurfaced some twenty-five years after her death, "the skeleton effused a wonderful fragrance," and "the cloths which wrapped the head were soaked with what appeared to be a soft liquor, much like the 'oil of Provence.' The brain was fresh, as if she had not even died." Elizabeth's

---

[6][The deposition by Isentrud von Hörselgau was made before a papal visitator during the process of Elizabeth's beatification. —*Trans.*]

[7][Wonder of the World. —*Trans.*]

first biographer and contemporary, Caesarius von Heisterbach, confirmed this phenomenal presence of a wonderful fragrance based on the reports of eyewitnesses:

> Three days before the corpse was to be moved on May Day, Prior Ulricus [probably Ulrich von Durne, a blood relative of Rupert von Durne, who was once Wolfram von Eschenbach's guest at Wildenberg Castle and sang a wonderful sonnet of Parzival, the Grail, and Provence], accompanied by seven monks, entered the chapel's catacombs late in the night and locked the gate. Scooping away the earth of the grave, they opened the coffin, and were immediately met with an extraordinary fragrance.[8] They separated the head from the body, removing all skin, hair, and flesh with a knife, so that the saint would not look too frightening.

Three days later, Emperor Frederick did his pious work. During the following centuries, the knights of the Deutscher Orden at Marburg, in whose care the relics were entrusted, permitted the balmy oil that dropped incessantly from the bones to be collected and sold as an expensive cure against every conceivable disease.[9] Yet the worst and most woeful was yet to come: *aux frontiers de la mort* (from borders of death).

At Eisenach in 1250, Elizabeth's eldest daughter, Sophie, induced Count Heinrich von Meissen to swear an oath upon a rib of her mother. In the same year, Duchess Anna von Schlesien, a daughter-in-law of St. Hedwig, who was an aunt of Elizabeth, presented another rib wrapped in gold and silver to the monastic church at Trebnitz. Around this time, an arm of the saint was shipped to Hungary, Elizabeth's homeland. In the seventeenth century, a certain Winkelmann, who lived in Altenburg,

---

[8][The wonderful fragrance that envelops the remains of certain saints is fact. The same phenomenon has been recorded in Nevers, France, where the body of St. Bernadette was known to have emitted a beautiful aroma. This has been documented in a little-known book by Dr. Hubert Larcher, *Le Sang, peut-il vaincre la mort?* (Paris: Gallimard, 1957), republished in 1990 as *La mémoire du soleil.* —*Trans.*]

[9][The Deutscher Orden, German Order, or Ordo Teutonicus, was a religious order of knights that was involved in the colonization of eastern Europe. They still exist as a monastic order, and their insignia is the Iron Cross. —*Trans.*]

near Wetzlar (and whose activities were revealed in a pamphlet titled *A Description of Hesse*), offered for sale—in addition to relics of Elizabeth's youngest daughter, Gertrude—the saint's hand adorned with gold and jewels! Then, Walther, a provost resident in Meissen, declared that he had a finger of the saint in his possession! What had happened? Well, you don't need much imagination: The German lords had sold off the saint's body, piece by piece.

In the sixteenth century, Holy Roman Emperor Charles V accused the landgrave of Hesse, Philip I (who was known as Philip the Magnanimous and who was a member of the Deutscher Orden), of robbing and hiding Elizabeth's bones for which the church in Marburg had been especially built (probably in 1283). Amazingly, Philip found the remains of his famous ancestor, although the German lords had been selling her relics for three hundred years. Yet he wrote the emperor:

> St. Elizabeth was a commendable and blessed-by-God princess of Hungary. His Highness [meaning Landgrave Philip] has found that her relics created so much ungodliness that various sinners have come to doubt if she ever existed. As a consequence, her remains are not buried together, but instead are separated, with a leg here, another there, and other bones in St. Michael's graveyard near the German House at Marburg.

The remains had been dispersed and reburied by the landgrave. Sometime later, Philip was betrayed and imprisoned in 1547 by Catholics during the Schmalkald War.[10] Yet as a member of the Deutscher Orden, Philip was still held in esteem by the emperor. It was said that he would be brought to Spain and imprisoned there for life if he did not release the bones of the saint. Then, on July 12, 1548, "a head, with a jawbone; five tubes, both small and large; a grater; two shoulder bones; and otherwise a broad bone" were delivered to the German lord. These bones were reburied yet again in Elizabeth's church.

---

[10][The Schmalkald War was fought between the Catholic forces of Emperor Charles and the Protestant German princes under John Frederick, elector of Saxony, and Philip of Hesse between 1546 and 1547. The Protestants were defeated. —*Trans.*]

Time passed until the year 1625, when the following happened: In Marburg, Landgrave Ludwig V had a piece of wood removed from a bedstead that allegedly had been Elizabeth's bed. He wanted to produce a staff as a gift for the pious infanta Isabella in Brussels. A similar gift was made for Ludwig's son, George II, the elector, and archbishop Ferdinand of Cologne. When the Thirty Years' War raged and went dreadfully badly for Hesse, this same George II sent a letter in which he instructed a certain president of Bellersheim to dig up the grave and send him what was still left of Elizabeth's bones, because he wanted to use them for a secret purpose that would do "him and his country a great blessing." Bellersheim responded to this missive. The bones were dispatched to the landgrave, who gave them . . . to the elector and archbishop Ferdinand of Cologne. In the year 1636, Landgrave George converted to Catholicism. This was his "secret purpose."

Now these relics (for some time no longer genuine) were kept in Cologne. But, as my original source infers, "the lord elector seems to have again engaged in business. They [the bones] reemerged this time in Brussels, where they were handed over by Isabella (who was still a child) to the Carmelite cloister. There they were lost during the French Revolution." Elizabeth's head was saved, however, and was found in the Jacob Hospital in Besançon. Conversely, the master of the Deutscher Orden stated that the authentic remains of the saint had never left the walls of Elizabeth's church: In 1718, Elector Franz Ludwig von Trier, the order's master at that time, said that knowledge of the hiding place of Elizabeth's bones was "obtained through verbal tradition in the surroundings of the German master." All the same, by the sixteenth century there were ten times as many bones in the West than Elizabeth could have had in her body. Before I close this section, which I felt obliged to write, although disgust has guided my pen, I have to relate the following: Elizabeth of Thüringia, who never belonged to Lucifer's courtiers, allowed the curse of the Lord of Hosts to wash over her, just as Isaiah threatened Lucifer and his angels. Elizabeth was not buried like others.

— *Giessen* —

On a workday, I was in the church where I was confirmed years ago. Called John's Church, it is a Protestant place of worship. When he was a young man, my father saw it under construction. As in my youth, I tiptoed through the deserted nave of the church, my steps echoing hauntingly. I climbed the broad stairs to the organ and from there went up the steep, spiral stairs past the four balconies under the pointed, multisided spire to the great clockwork. I will never forget how I stood there with my schoolmates during the world war, listening to a distant, dull, ever-rolling thunder that would not end. The sound was from the battle for Fort Vaux on the Western Front. In that desperate time at the end of the war, I gathered beechnuts near Buseck for oil extraction, nettles near Krofdorf for the production of fabric, and flour and milk once a week from a mill near Wetzlar for my sick brother. In Giessen I listened day and night as prisoners of war, mostly French and Russians, shuffled through the streets or as our troops marched past in endless ranks to the Front or returned from it seeking only the hope of health.

I recalled my student days at Castle Gleiberg, when, without embarrassment, I carelessly raised hell in taverns. Then I thought of Konrad von Marburg as he sat on the back of a donkey, riding through the same countryside that anyone can admire from the tower of John's Church.

Because he had burned so many heretics, he hoped that the pope would beatify Elizabeth speedily. This, however, required proof that the bones of the woman decaying in a Marburg churchyard had indeed been responsible for miracles. Inquisitor Konrad thereby pursued a proven strategy: He created a correlation between Elizabeth's beatification and the eradication of the *virulentum semen hereticae pravitatis,* the "poisonous seed of heretical wickedness." He hoped that her beatification would rebuke the heretics, who rejected any sort of veneration of relics and supernatural miracles. To this end, he rode through the country and collected testimonies of miracles from the people who trembled before him. Finally, he wrote a report titled *Relatio authentica miraculorum a Deo per intercessionem B. Elisabeth Landgr. Patratorum,* Miracles Implemented by God through the Intercession of Blessed Landgravine Elizabeth. He began the report with this address: "To our very Holy

Father and Sovereign Lord Gregory, the highest pontiff of the Holiest Roman Church." Then he wrote:

> [I]n the parts of Germany where the right faith reigns, the poisonous seed of heretical wickedness has begun to sprout. But Christ cannot tolerate that his flock is tested by the strength, and obstinacy of the heretics who should be smashed to pieces . . . [*lacuna* in my text] . . . has immediately our marvelous faith the truth . . . [*lacuna* in my text] . . . through many miracles and good works to his glory and to the honor in memory of the blissful Lady Elizabeth, former landgravine of Thüringia, which have occurred in abundance and openness.

The beatification of Elizabeth took time. Konrad did not live to see it.

On the strength of the visitator's report, the Holy Father must have regarded the inhabitants of Lahngau and Hesse (whom Boniface once identified as idiotic) as heaven's suddenly chosen people. In Giessen, an affluent heathen testified under oath that his daughter, whose whole body was afflicted with draining abscesses, was healed by calling out to the dead landgravine. Heinrich von Gleiberg confirmed that he had overcome a difficult digestive illness through the intercession of Elizabeth. Someone from Krofdorf whose face had been eaten away by worms convalesced when he packed on his face the earth from Elizabeth's grave. In Buseck, a girl lost her nearsightedness. A woman from Wetzlar stated that her son had been cured of blindness in one eye. Near Densberg, which is perhaps the Dünsberg next to Giessen, a warrior named Degenhard who fell into enemy hands around noontime was able to free himself from his chains and flee into the forest after he had fervently prayed to the Almighty in the sacred name of St. Elizabeth. The warrior, however, seems to have been rooted to the spot. Something held him back, and *Degenhardus subito suo domino fuit restitutus*, Degenhard was suddenly returned to his master. Whether this Dominus[11] was Degenhard's own field commander or that of the enemy, I am not able to say. Degenhard, that faithful Christian warrior who thanked Elizabeth for loosening his chains, stood before the forest

---

[11][Lord. —*Trans.*]

and could not enter it. Why? Because neither the Lord of Hosts nor the Ruach nor Jesus and Mary nor Konrad von Marburg nor Elizabeth reigned in the German pine forest, with its charms and miracles! The lord of the free forest was Tiubel, as old chroniclers called the devil. They could also have called him Lucibel or Lucifer.

Around noon, Tiubel would have had free run of the forest. Heinrich von Falkenstein, a knight whom I have already mentioned, wanted "a look into the dark world of the hereafter." At noon, a sorcerer led him to a crossroads, drew a circle, and warned Falkenstein to forsake this spot at his peril. Neither should he give or receive gifts. "Then a howling storm arose, floods roared nearby, and frightening shapes appeared. Finally, a darkened form, as tall as a tree, stepped from the forest. It was the devil. The knight engaged in a discussion with him. Tiubel demanded gifts: a sheep and a cock. The knight refused both and did not leave the circle. Afterward, he became deathly pale and never again regained his healthy color." From then on, as is said, he was pale like a Manichaean.

From the tower of John's Church I also saw Frauenberg Mountain. In its vicinity, Lord von Dernbach, the Westerwald knight, cornered and killed Konrad, who whimpered for his life before he died.

~ SIEGEN ~

Along a pilgrim's path that leads uphill from a small village called Herkersdorf are twelve stations. At each stop, multicolored pictures describe the tragic story of Jesus of Nazareth. On a basalt crest that rounds off the way, a mighty wooden cross juts out of a druid stone. At the thirteenth station, a niche is carved into the rock, and in it stands Mary with her child. She is made of plaster and is painted in loud colors. In the past, when a climber walked here, he or she passed the house of Hekate and walked to the stone of Trute. These are the pagan names.

From the loftiness of the Trutenstein, climbers can marvel at the beauty of Germany. All around are mountains, hills, forests, meadows, even cities, and silvery, glittering watercourses. Sunshine and cloud shade play over the area, and the wind sings her beautiful song. When the midnight wind or morning storms blow, they tell the heroic tale of Siegfried, who, as the saga of the Norwegian Thidrek relates, learned the blacksmith's trade from the dwarfs of Balve in the depths of the Sauerland Mountains. Somewhere in the east, where the beautiful rolling heights are tinged blue, our radiant hero killed Fafnir the dragon upon the Gnitaheide. An Icelandic abbot named Nicholas, who made a pilgrimage from the north to Rome seven hundred years ago, met this pagan warrior on his journey between Kaldern on the Lahn (which sports yet another Siegfriedsloch) and the old Horohûs near Niedermarsberg, where Charlemagne razed to the ground our famous ancestral sanctuary at Externsteine because the Irminsul, or Tree of the World, was located there.[12] There were several of them. Wasn't one located in the vicinity of the Trutenstein, near Irmgarteichen or Erndtebrück? Irmingardeichen and Irmingardebrück are names from many, many years ago.

---

[12][Horohûs is another variant of the falcon-god of the pharaohs, Horus. Irminsul was a holy tree named after Irmin, the Teutonic war god; it was the symbolic Tree of the World. The German archaeologist Wilhelm Teudt (1860–1942), author of the study *Germanische Heiligtümer* (1929), believed the Irminsul was located at the Externsteine in Lippe. His findings, however, were based partly upon his "paranormal" faculties and fell into disrepute. To add to the confusion, in the early 1990s, Dr. Heribert Illig, in his book *Das Erfundene Mittelalter* (1996), cast into doubt the entire existence of the Frankish emperor Charlemagne. —*Trans.*]

In the south, the Feldberg, Altkönig, and Rossert Mountains rise toward the sky; they are the highest peaks of the Taunus range. A beautiful group of rocks crowns the Feldberg: the Brunhilde rocks. Here, the Valkyries rested between flames only to be awakened by Siegfried's kiss. It is not far fromTrutenstein to Herkersdorf and from there to Siegen. Wieland lived in Siegen, or so believed another child of the twelfth century, the Welsh chronicler and chaplain Geoffrey of Monmouth. In all probability, the nearby village of Wilnsdorf has to thank the blacksmith of the blacksmiths for its old name—Willandsdorf.

The expansive view of the Trutenstein extends toward the southwest, all the way up to the Seven Mountains on the Rhine. Poets have compared these seven peaks to giants or kings, yet the most beloved of these peaks, the wonderful Drachenfels, is none other than the Drekanfil of Scandinavian lore. According to fable, King Drusian once lived there. Further, Dietrich von Bern's wife, Godelinde, who was the daughter of a king of the Drachenfels, faced a hard struggle there with the giants Ecke and Fasolt. Löwenburg is hardly less interwoven in legend: The Ölberg, or the Petersberg, is where there existed a ring wall, the Lohrberg, which, as some claim, owed its name to Laurin. The Wolkenburg and the Nonnenstromberg complete the count of seven. Thus, the mountain chain bears its numerical name justifiably.

An immeasurable forest area designated by geographers of antiquity as Silva Orcynia (Orcynia Forest) and mentioned by Caesar as Silva Hercynia (Hercynia Forest) stretches out around Herkersdorf. Beginning at the source of the Theiss, it extends beyond Westphalia and the Harz region of Lower Saxony, toward the north, accompanying the Rhine from Schaffhausen to Speyer. The Greeks and later the Romans believed that Hades, the guardian of the land of the dead, and Demeter, Mother Earth, ruled in this forest of Hekate. People came here and were allowed to return again. The forest, supported by trees and canopied by heaven, was the temple of the gods.

Similarly, the Teutons called their goddess of death Hel or Holda, after Hekate. The works of the goddess were not frightening for them, for she sent them good-natured and graceful trees, leaves, blooms, and fruits. Therefore, the ancient Germans believed the first man had grown into a tree whose roots reach to Lady Hel. If a man dies, his body must move on the Helweg to Hellia[13] to build Hel's house, which lay "deep down toward the north." There, to save himself from a second death, he could pick succulent fruits—similar to the fruits of the Hesperus Garden picked by Herakles, the Greek hero whom the Romans admired as Hercules for his acts of courage. Even today, there is a path in the forest of the Hekate that some still call the Helweg.

For everything, including the stars and people, Hel is the great mother, child bearer, and grave. As the year passes and the sun moves on, life is ended and people are received unto her. Yet everything rises anew, enlivened in a new life because Hel is, as the ancients taught, mistress of the life-giving waters from which the sun emerges, rejuvenated. The apples of immortality also belong to her—and Lady Hel is also death. Therefore she cannot reign anywhere other than in the wintry north. The closer we go to the north, the more miserable the trees become, the more meager is the grass, and the more pale are the flowers. Finally, presiding are snow and ice, which never yield because the sun never shines.

In the internal realm of Mother Earth, under the roots of the Ash Tree of the World,[14] which is also called the Tree of Life, lies the spring of destiny, the Udrbrunnr, which Odin consulted to gain ultimate wisdom.[15] In the deepest corner of Lady Hel's house rests the mystery of all mysteries—and at the same time its solution. The "Lord All-father" Odin whispered this remedy, contained in only one mysterious word, in the ear of the dead Baldr before he was placed on briarwood for cremation.

Lady Hel is death, not life, although everything that lives sprouts from her. Just as each wife remains without a child until a male loves her, Lady Hel also requires a husband. Together, they celebrate a woman-earth and man-sun wedding, so that their marriage can produce a child: life. To embrace the goddess of death, the sun god goes to her, who is the earth. On the night of the winter solstice, both celebrate the "holy

---

[13][Helweg refers to "light path" and Hellia refers to "the underworld." —*Trans.*]

[14][In Norse the Ash Tree of the World is Yggdrasil. —*Trans.*]

[15][The Udrbrunnr told Odin that he would die in the Götterdämmerung, or twilight of the gods known as Ragnarökk, a victim of Fenriswolf, a mighty demon who appears as a wolf. —*Trans.*]

marriage." Defeated by the force of the male god, Lady Hel gives herself to him and becomes an expectant mother. When they plowed and sowed their farmland, Anglo-Saxon farmers would shout the words "Salvation be unto you, earth, the mother of man! Shall you grow in the embrace of God and satisfy yourself with fruit of man!"

Hel is also love, the force that brings forth new life, although all living creatures carry death within them. It is love that encourages a woman to find her man, and love that occurs when a mother nurtures her children. Great is the love of the Great Mother!

From the Trutenstein, it is easy to see the heights of the Westerwald. As my guide informed me, the Ketzerstein[16] and the Hohenseelbachskopf are both shrouded in legend, yet I could learn only the legend of the Hohenseelbachskopf: Long ago, the castle of the knights of Seelbach stood on the top of the mountain. It was secure, and the lords on the Hohenseelbach, who called themselves "friends of God and enemies to all the world," did little to determine the public peace, which was well known at that time. One day, the German emperor ordered Archbishop Baldwin von Trier to throw out the Seelbacher knights. Baldwin laid siege to the castle for an entire year, but with no success. The lord of the castle told his lady that just as it was impossible that the beech tree before their castle would turn to stone, the archbishop would never emerge victorious. Nevertheless, the besiegers succeeded and conquered the Hohenseelbach stronghold. In the year 1352, the beech turned to stone. As the lady of the castle on Hohenseelbach had foreseen, with that the contest was lost. She asked the archbishop whether she could take her bridal treasure with her. The Trier bishop thought that she meant her jewels and permitted it. She could, however, take no more than what she was able to carry—so she took her husband and carried him to the base of Zeppenfeld.

It is said that the castle stood in ruins up until the end of the eighteenth century. Now the ruins have disappeared. Sometimes—but only at night—it is still possible to see the whole castle as it once was. At the right hour, a ghostly cavalcade of knights in armor gallop up the castle path, with the lord and his faithful lady at the fore. Outside the gate they

---

[16][Heretic's stone. —*Trans.*]

look for the freshly revived beech, but find it petrified. And as fast as they arrived, the ghosts disappear again. The lords of Seelbach called themselves Friends of God. They might have been German Cathars. Indeed the aristocracy of the Free Dominion of the Westerwald was once loyal to them. There were the counts Sayn and Solms, who were targets of the attacks of Konrad von Marburg. There were also the lords of Wilnsdorf and the knights from Dernbach. These are said to have been the ones who killed the vile magister Konrad. Friends of God. . . . The opposite of this is "slave or servant of God." The Westerwald knights were friends of divinity, grew into iron, and were servant to no one! In addition, in Germany at one time there were true knights. I am sure of this!

German heretics were accused of the following:

[W]hen an initiate attended a heretical assembly for the first time, he was obliged to kiss a toad on the rear end. Sometimes the animal looked more like a goose or duck as large as a baking oven. Then an incredibly pale man with the blackest eyes in the world would approach the new member, who would then kiss him on his ice-cold skin. With each kiss, the Catholic faith would slowly vanish from the new member's heart. Then all the participants would sit down to a meal. Suddenly a black cat as big as a dog would climb down from an ever-present statue. As the cat moved backward, first the initiate, then the master of the assembly, and finally all those "who are worthy and perfect" would kiss the animal's rear end. The imperfect ones and those who felt themselves unworthy would then receive peace from the master. After everyone had taken his place again, songs were sung and the master asked his neighbor: "What does that mean?" The unworthy ones received peace from the master whereupon the neighbor answered: "The highest peace" and another added, "And that we must obey." Then all lights were extinguished and sexual intercourse took place. The torches were then relit and the members took their places again. A man stepped out from a dark corner. He shone like the sun from the head to the haunches and illuminated the entire area, but from the hips down he was as black as the cat. The master grabbed a shirttail of the clothes of the initiate and said: "Master, I give unto you what

I have received." Whereupon the luminous man answered: "You have served me well; you will serve me yet better. I surrender your cares, which you have given unto me." Thereupon he vanished. Each year, around Easter, the members of the sect receive the communion Host, carry it home in the mouth, and then spit it into the toilet pit to express their contempt for the Savior. They state that God had unfairly and traitorously thrown Satan into hell. In the end, he will overwhelm God and bring blessedness. All that pleases God must be avoided; all that he hates is to be loved.

"This transparent web of fabrications," as it is called in a book about Pope Gregory IX from which I extracted this report,

nevertheless found credibility everywhere and excited almost to insanity the gullible old man who sat at that time on the papal chair. Pope Gregory answered that he felt himself inebriated as if from absinthe, and actually sounds in his letters like a raging lunatic: "When the earth found itself pitted against such people, and the stars in the sky did not reveal their fiendishness so that not only people but also the elements united for their destruction and exterminated them to the eternal dishonor of the peoples of the earth, without any consideration for gender or age, then would be a sufficient punishment for their crimes! When they could not be converted, then people had to resort to the strongest means; against wounds which cannot be healed by mild means, fire and sword must be used."

Almost immediately, on June 10, 1233, Konrad von Marburg was instructed to preach a crusade against Luciferianism. The archbishop of Mainz as well as Bishop Konrad von Hildesheim received instructions to muster all their forces in order to exterminate the wretched ones.

But the wily judge Konrad could not implement the order. Twenty days later, he was killed in the vicinity of Marburg. Apparently, Konrad, who had never spared anybody, pleaded for mercy. It was in vain. "A chapel was erected in his memory in Kalleln, near Marburg, at the presumed location of his murder. His corpse was brought to Marburg and buried alongside that of St. Elizabeth. When her bones were transferred to the magnificent church of Elizabeth, his were also reburied there."

When Konrad von Reisenberg, the bishop of Hildesheim, preached a crusade against the Westerwald, Landgrave Konrad of Thuringia and Hesse implemented his sermon. The old *Hessian Rhyme-Chronicle* reports on it briefly but concisely:

> *In this county, in Konrad's time*
> *Many heretics abounded.*
> *Count Heinrich von Sayn was one.*
> *Indeed, he however converted.*
> *Also understood the times were*
> *Knights, priests, and awful people.*
> *Thereupon several turned themselves around*
> *Several to be burned with fire.*
> *Landgrave Kurt destroyed in the land*
> *All heretic schools where he found them.*

~ RUNKEL AM LAHN ~

I arrived in this small town last night by the light of the full moon. People and animals were sleeping. My cleated boots resounded on the cobblestones. Water rushed over a barrier. Like a tremendous black stone wreck, the old castle towered above the houses. The town smelled of linden trees.

Runkel owes its existence to Roland, that hero who entered the Pyrenean valley of Roncesval and who died a heroic death there. He "was guided by his sword Durendal as if only it could accomplish bravery. . . . Once Roland had died, a great light appeared in the heaven."[17]

Roland certainly belonged to Lucifer's courtiers, as did his lord, King Charles—not that Frankish king and emperor, but the "great Charles and lord" in the Nordic heaven: Thor. The town smells of linden trees, roses, and all the flowers that fill Runkel's gardens. There is also the smell of hay in the meadows, and the fields of grain wave in the light wind. A lark soars jubilantly toward the heavens. From a nearby forge, you can hear the beating of an anvil. Under a jasmine pergola, where I am writing this, a colorful butterfly floats past. The Greeks called it *psyche. Psyche* also means "soul."

Like the sea, the fields of grain undulate. Children in this region were shown the undulating fields of grain and were told (to frighten them): "The evil grain-mother will come! And if she gets you, then you must suckle her wooden breasts." The Greeks called Mother Earth their "grain-mother," Demeter. In Germany, she was formerly called Lady Herka or Lady Hel. Her home was the forest or the field and her breath was the wind. People loved her because she was a lovely Venus. Tannhäuser became her lover. Yet Mother Earth, Hel, is also the cool night and murky death. Death is a cool night, and it sings a beautiful German melody by Johannes Brahms. Although the sun bestows life on its own, the night allows the trees and plants to grow. Only the moon, the stars, and the animals are witnesses to this miracle. So it became understandable to me why the Argonauts had to sail into a harbor of Venus to find the golden fleece. They wanted to put their increasingly

---

[17][*Song of Roland.* —Ed.]

divine nature to the test. This spiritual growth was quite comparable to the development of trees. When those Viking-like Greeks sailed over the ocean "on north winds," they carried an oak plank, which was symbolic of the fact that we have to be rooted to the earth, the Mother, to grow upward in the light and stretch ourselves up to the stars. Among mankind there are creatures and heroes in the forest that grow into lowly trees and giant trees. It is up to us to become what we want to be.

The Great Mother, vulgarized as the evil grain and grandmother of the devil, wipes away her tears from those beautiful eyes and quite often laughs, as the golden yellow fields of grain in the Runkel subdistrict are bathed in sunshine. From now on, she will endure fewer injustices, and she will again become the Beloved Lady.

Is the word *heart* derived from Herka? If so, then Parzival's mother, Herzeloyde, is the epitome of the suffering Herka. Parzival left his mother and found the Grail on a mountain after a long odyssey. As the chronicle *Halberstädter Saxon* stated, Lady Venus resided in this mountain. The Grail seeker had made his way from the human mother to the divine mother. One had brought him into the world, while the other assimilated the knight into herself. Parzival had finished the cycle, which, on this side of the Grail Forest, is called life, and was made king. His eyes gazed upon the stone of light before which earthly radiance is nothing. This stone would be borne by a queen. Let us not forget that Lady Wisdom, the mother of the heavens, keeps the philosopher's stone! Let us remain faithful to this woman and not say: "Woman, what for work you have given me. . . !"

When Tannhäuser left Lady Venus, the unfortunate knight began a pilgrimage that became an odyssey. In Rome, he became aware of his mistake, and returned to his Venus in the mountain, where a Round Table awaited him. There he was bitterly missed. As king of the fairy realm, he would deliver the goddess from her anguish.

There was once *une comtesse qui depuis devint fée,* a "countess who then became a fairy." A courtly work of poetry in Old French tells that she was the wife of King Huon of Bordeaux, who should be familiar to us from Wieland's poem *Oberon* or Carl Maria von Weber's romantic opera *Oberon.* This countess undertakes a long odyssey with her husband through the lands of Commans and Foy to the *bocaige Auberon,*

Oberon's magic forest. Afterward, the two are borne over an expanse of water by a fisherman who had transformed himself into Apollo's fish: a dolphin. In the midst of the magic forest is a castle. There, Oberon reigns as king. Like Anfortas or Arthur, he also suffers from a terrible wound. Yet he cannot die until a young king takes his crown and spear, the symbols of sovereignty over the fairy realm. Huon and his wife are to be crowned. Oberon bids farewell to the fairy world and dies. His body is kept in a shrine floating in air.

Once there was a countess who became a fairy. Her name, so the old poem goes, was Esclarmonde. The lands Commans and Foy, mentioned in the old poem, are in fact the Pyrenean districts of Comminges and Foix, where the Cathar castle Montségur rises atop a mountain that belonged to the heretical countess Esclarmonde de Foix.

There was another suffering king and father. Although resembling a god, he would be blessed only when another became king in his place. This suffering king knew nothing about that God of the Jews who jealously guarded the fact that "he is the Lord and otherwise no more" and that his only son, Jesus, who was called Christ, had been forsaken and surrendered to those suffering instead of suffering himself. His son would have suffered and did endure death upon the cross because of the inadequacy of man made by God in his own image on the sixth day of creation. Yet he had pronounced through Moses the curse of all those who would hang on the cross. God who also created evil had condemned in advance his only begotten son! He regretted that he had created man.

This divinity, which is not biblical, wants to be redeemed. It must be redeemed, in order to be divine. The savior has to come from man. What would God be without man? The divinity suffers, because everything is not in order with the world. If man creates order in the world, then the observable part of the essence of divinity, nature, is brought into harmony with the unobservable part, the center of power. As if between magnets, God "floats." When both power currents, the positive and the negative, are equally strong, divinity can rest in itself. This rest, however, has nothing to do with stagnancy. Flowing power lets the redeemed and what is invisibly becoming divinity remain in equilibrium—and thus visibly generate a younger God.

In the old legends and sonnets of chivalry, a younger God reigns over barons and fairies and over knighthood. The life that it leads is different from that led by human creatures. The world in which it lives is not the earthly vale of tears, but an earthly Paradise controlled by a crown, protected by a spear. Only he who remains alert and fights to protect can keep the crown and remain in the earthly Paradise, until, redeemed by youth, he can insert himself into the stream of cosmic power. Up to this point, he lives—but his life is a labor of interpretation and respect for the law and the successor of that God who "floats" in the sky: the sun. His life is a life of loving service. Minne, which is "commemoration," makes the equivalent of earthly Gods all those *irdische göte gnôz,* those who forget neither their past nor their goal, as the song of *Der Wartburgkrieg* goes. The Minne found consolation in the remembrance of man's origins: He who serves love recognizes his final goal. If a man received the consolation of the Minne (this consolation presupposes quests and mistakes and struggles), he could wear a new coat and become a child of God. From then on, he was united with the cycle of creation and with all that crawls and flies and grows and dies. He penetrated with his spirit—to which faith cleared the eye—even the trees and wellsprings whose murmurs and channels he now understood. He would himself become a tree spirit or a water nymph. He even comprehended the nature of stones.

True chivalry and true Minne were accessible to everyone. Nor was it necessary to call yourself "count" or to have much money. The only condition: You had to be a pure one, but not a bastard. For this reason Feirefiz, Parzival's half brother, could not look for the Grail, though it had passed right before his eyes. True gods want a youth who demands his birthright tempestuously and yet is true to the law. This youth replaces and therefore "redeems" the divinity who is becoming old.

I wrote this on a splendid Sunday at Runkel on the Lahn while the Corn Mother wove and the Sun Father shot his arrows. Before me lies an old book. On a yellowing page to which it is opened appears the following sentence: *Runcarii vocantur a villa.* Runkel was named after the German Cathar Runcarii (or, as I also read, Runkeler). On the other hand, Jakob Grimm supposed that the people of Runkel carried short swords called *runco,* which explains why they adopted this name.

~ Cologne ~

The transcription of the old official seal of Cologne reads: *Sancta Colonia Dei Gratia Romae Ecclesiae Fidelis Filia*, "Holy Cologne, faithful daughter, by the grace of God, of the Roman Church." Pope Innocent III, the chief architect of the crusade against the Albigenses, considered Cologne more illustrious in fame and splendor than all the other cities of Germany. Further, a chronicle from the eleventh century christened the city *caput et princeps Gallicarum urbium*, "chief and prince of the Gallic cities." Cologne was Roman during ages past and was forever Roman.

As Colonia Agrippinensis, the city had been pagan Rome's main fortress, weapons depot, and headquarters for a major field commander on the Rhine. It had all the attributes necessary to Rome: capitol, temple, amphitheater, and aqueducts—even Caesars. Then one day, Frankish and Christian bishops arrived, and Cologne remained "Roman." In the ninth century, the Normans destroyed the city. Did these northern enemies of the south wish to undermine Roman authority on German land? In all probability, as religious chronicles may have overstated, Cologne would have remained a heap of rubble after this devastation had the Church not taken it upon itself to help the town recover. Nevertheless, a majority of the Cologne citizenry, above all the weavers guild, was not by any means satisfied with the authority of the Roman priests. Some chroniclers bitterly complained that "only rarely have the citizens accepted with gratitude the advantages and privileges which the bishops indirectly and directly allow to be apportioned unto them."

In the eleventh century, under Archbishop Anno, the citizenry began to conspire against the Church. Before eventually becoming a saint, Anno knew no mercy with the rebels. On his instructions, all lay judges in Cologne had their eyes poked out. Only one judge was spared so that he could escort the others home. Yet about hundred years after Anno, Archbishop St. Engelbert, who became a pillar of the Church and linchpin of Germany, had his own trouble with the citizens of Cologne. He knew, however, that the nobility and service men were so intimidated that nobody dared revolt against him. So the execution flames blazed in Cologne!

In his *Miraculous Dialogue,* the Cistercian monk Caesarius von Heisterbach wrote:

> One day, heretics were seized in Cologne. After an initial investigation, they were transferred to a secular court and condemned. As they were brought to the fire, one of them, Arnold with an unknown surname, who was referred to as the "remaining master," requested bread and a bowl of water. When someone wanted to fill the request, the authorities advised against it, because the devil could very easily conjure something which could cause offense and perdition. As I, Caesarius von Heisterbach, can judge, based on the testimony of another heretic who was held for three years by the king of Spain and then burned, Master Arnold intended to incite a blasphemous communion for the eternally damned. The heretics were led from the city to a place near the Jewish cemetery that was surrendered to the fire. When these people were already glowing intensely, many heard and saw how Arnold applied his hand to the half-burned heads of his students and spoke: "Be firm in your faith, because today you will be with Lawrence!" Among them was a beautiful maiden who was likewise devoted to the heresy. Because many pitied her, one took her from the fire and promised to marry her or deliver her to a convent if she converted. Yet she spoke to those who held her: "Say unto me where that seducer lies?" When they showed her Master Arnold, she fell over the body of the false teacher, veiling her face with her garment, and she ascended with this into hell.

Master Arnold and his faithful must have been some very strange heretics indeed if they were so anxious (already roasting in a fire ignited by Catholics) to join "Lawrence" in Paradise, in the custody of Catholic saints. After he became deacon in Rome, St. Lawrence is said to have been placed on a glowing gridiron by the heathens there and martyred in AD 258. He is regarded as the patron saint of libraries and librarians. Why should he have also been the patron saint of heretics, especially those condemned to be burned to ashes? Caesarius's report raises still more questions: Since when does one *ascend* to hell, and why were the Cologne heretics burned near the Jewish cemetery?

St. Hildegard von Bingen once visited Cologne and spoke before the entire clergy of the city. Yet she did not speak about the sweet love of God, to which she had dedicated so many poems; nor did she talk about heaven, toward which she so earnestly strove. Instead, she lectured on the hiding places of the heretics and informed her audience of devout priests that in order to capture this riffraff of the devil, the workshops of the weavers must be searched—and thoroughly. The art of weaving arrived in the valley of the Rhine from Friesland, to which the island Helgoland also belongs. Therefore, it was no coincidence that the Stedinger were so cruelly exterminated in Friesland[18] while at the same time a hunt for heretics was undertaken against the people of Cologne and the Albigenses. It was also no coincidence that the Provençal Cathars were often called Tisserands—weavers!

Sacred weaving!

At the whizzing loom of the earth, the spirit sits and knits the clothes for the living divinity. To weave is to be. Under the ash tree of the world, the Nornen, the Weird Sisters, wove the thread of fate.[19] There are three of them: The eldest is called Urd, which meant "weaver" in pagan times. She attaches the first knot of the fabric, which will spin farther to Hel. Laurin, the dwarf king, also wove a silk thread, which he used to enclose his paradisal rose garden. Weaver's ship, you follow the path, which you must follow, back and forth, until the cloth is woven. Weaver's ship, you define the cycle that each individual action must fulfill. Therefore, among the people, you went by the name of Radius, for those who originally spoke Latin.

In 1133, a farmer from the town of Indien (today Komelimünster, near Aachen) built a ship in the forest and equipped it with wheels. Members of the weavers guild wanted to transport their ship to Aachen. On the way, a collection was taken from everyone, excluding the weavers, who touched the ship. As the ship journeyed to Aachen and passed by Maastricht, it was outfitted with mast and sail, and in Saint Trond

---

[18][This refers to the Stedinger Revolt in Friesland (AD 1233–1234) and the crusade that Pope Gregory IX mounted against the Stedinger "heretics." —Ed.]

[19][The three Nornen, or Weavers of Destiny, were Udr (what was), Verdandi (what will be), and Skuld (what should be). They worked under the Yggdrasil, the sacred ash tree, and appear in Shakespeare's *Macbeth*. Their Greek correspondents were the Moire. —*Trans.*]

near Lüttich the weavers of the town guarded their ship day and night, filling it with all kinds of equipment—though what exactly it was filled with has not been passed down. Minstrels then encircled it and struck up a dance. The merry chaos lasted twelve days, until finally the authorities intervened. They dared not burn or otherwise destroy the ship in the belief that "the place, even if only ash were to remain of it, would be disgraced." Therefore, the vessel was caulked so that it could be transported to a place in the nearest vicinity without much commotion or the authorities' need to resort to the force of arms.

In a cave in the Sabarthès, I found a symbol from the Albigensian era. It depicted the ship of the dead with the sun for a sail—a sacred ship! When Apollo descended to the world, Zeus gave him a golden mitre, a lyre, and a chariot harnessed with swans. Then he sent him to Delphi, where Apollo was to promulgate the law to the Greeks. Akin to a star, Apollo navigated his swans to the land of the Hyperboreans, and his radiance penetrated to heaven. The journal of navigational tables forged from precious gold by Hephaestus-Vulcan, the son of Venus, saw him through the journey. On the surface of the water the deity slumbered. The Athenians dedicated their Parthenon to Athena, the virgin goddess of wisdom, who was a weaver and manipulator of the spindle. A saffron cape hoisted as a sail on a parade float was solemnly carried to the Acropolis every four years by the highest officials of the Athenian state and there was offered to Athena. Noble-born Athenians intricately embroidered the sail with the representation of the clash of the Titans: when the gods and Titans waged a war over the mountain of Olympus.

Athena, the divine maker of the saffron-colored carpet of life, also protected the handiwork of the forge. She owed her divine existence to the moment when the blacksmith Hephaestus or, as others taught, the fiery Prometheus split from the head of Zeus. Thereby was Athena born. On the Acropolis her combat-ready spear always flashed, symbolic of the fact that without combat readiness and courage in the face of death, life is forfeited. When the Athenians carried the coatlike sail and spear to the temple mount, they also carried the banner of a raven, woven by the noblest daughters of the city, to span across the mast of the holy ship, which was left to the driving wind of fortune at the beach on the edge of the sea, so that it would sail to wherever it wished. Holy ship!

The most famous Hellenic heroes navigated the seas aboard the *Argo,* which was perhaps an *arca,* an ark. They sailed to the north. Jason was the ship's captain. Orpheus, the sons of Zeus, Castor and Pollux, and Hercules were his companions. Placed on the bow of the ship was a talking oak plank fetched from Dodona, where Greece's holiest oak spoke wisdom. The Argonauts had to withstand terrible hardships throughout their journey, until they found the goal for which they had traveled: the golden fleece of divinity. In the Middle Ages this was considered akin to the philosopher's stone.

Wieland the blacksmith embedded himself in a tree trunk and let his fate befall him. He hoped to be exonerated in this "ship" (like an Argonaut). The smith had been lamed by King Nidhag, which forced him to seek revenge. Earlier, Wieland and his two brothers, Schlagfidr and Egli, had surprised three swan maidens who "chose the ones who died in the battle" in the Myrkwid, or "dark forest." These swans were the Valkyries, who were dedicated to peace. On the banks of Wolf Lake, they took off their swanlike feathery gowns that were spun of white linen. Stealthily, the three brothers took the swan gowns and led the three virgins home as their wives. One day, after seven winters had passed, the women were driven deep into Myrkwid and never returned. Wieland's pain at his wife's disappearance became so great that his son, Wideke, wanted to abandon him: "Father, I do not want to become a smith! Give me a good stallion, a sharp sword, a strong spear, a new shield, a hard helmet, and a shining coat of mail so that I may take off and seek a good lord—he with whom I will serve and ride, so long as life is granted to me!" Whereupon his father asked to where he intended to ride. "To the land of the Amelungen, to Dietrich von Bern. . . !"

In the eighteenth century, the people from Berkshire in the south of England said "Wayland Smith lives in a stone." Holy ship and holy stone. . . . Chiron, the ferryman of the dead, uses his boat to transport the souls of the deceased across the Styx to the underworld—across an expanse of water, which makes everything pure. In Nordic myths, this underworld is called Glasisvellir or Glasislundr, which can mean "glass site" as well as "amber country." (Tacitus equates the Germanic word *Glas* with "amber." The Romans called it *glesum* and the Greeks *elektron.*) The Friesian island known as Helgoland and others in the North

Sea were also known as the islands of the dead. The Roman historian Pliny calls them Glesiae or Elektrides. They were the *insulae vitreae,* the glassy islands of Celtic tradition, where King Arthur dwelled. Arthur means "great bear."

On a small but seaworthy ship, Pytheas sailed from Marseille toward the midnight sun. He landed, as he intended, on the island of Thule: in amber country. Pytheas was a philosopher and a friend of wisdom. What use is wisdom if the final, divine mysteries are ignored? Pytheas probably carried amber in his hand as his ship entered the port of his hometown after his historic journey. In his own way, he was an Argonaut. Indeed, like the heroes of the *Argo,* he sailed to the north and may have brought back a golden yellow stone. I am sure that he sat before this stone and inspected it as thoughtfully as Hamlet contemplated the skull of his ancestor. The prince of Denmark asked what life is and why humans live. The questions he posed were those that provoked Lucifer's fall from heaven. I am certain that distress did not and would never frighten Pytheas, even if he had known about Jehovah's curse. Pytheas held a golden yellow stone. For him it was the philosopher's stone . . . the golden fleece!

In a boat pulled by a swan, Lohengrin went to the needy and brought them the glad tidings of the Grail, the stone that fell from Lucifer's crown. He also forbade people to question its provenance, but only his own! He did so for a reason: he was not human and, if humans recognized him, he had to return from whence he had come.

Europe was not purified when the Cologne Cathars were tracked down, seized in their workshops, and burned. That cremation near the Jewish cemetery was mockery. Instead of the biblical words Jesus spoke to a thief on the cross, "Today you will yet be with me in Paradise," the Cathars, or at least the Cologne archheretic Arnold, used the comforting words "Today you will be with Lawrence!" But Arnold couldn't have meant St. Lawrence, because most saints felt for heretics only hatred— not understanding or forgiveness—while they were still on the earthly side of misery. There is no reason to think that they would have felt otherwise in heaven. What Pope Gregory, sometimes called the Great, once said about the joy felt by the righteous of heaven at the sight of the agonies of the heretics would have also been valid for the saints. These agonies multiplied the divine desires of those dwelling in Abraham's fold. So why should St. Lawrence, who accepted a martyr's death to attain heaven, have been mentioned as a protector of the infernal ones?

Even if the account of Pope Gregory is incorrect or Lawrence had recognized that heretics were people who were not what his Church had taught, what clearly emerges from Caesarius's account is that the Cathars of Cologne hoped to dwell with "Lawrence" in that place which the Catholics of the thirteenth century regarded as hell. Yet it was necessary to ascend to this otherworldly place. Consequently, it could not be hell, the place where Jesus was driven down after his resurrection, only to ascend to heaven finally and sit at the right hand of God, as the Christian profession of faith maintains. That Lawrence whom the heretics awaited was Laurin!

— HEISTERBACH MONASTERY RUINS —

Seven hundred years ago, the famous monk and medieval chronicler Caesarius von Heisterbach wrote his principal works *Dialogue of Visions and Miracles,* the *Life of the Holy Landgravine Elizabeth,* and, at the request of the inquisitor Johannes, who was a well-known torturer of heretics, the writ *Against the False Doctrine of Lucifer.*[20] There are many things to recount concerning the monks and abbots of this abbey, its growth, and its flowering.

Before setting up a monastery in the valley of St. Peter, fourteen Cistercian monks had sailed down the Rhine on an April day in 1188. They wanted to settle in the Seven Mountains, around the abandoned monastery of St. Maria on the Stromberg. Suddenly, as the choncler Caesarius relates, they saw a circle in the sky that enclosed seven suns. That seemed to be a good omen because they believed that a circle signified the holy spirit and the seven signified the seven Christian gifts of grace, which, from then on, would illuminate the disbelieving and heretical land.

Finally, they arrived on the Stromberg. Fifty years earlier a knight had established himself here as a hermit. Around his hermitage had assembled a flock of believers who, like him, "had escaped naked from the shipwreck of the world" and founded a monastery. Promoted and protected by popes and Cologne's archbishops, who, in the area surrounding the monastery, were building one small castle after another, they tried to preach the gospel. It was not told to what extent they succeeded. What did reach us, however, is the fact that after the death of the hermit, the cloister was abandoned because of the altitude of this dwelling place on the mountain. With the archbishop's permission, the monks founded another monastery—but what concerned those fourteen Cistercian monks who took possession of the abandoned monastery on the summit of the Stromberg was the rough climate, the deficiency of the dwellings, and the difficulty of providing for themselves because of the high altitude. All this made them dissatisfied. They wanted to escape.

---

[20][Caesarius von Heisterbach (1180–1240), master of novices at the Heisterbach monastery, was one of the most widely read authors of the Middle Ages. —*Trans.*]

Yet because of a dream he had, the abbot believed in this mission and had to hold back the friars by persuasion and punishment: He dreamed that, holding the cross, he had boarded a boat along with a crowd of white men. A fast current propelled the boat into the choir of a church, and only by skillful steering could he prevent the boat and crew from smashing into a column. Therefore, all of the monks remained on the Stromberg. Finally, however, even the abbot was no longer happy up there, and, in 1191, the monastery was moved to the foot of the mountain, to the valley of St. Peter. The church on the summit remained the monastery's place of worship.

One day, the Cologne archbishop, Theodericus, saw to the beginnings of construction of Godesberg Castle. For some time, the chapel of St. Michael had stood there "because of the holiness of the place," and nobody had dared to construct a castle. But when the constuction commenced, the Archangel Michael was allegedly so enraged about the building that, with outspread wings, he had flown off to the chapel on the Stromberg with a reliquary shrine from the chapel on the Wudinsberg (Wotansberg), as the Godesberg was still called.

~ Bonn ~

Earlier, our students sang the drinking song *Mihi est propositum in taberna mori,* "My Idea Is to Die in the Tavern." The song was written in the thirteenth century by a wandering cleric named Nicholas, who was called the *archipoeta.* Caesarius von Heisterbach recalled that Nicholas once fell ill with a high fever in Bonn and believed his last moments had finally arrived. Penitently, he banged on the door of the Heisterbach abbey and asked for shelter, which was given. For a while, it was believed that he had become a monk with a great sense of atonement. He was hardly recovered, however, when he pulled off his cassock and threw it away contemptuously. Then he escaped. Jakob Grimm compared this archipoeta to a tamed beast that was suddenly freed in the wild forest.

Nicholas reminds me of three famous characters: First, I recall troubadour Peire Cardinal, whose father wanted to make him into a clergyman. Instead, he became a heretic and one of the most famous wandering minstrels of the Minne.

Second, Till Eulenspiel: Although he couldn't stand monks and nuns, when he felt miserable and depressed, he became the doorman of a cloister for a few days. What Till was up to in his capacity as doorman, archpoet Nicholas also would have done: He let wandering scholars and minstrels into the abbey and showed them what was in the kitchen, then he escaped with his guests. In the end, Till fell headfirst into the grave. Third, Nicholas reminds me of Shakespeare's Lord Falstaff, that famous glutton with a fishlike thirst who traveled English roads, letting "the devil ride from his fiddle bow," and who drowned his sadness because no virtue in the world remains in champagne. Yes, "that villainous, abominable misleader of youth, Falstaff, that old white-bearded Sathan": He enjoyed his life with a zest that can be compared to the weaver's ship, and when he died, he went to "Arthur's bosom." The hostess of the East Cheapside tavern where Falstaff drank himself to death knew that "Arthur's bosom" was not hell. She, Mistress Quickly, stayed with Falstaff in his last hours, "until he was as cold as any stone." I will return to Sir Falstaff a bit later, because he was a heretic.

— Asbach in the Westerwald —

Near this tiny place is another hamlet called Wambach. Because both names recall the Asen and Wanen, the divine caste of gods of Germanic mythology, I decided to make a detour. The unexpected coincidence was golden in another way because at harvesttime, less than one hundred years ago, in 1830 to be exact, a farm girl unearthed a precious gold coin with the inscription *Lysimachos Basileus,* King Lysimachos. (Lysimachos was one of the most courageous field commanders of Alexander the Great; after Alexander's death, he became king of Thrace and united Thrace with the adjacent portion of Asia Minor in an independent empire. From 288 BC, he was able to share domination over Macedonia with Pyrrhus, the king of Epirus and the warrior who vanquished the Romans. He fell in a battle with Diadochen Seleukos, who had become the king of Babylonia.) The coins were eventually handed over to the Prussian crown prince Friedrich Wilhelm and can still be admired, unless I am mistaken, in the coin collection in Berlin.

So a small coin opened a bridge to ancient Macedonia in the little town of Asbach. I stop and reflect on the fact that this is truly exceptional.

Alexander the Great, you also belong to Lucifer's court! Wolfram von Eschenbach praised your wisdom in song because you were a knight and Isaiah cursed you in the name of his Lord of the Hosts.

You wanted to be seated upon the "mount of the congregation, in the sides of the north" because you tried to storm the walls of Paradise, which some placed in Obarkia in the far north, the land of temporary darkness and long winter nights. According to legend, even as an arrogant youth, you wanted to fly with two griffons high over the clouds to the heavens. You wanted to be the same as the gods and you boisterously demanded entrance to Paradise, shouting stridently, "I too am a king!" And you let the priestly caste of the Siwa Oasis name you a son of Zeus: Amon. Your father, Philip, whose name means "horse friend," believed that these animals were sacred. You must have asked, "Why have you created me?" or, as your father's son and king of Macedonia, you wouldn't have accomplished your duty to unite the Aryans. Your mother was Olympian. You asked yourself, "Why was I born to my mother?" Because you wanted to become an Olympian, you became immortal.

During one of your father's military campaigns, an eagle flew into his tent and laid an egg upon his shoulder. The egg fell to the ground and broke and a snake crawled out. At the same instant, Olympus's messengers arrived with news of your birth. The midwife was the serpent!

You died young, Alexander, and, if the reports are to be believed, with a smile upon your lips. Your corpse was laid to rest in a magnificent sarcophagus, although according to your last will, your hands were outside. They pointed at and were filled with earth. I know what you wanted to say: You wanted to ask the Creator, "Why have you created me from the earth?"

In the end, they laid you to rest in the city that you built in the Nile Delta, next to the Homerian Pharos, the city that still bears your name: Alexandria. Your last resting place was shown to those who wished to see it. As fanatical Christians demolished all temples in your Alexandria and, in a church, tortured to death the philosopher Hypatia, your sarcophagus vanished. You fell from the skies, Alexander, but you entered the enlightened realm of Lucifer, the Light Bringer. Your realm was called Olympus. We call it Asgard, Walhall, rose garden, and Mont Salvat. The Jews cursed it as Gehenna, and the Christians fled in terror from it—they called it hell. According to a shaveling named Lamprecht, a raging savage who was torment incarnate, during your lifetime hell reigned supreme over heaven and earth and could never be filled. Finally, it was written in *The Solace of Souls,* an orthodox medieval devotional book, that you, great Macedonian, were "violent to all people": "Now he is in the power of the devil. For a short time, he was happy; now he is miserable for eternity. He created an empire but now is poor forever. Nobody attested to his goodness, so now he is filled with hell's fire. He had great and worldly pride, but now has only shame. He didn't want to follow the commandments of our Lord, so now he must obey the devil in hell." We know, however, that Lucifer, who suffered injustice, greeted and kissed you, great Alexander.

As Pytheas sailed out of Marseille to the land of amber and the island of Thule, Alexander the Great stood in Gordion in Asia Minor before the sacred cart of Zeus. I prefer to believe that it was in the same year, 334 years before the birth of Jesus of Nazareth.

Alexander observed how the yoke and shaft of the cart were bound with a mind-boggling knot. Until then, no man alive could untie it. But Alexander wanted to fulfill the prophecy that was spoken by Pythia in

Delphi: He wanted to become the king of Asia. Apollo had given him wisdom because he had a strong will. In both hands, Alexander took his sword, the sign of his royal power, and split the knot in two.

It was the Phrygian king Midas who had tied the knot, because Apollo had cursed him. Instead of listening to Apollo, Midas had followed Pan. Everything he touched had turned to gold, and instead of human ears, he had donkey ears. Did Alexander know Midas's secret? We can only guess the answer, but when upon visiting the early Christian catacombs in Rome, we can see Jesus of Nazareth depicted with a donkey head and can even see a donkey instead of a person hanging from the cross. We can also see that the pope has gold coming from all over the globe.

Pytheas sought the divine wisdom of Ariana, and Alexander wanted to be the king of kings of Asia and Iran, which is a new Ariana. Both sought, and seeking led them to the same goal: to prepare himself for the passage to divinity. With his sword Pytheas realized the necessity to be forearmed and Alexander knew the will to victory. Both needed partners and oarsmen, generals and soldiers. Pytheas had to overcome the skeptics in his city and, while on the high seas, he had to overcome the ocean waves, the storms in Biscay, the fog in the North Sea, and the worrisome question: "What next?" A whole front of Macedonian cynics was ranged against Alexander, and beyond the Hellespont were the sandstorms, deserts, mountain frosts, torrential rivers, and enemy armies as well as the probing question: "What then, when I am no longer?"

For Midas, the man who tied the Gordian knot, everything he touched turned to gold. Apollo cursed him because he placed Pan's sonnets over Apollo's songs, Catholic sonnets over those of the Hyperboreans. Properly translated, *catholic* means "world encompassing," whereas Hyperborean means "Nordic." Clearly, Midas had given the north priority in the tangled world, and the knot was tangled. Only an Alexander could untangle it—through action. But action that leads to victory sits next to the *will* to action. Alexander's insight was Apollonian in nature: Like the sun god who was at home in the land of the barbarians, near and over the numerous stars, some more brilliant than others, Alexander chivalrously prevailed. The king of northern blood came and conquered his dominion over the king of kings of the Arian caste: Darius. Every struggle was a challenge for him, and every puzzle was a challenge. To win, man needs weapons. Alexander took his sword, just as Siefried took his Balmung, Dietrich his Eckesacks (magical swords), and Ornit his rose, and cut the Gordian knot. In this way, he untangled Midas's knot and dominated the world. So his blood showed him the way.

Pytheas was of the same blood as Alexander. His nature sent him north to search for the answer to the questions "From where?" and "Where are we going?" Prior to Pytheas's journey, Heraclitus had guessed at the heliocentricity of the world, just as the high priests of Apollo announced Apollo's message, while still others made a pilgrimage to Delphi to see a stone where Apollo had killed the snake, Pythos. Pytheas knew all these puzzling questions, but he still had to resolve them! As the sun god Apollo traveled to the land of the barbarians to gain strength, so Pytheas traveled in his boat to the land of amber and Thule. In his own way, the Massilian sailor cut his own Gordian knot, and discovered the beginning and end of his world. Insight drew Pytheas inexorably to the north. Alexander resolved his greatest challenge through action—yet action, which leads to victory, demands insight (and how could it be otherwise?). As a consequence, Alexander had to combine perception with action. Did he gain this insight among Greece's wise men, possibly Pytheas? His teacher was Aristotle.

I am traveling across the country, seeking knowledge of a stone that fell from Lucifer's crown. It is an antiquated and foolish project, some would say—and some do say it.

A gold coin that a farm girl found more than one hundred years ago took me to Asbach in the Westerwald, a small German town. I pondered Alexander and Pytheas and continue to ponder Aristotle. I am happy; in a way, the circle is closing, although not fulfilled because Aristotle *kunt maere von dem agetstein,*[21] as Wolfram von Eschenbach says in *Der Wartburgkreig.* Like Aristotle, he knew about the stone that fell from Lucifer's crown.

I will return later to Aristotle and Alexander and the Claugestiân stone, from a land that "never saw a Christian." Even at midnight, the stone shines brightly. In the end, the old duke of Meran, Berchther, King Rother's companion, wore it on his helmet.

---

[21]["knew what to do with the agate stone." —*Trans.*]

~ Goslar ~

In a sermon preached in 1220, Heinrich Minneke, provost of the Cistercian cloister in Neuwerk, asserted that there is a lady in heaven who is even greater than the Blessed Virgin Mary, and that her name is Wisdom. Did it come as any surprise when Minneke was charged with heresy by the bishop of Hildesheim? After all, the provost saw Lucifer begging forgiveness from the Almighty. The bishop of Hildesheim, a town that prominently displayed a thousand-year-old rosebush, was Konrad von Reisenberg. Pope Honorius III had entrusted him with the bishopric during the lifetime of his predecessor.[22] In France, he had helped preach the crusade against the Albigenses, and now he brought his rich experience to Germany. Rome had good use for such a man in the Harz region. For a long while, this area had brimmed with heretics. In fact, 170 years before, in 1052, it was already well known that the inhabitants of Goslar would rather hang than kill a chicken. Apparently, early on they had been influenced by Manichaeism, a creed that Rome despised. It is truth that Manichaeans forbade the killing of animals, so as not to offend the law of reincarnation of souls.

Bishop Konrad was an Upper Hessian by birth. Accompanied by a prelate, he traveled to Goslar to clear up the Minneke case. After the Neuwerk nuns had—against their will—implicated the accused in their depositions, the bishop ordered him henceforth to teach only the "correct" belief. Heinrich Minneke, however, never stopped praising divine wisdom and Lucifer's forgiveness. Now far too flagrant for the bishop of Hildesheim, the provost was summoned before the bishop's tribunal, stripped of his position, and sent back to his monastery. (Minneke belonged to the Praemonstraten order.) The bishop ordered the nuns to find another prior—this time an uncomplicated one. Neither Minneke nor the nuns followed the instructions of their bishop, who protested directly to the pope. But the courageous nuns of Goslar also protested to the Holy Father, though they seemed uncertain of the pontiff's powers of judgment, for they took the precaution of writing a letter to Emperor Frederick II, explaining that the Neuwerk monastery had blossomed like

---

[22][Pope Honorius (born ca. 1227) was a former tutor of Emperor Frederick. —*Trans.*]

a lily under Minneke's direction. In their eyes, jealousy motivated the bishop of Hildesheim, who, apart from the imperial rights over the case, wished to damage the Neuwerk monastery. To them, their prior was a pious man who wanted only the best for their monastery, while the bishop of Hildesheim was only holding Minneke in a bad light under the undeserved accusation of heresy.

At his Ferentino court, the emperor gave the nuns' letter to the bishops in attendance. Naturally, they supported the assessment of their colleague in Hildesheim. In their view, as they stated, the Neuwerk nuns were so partial that they seemed to have gone mad. They informed the Goslar nuns that it was high time to be reasonable: Obey the bishop and observe the rule of St. Benedict.[23] The pope did not answer differently: To him, Minneke was a rotting appendage that had to be amputated from the body of the Church, a dispensable man whose replacement was a necessity. He was endangering souls and placing the Neuwerk cloister in a bad light. They should all be happy at Minneke's recall.

Shortly after this, Bishop Konrad had the heretical provost arrested. At this time, Minneke himself wrote directly to the pope. He complained that he had been thrown in a dungeon without ever confessing or even being charged with heresy. He pleaded to be heard properly; he asserted that his arrest was an error, but if it could be proved that he had persisted in speaking against the unity of the Church, he would stay in prison for the rest of his life. The pope was so impressed with his letter that he ordered the bishop of Hildesheim to try the prisoner before a court of papal legates, theologians, and the grand inquisitor of Germany, Konrad von Marburg. On October 22, 1224, the synod gathered in Hildesheim. Minneke was charged and, after a long trial, condemned for heresy. He was stripped of his office and cursed and his priest's clothes were taken from him.

Heinrich Minneke was burned alive as a Manichaean and Luciferian. He claimed to be a friend of wisdom and philosophy, but if we have been correctly informed, Minneke belonged to those heretics who were already quite weakened by a belief in Christian salvation, even if this

---

[23][The Rule of St. Benedict is the principal guide to Roman Catholic monastic life. It was written by Benedict between AD 530 and 560. —*Trans.*]

was not very Roman Catholic in nature. For him, Lucifer was a fallen angel who one day—the youngest day—would be forgiven by God and subsequently redeemed.

To play with words is a dubious game. I cannot at all see any real link between Heinrich Minneke's incineration as a Manichaean and the Minnesingers, who were also influenced by Manichaeism.

Heinrich von Reichenau relates the following events of 1052 in a south German historical treatise:

> The emperor [Heinrich III], who was spending Christmas in Goslar, had a certain heretic hanged on the gallows with the general agreement of the populace to stop him from teaching heresy and infecting more people. Apart from teaching the terrible ideas of the Manichaean sect, the heretic had refused to eat any meat. In full sight of the gallows, the heretic refused to kill a chicken, and in the thirteenth century this was accepted as certain proof of heresy.

The heretic's refusal to kill a rooster was quite understandable because a rooster was sacred to Apollyon, as John calls the diabolical blend of Apollo and the Antichrist in the Apocalypse. It was a bird that also would have pleased the German Tiubel when he presented himself at the forest's edge at midday, as trees cracked and the wind howled. Even if today many still look askance at vegetarians, there is a certain sense about Goslar's vegetarian heretic, and he hurt no one. It is surprising, then, that others demanded that he be hanged or burned. The number of ascetic heretics was very small, according to a Catholic historian. Why, then, should exceptions be presented as generalized truths? I haven't strayed far from the preposterous reports concerning Landgrave Hermann, the father-in-law of St. Elizabeth: "He ate neither herring nor smoked fish and drank neither beer nor mead," which the Cathars did with gusto. I think we should leave to the meticulous investigation of armchair detectives the menu and drink of medieval heretics or Catholic faithful.

The founder of the Manichaean sect to which the Goslar heretics belonged was Mani. It is asserted that he was born smiling. I find this archheretic more attractive at his first breath than all the other sad-faced creators of religions. I cite from a well-known essay on Mani's life and work:

> He must have been a visionary and highly-gifted poetic personality, a fiery orator and an unparalleled artist. Mani's respect for art must have been due to his Iranian heritage. As the offspring of the ancient Ashkanian and Arshakuni castes, he was, in this regard, an authentic Persian who considered poetry, music, and the arts to be the most precious and pure of all noble undertakings.

We must also remember that an English language *Literary History of Persia* described the Manichaean joy in the creation of the beautiful as one of their major characteristics. Like the Hellenes who cultivated their *kalos k'agatos* or the Provençales who loved their *bel e bos,* the Manichaeans developed the beautiful and good and arrived at a gay Savoir.

Mani, who arrived smiling into this world, descended on both his father and mother's side from the royal Parthian house of the Arshakuni (Askanija, Baskanija), which was founded in 256 BC by the Scythian king Arsarces I. This king had led his armies into the northern Iranian region of Parthia, where the ancient Persian religion had endured in the hearts of the Persian people and constituted a dam against Hellenism (which we should understand as the Near Eastern variety), Roman power, and the creeping influence of Judaism. It would be going too far to describe here the history of the Parthians and their kings or Manichaean morality and its doctrine, but it is a fact that Mani, the Ashkanian, was an Iranian-Aryan who rejected the Old Testament and the divinity of Jesus of Nazareth. In AD 275, he was crucified on the orders of Zoroastrian priests. His body was skinned, stuffed, and hanged at the gates of Babylon as a gruesome warning. Long before Alexander had died there and soon after the death of Mani, the followers of Muhammad would conquer the city. Manichaeism seemed dead; but just a few years ago, the deceased Parsi seemed to have returned from the dead. As I leafed through my files, I came across the following newspaper clipping:

A short while ago, scientific journals and newspapers reported the sensational discovery of an original manuscript by Mani, the founder of a Persian religion. Crucified in 275, his followers hid his writings in fear of discovery. The seven volumes that were discovered in Fiume are scientifically and historically priceless. Dark brown, moldy, dusty, and torn, the treasures, which are like a piece of rotting tree bark, lie before Dr. Ibscher, a Berlin handwriting expert. With the help of a magnifying glass, tweezers, and an air brush, Ibscher must lift each page and place each little piece between glass plates. Resorting to other methods such as the use of chemicals is strictly forbidden, because it could destroy the handwriting on the pages. Dr. Ibscher estimates the time required for the full restoration of the text to be at least ten years. And how long will we have to wait for a translation?

The article appeared in 1935.

Another clipping from the same year asks, "Has the Grail Been Found?": "A cup believed to have been used by Jesus during the Last Supper has been found by a British archaeological expedition in a cave in the Orontes Valley between Antioch and Harim in Syria, in the vicinity of one of the oldest Christian churches in existence. The cup has been taken to London for careful scientific examination." I have never heard another word about his Grail and I doubt if we will ever hear of it again.

Finally, there are amazing similarities between Manichaean-Iranian and Icelandic poetry. I think we can exclude the explanation of coincidence. Nor did Manichaean missionaries evangelize in Iceland. Maybe, however, the Provençal troubadours who fled Rome's inquisitors reached the land of the *Edda,* where they found their spiritual brothers in the skalds and transmitted to these singers and storytellers some of their Manichaean concepts. Or did the troubadours, skalds, and Manichaeans drink from the same well of Norse wisdom?

At any rate, my journey in search of Lucifer's spirits, who were in no way bad ghosts, will almost certainly take me to Iceland.

~ HALBERSTADT ~

It is Christmas. Before visiting my friends who invited me to Christmas Eve, I decided to wander through the town. Through the windows of the old town I saw some beautifully decorated Christmas trees glowing in candlelight. I could hear the happy laughter of children and feel the passion of the fathers and mothers. Both sadness and happiness overwhelmed me. The bells began to announce the celebration, the ancient festival of light of the middle of winter. The sun god Helios-Apollo, Mithra, and even Chronos, the father of Zeus, were all born on this day, and time again they are born of a virgin mother. At midnight in the church of this old town, the choir will resound: "Today is born the lord, who is Christ the Lord, in the City of David!"

Lucifer could easily complain that mankind has turned its back on him, for long ago, his birthday was celebrated on this date. The Light Bringer suffered and nobody remembers him—except I! Some twelve paces beyond the entrance to the town's cathedral, I will touch with my hand a stone that fell from the heavens. According to legend, the devil was so upset over the construction that with this stone he bombed the half-finished church in order to destroy it. He just missed, goes the story. The stone is called *Teufelstein*.[24] Oddly, the devil threw it from the heavens!

How contradictory are Christians! In Cologne, they had burned at the stake heretics who should *ascend* to hell, while Isaiah placed hell at the bottom of all. And here in Halberstadt, the devil supposedly threw a stone from the heavens when, as we all know, he is the lord of the depths of hell. Christians will believe anything!

When I stand before the mild irradiance of the teufelstein, which found its way, undisturbed, through the stars in their divine firmament, I am forced to think of the Grâl, the stone that fell from Lucifer's crown and was won by Parzival. Further, I cannot forget the Grâl messenger Lohengrin, whom some called the Light Bringer Helias, which means Helios. In the depositions of the Inquisition, I read that the Cathars were awaiting an apparition, and according to the fifteenth-century *Halberstädter Sachsenchronik,* "the chroniclers believe that this youth,

---

[24][Devil's stone. —*Trans.*]

Helias the swan knight, came from the mountain where Lady Venus resided with the Grâl." When I visit the devil's stone, I will also think of Apollo, that light bringer who is born to a virgin every winter solstice in the land of the Hyperboreans and is carried to mortal men by swans in order to bring the law to mankind. Names are more smoke and thunder when they belong to divinities. After all, it is Christmas.

~ BERLIN ~

As I walk down the wide and long streets of this city and look at the bustling people, when I look from the room where I live into the big patio of the apartment building and observe the exhausted people who almost never leave their apartments or who leave them only briefly, I am filled with pity. They don't know how deep and beautiful life outside can be—in the mountains, on the plains, in the towns and villages and hamlets. Bitter is the fact that most big-city people would never exchange their desert of cement houses for what they call contemptuously the provinces. Not for a second will they leave. They are condemned to extinction.

I again attended Richard Wagner's musical dramas *Parsifal* and *Lohengrin*. When I saw the doves on the costumes of the Grail knights, I thought of that tiny clay dove that an old man showed year after year in Lavelanet in the Pyrenees. When Lohengrin sang his tale of a castle "in a remote land, far from your steps," my mind wandered to Montségur, that Pyrenean rock with its marvelous citadel in whose ruins clay doves were unearthed. After the performance of *Lohengrin,* I returned home on foot with a friend. It had just rained. The street's wet asphalt mirrored the lights of the street lamps and the headlights of the cars and, even more, the bright lights beaming from the shop windows and the department-store window displays. In short, the night had been turned into day. The air was laden heavily with the smell of gasoline and artificial aromas that are mistakenly called perfumes. The roar of automobiles and the chatter of the city's inhabitants boomed in my ears. I thought that my old professor of religion was right: Hell is nothing other than the absence of God. In the big city that is so proud of the title "world metropolis," God goes silent quickly. To live forever in such a place would be like being banned in Gehenna.[25]

I spoke of these thoughts to my companion. He became a pastor early on, but one day, he gave up preaching biblical fairy tales from the pulpit and, trying to prove that they had actually taken place, began to write for the German spirit. Now he tells his congregation that what he preaches is the word and revelation of God—but of a God other than

---

[25][Gehenna or Gehenom or Gehinom is Jewish hell or purgatory. The term also appears in the Qu'ran. —*Trans.*]

the one in the Bible—and whoever wishes to listen to this God shall hear him.

Finally, we sat at a round table in the soft light of the lamp. My friend read aloud passages from the manuscript of his new book, which he has called *The Birth of the Millennium:*[26]

> The time has come to hand over all power to the strong. Only in this way, can the "sins" of the world die, because sin is weakness. Strength is the recognition of the law, the self in all its facets with all its limits and perceptions. Strong is he who is the lord of himself in relation to society. The aspiring have rebelled and demand the fulfillment of their duty. The religion of redemption is dead. The religion of strength has been born: That is the law.

He continued:

> The history of this lost law is short: The people of the north brought the unwritten law to the tired, decadent city-states of the south that had given up their blood and morality in democracy. As the people of the north stood before the exposure of the law and saw the consequences of democracy and examined its basics, the teachings of the cross swept over them. Poignantly, the northerners realized that they could give structure to the teetering ancient world, decaying under the influence of Oriental Hellenism. The old world was educated but tired. The prophets of Apocalypse preached fear. As a consequence, the old word's essence was fast dissipating. In its last frenzy, it committed a crime. At this apocalyptic moment, it announced its grim teachings. Sustained was the din of the death march of the young people of the north. The Orient held the cross aloft and overshadowed the young people. Although their young bodies were willing to fight under the foreign sun, their souls were defenseless against the poisonous teachings of the Orient. Despite

---

[26][Rahn's friend was Kurt Eggers (1905–1943), a German author and a National Socialist cultural writer. He volunteered for the Waffen SS and was killed in Russia in 1943. According to Rahn biographer Hans Juergen Lange, Eggers was in part responsible for Rahn's suicide when he refused to give him his passport to flee Germany in 1939. —*Trans.*]

enriching the world with its youth, the north was poisoned. The cross prepared its attack. Defeat became the gospel—a belief that damned the strength of will and praised surrender. The old world sucked the blood of the northern peoples because their spirit was too childlike: Its will was not properly focused and its actions were not planned. So the people of the north lost the law. With their calculated experience and hatred of the God-fearing, the prophets of defeat overcame the joy of the living and the bearers of the will. Goodness and honor stopped the young from killing the old, so that they should live among the young and teach. Lessons took the place of action. Because the law was lost, nations lost their sense for following a course and for arrival, life, truth, and greatness. More than once, the silence of the cemetery reigned in the north. But the will to life of the Germanic peoples was so strong that, time and again, it grew in the light. The much-accursed law broke the deadly policies of the cross—only to be covered up at the decisive moment.

So it is, I thought. We should not forget that there were wars against heretics, so-called crusades against heretics. We should never forget this. And my friend continued:

Groups of the weak-willed have erected a dark and somewhat secretive idol: destiny. Destiny once played an important role in the world of northern ideas. Destiny stood as a law over the being, and consequently stood outside the natural order of things. The life of an individual, his clan and his people was enclosed in destiny. To believe in destiny meant to believe in the validity, value, and sense of life. A believer no longer feared death.

His actions were based on the knowledge of the validity of the law that not only survives individual life but forges—exactly through action—those links in a large chain that reaches into the eternity of a people. Whoever believed in destiny recognized his own responsibility for his life, but was also aware that a chain is only as strong as its weakest link. Destiny was not a secretive, threatening power, but the basis of legality. Whoever consciously trod upon the road of life as a believer in destiny could not tire of struggling with the desire to survive. The knowledge of the validity of the law protected the believer from doubts and insecurity and gave him dignity, the unique and admirable quality of paganism that seems so far from the religions of redemption and seems unattainable. The belief in the validity of this concept of destiny means that mankind utters a happy "yes" to life and death despite all the obvious senselessness of everyday life, and allows him to praise the sunshine despite the fog, night, ice, and snow. To believe in destiny means to live heroically. This attitude can be discerned in the sagas and ballads, as long as we have the insight to see the real meaning of the sonnets through the false works that were created over time.

What did I have to say his words? asked my friend.
"I say yes, an unconditional yes. Read more." I listened:

The believers in destiny were bound to unity at every manifestation of the law. They knew the natural laws governing the stars and observed life in all its forms. These people could honestly say that they could understand the language of the animals or the rustling of the forests, the singing of the fields and the clap of thunder. They understood the all-comprehensive law. Because the strong were marked by destiny, they were victorious. In this way, the songs of heroes praise the struggle for life. What was everyday life against this? Nothing worth talking about, just sheer irrelevance.

Lucky to have found a fellow seeker, I started to talk about Lucifer and Lucifer's court; the restlessness of Pytheas; the self-discovery of Hercules, Parzival, and Tannhäuser; the earthly Paradise of the Grâl; the rose garden; the gay Savoir of the troubadours and Cathars, whose destruction was the work of the cross. Our conversation continued as the night slowly turned into day, until sunshine burst into the room. As we greeted the sun, it was already shining over the roofs of the huge city. In the middle, as if it cut the sun in two, was the spire of a church. I said that the church was like a sun column in which the Prophet Isaiah and the children of Israel were as hated as the proud Lucifer. As it is written in the holy scriptures of the Jews:

> And his eyes for the holy one of Israel . . . and he shall not look to the altars, the work of his hands neither shall respect that which his fingers have made neither the groves or the images [idols of Ashera; Ashera is Artemis, Apollo's sister, the Moon goddess] nor the sun . . . At this time the Lord will seek a place for his armies in the highest . . . then the moon shall be confounded, and the sun ashamed, when the Lord of the Hosts shall reign in Mount Zion and in Jerusalem and before his ancients gloriously . . . And it shall come to pass in the last days that the mountain of the Lord's house shall be established in the top of the mountains . . . and many people shall go and say, come ye and let us go up to the mountain of the lord, to the house of the god of Jacob . . . and he will teach us his ways, and we will walk in his paths for out of Zion shall go forth the law and the word of the lord from Jerusalem.

Because the sun is not bashful but instead is smiling and shining, I was happy in the morning, loyal to our law that is not the law of Zion.

⁓ *WARNEMÜNDE-GJEDSER* ⁓

My ferry is plowing through the choppy waves of the North Sea. Very few passengers are on deck. Some doze, while others like me sit in the smoking room. Some time before, I stood on the stern and watched Germany disappear into the distance until Warnemünde's lights had melted into the moonshine that illuminated the ferry's wake, enveloping in tranquillity the air, steam, and ferry and even myself. The beacon of the lighthouse traced its circle. As I looked astern, my eyes fixed upon the Little Dipper and Big Dipper through the lasts and tackle blocks. At one time long ago they were known as Arktos, the Bear. Arktos will show us the way north, as it did for that daring sailor from Marseille, Pytheas, some two thousand years ago.

I am now traveling to Iceland. Only there can I hope to resolve the mystery of the midnight crown, the secret of Lucifer's crown. I am going to the land of the *Edda*.

⁓ EDINBURGH ⁓

Our ship anchored for a day in the harbor of Leith. In the afternoon, while coal was trimmed, I visited Edinburgh and enjoyed the fabulous view from the castle where Mary Stuart once reigned over Scotland's largest city, down to the sea, and over to the rough mountain peak of Arthur's Rock. Because I am on British soil, I should not forget to mention England's greatest poet, William Shakespeare, and in the same breath the Lollards, those English heretics who also belong to Lucifer's court. They were accused of teaching evil and—in a ballad composed by the staunchly Catholic Thomas Occleve about the most celebrated Lollard of all, Sir John Oldcastle—they were accused of "holding every knight for unworthy who busies himself with the Bible." In his lifetime, Oldcastle was reproached for preferring tales of chivalry to biblical scriptures.

Arthur was more important than Abraham or David to English heretics. He was a Parzival/Perceval who was more meaningful than Christ, a Dietrich who was more important than Peter. Priests burned or branded a key on heretics' foreheads for this reason.

The first record we have of a heretic presence in England goes back to 1160. Thirty farmers and their wives, all of German heritage and language (they were probably Flemish), left their homeland to escape brutal persecution by the west Frankish archbishop of Rheims and were brought before a bishop's council at Oxford. Because they openly confessed to being heretics, they were flogged and a key was branded into their faces. They were then chased into the fields, where (in the winter) they were stripped to the waist, whipped, branded, and left as helpless prey to a quick and miserable death. They ended with a Dietrich in their hearts and the key of Peter branded on their faces. I think, however, that the heart is more important to God.

Two hundred and seventy years later, the most famous heretic of England, the celebrated Sir John Oldcastle, was executed in a most barbaric way: He was hanged over a smoldering fire with an iron chain wrapped around his body, and he was roasted to death. In the end, he commended his soul into the hands of God. After an agitated life, he had eternal peace. An English monk dedicated an epitaph to the deceased that began: "that Dog of Hell, the archheretic and Lollard John Oldcastle, whose stench rose into the noses of Catholics . . . Sir John Oldcastle was a knight in peacetime and a strong man in battle." He went down in history because he was a heretic. Thanks to the king's favor, he was openly able to proclaim himself a Lollard. This explains why the clergy did not dare openly and decisively move to arrest him. First, they went after his chaplain, a man named John who had great success as a wandering preacher, casting an interdict on several churches in which he had preached. In 1413, they began an investigation into some books that had belonged to Oldcastle and that were found at a bookseller. Alas, nothing was turned up. Soon, however, the clergy went to the king with even graver charges: Not only did Oldcastle give shelter to nonordained priests, but he also encouraged them to go out and preach! The king gave him a strong warning, which prompted Oldcastle to take his leave of the royal court, retiring to Colling Castle, not far from Rochester in Kent, where he locked himself away.

Angrily, the king left the Oldcastle affair in the hands of the archbishop. Oldcastle ignored the archbishop's summons and did not allow any envoy entrance to his castle. He declared that he did not recognize any religious court. Nevertheless, he was publicly summoned, and at least twice the summons was nailed to the door of Colling Castle. Still, Oldcastle did not show up. Ultimately, he was forcibly brought before the religious court under the archbishop, who resorted to the authority of the commander of the Tower. Without answering the questions posed to him, Oldcastle offered to explain his religious beliefs. They were far less heretical than was thought. Obviously, and with some justification, the truth of all this was put into question. His interrogators demanded straight answers to their questions. Once pushed, Oldcastle explained that he had nothing for which to be sorry. He had to answer only to God and look only to God for forgiveness. "Those who wish to judge and condemn me will seduce themselves and wind up in hell. Be careful of them," said Oldcastle to the public. Then the religious court handed over the lord to the secular arm. Oldcastle became a prisoner in the Tower—but he escaped. For a long time he wandered in the countryside before he was captured and brought before Parliament. There, he was condemned to death for high treason and heresy. And Sir Oldcastle, who was called the "good lord" by the public, ended as I described.

England's greatest poet, William Shakespeare, was reproached by his

Protestant contemporaries for converting Sir Oldcastle, now a hero of the faith, into that obese, indebted, and womanizing Sir Falstaff. In his epilogue to the second part of the royal drama *Henry IV,* Shakespeare defended himself: "Oldcastle died a martyr, and this is not the man." Whatever the truth, Shakespeare certainly falsified the Oldcastle character by making him funny.

Today, it is generally accepted that Shakespeare's Falstaff episode in *Henry IV, Part 2* had as its model, in the spirit of the most hated and dishonest clerical traditions, the drama *The Famous Victories of Henry V.* Furthermore, as we can easily ascertain, "in Shakespeare's epilogue and other sources, the fat knight was in reality Sir John Oldcastle. The Puritans were upset that the author had made their honored martyr into a comical figure. In the second part of *Henry IV,* Sir John Oldcastle is introduced as a former page of the duke of Norfolk, Sir Thomas Mowbray [which in fact was true]. This was seen as an insult to Oldcastle, so Shakespeare changed his name to Falstaff."

We know how the Lollard and knight Sir John Oldcastle died. Before his terrible death, he said with a smile that he would go to heaven in a carriage and rise on the third day. A monk named Thomas Elmham took down Oldcastle's last words. I believe these words are authentic because I can read in Shakespeare's work how Falstaff, alias Sir John Oldcastle, died. The proprietor of the tavern was with him in his last hours. She reported:

> Nay sure, he's not in hell; he's in Arthur's bosom, if ever man went to Arthur's bosom. . . . 'A parted ev'n just between twelve and one, ev'n at the turning o' th' tide; for after I saw him fumble with the sheets, and play with flowers, and smile upon his finger's end, I knew there was but one way; for his nose was as sharp as a pen, and 'a babbl'd of green fields. . . . So 'a cried out, "God, God, God!" three or four times. Now I, to comfort him, bid him 'a should not think of God; I hop'd there was no need to trouble himself with any such thoughts yet. So 'a bade me lay more clothes on his feet. I put my hand into the bed and felt them, and they were as cold as any stone; then I felt to his knees, and so up'ard and up'ard, and all was as cold as any stone.

Like Sir Oldcastle, Falstaff did not go to hell. Nor are the two resting in Abraham's lap. (My Falstaff expert says that the uneducated tavern keeper meant Abraham's lap.) After death, Falstaff and Oldcastle went to King Arthur, the king in the north who is named Artus. He keeps his carriage ready to transport them to Lucifer's kingdom, to the lights of the Asphodelos fields. The northern Germans called him Thor, "strength of God," or just the Great Father. Oldcastle loved books of chivalry that praised Arthur, Artus, and Dietrich, but not the Old Testament.

Not surprisingly, the other Sir Oldcastle, Falstaff, didn't trust Jews. When he swore an oath, he would say: "or I am a Jew else, an old Ebrew Jew." Falstaff did not believe that life was a vale of tears or (equally senseless) a bowl of cherries. Perhaps, like the Cathars, who saved the wisdom of weaving and the weaver's ship in the Middle Ages, Falstaff thought life was similar to a weaver's ship.

Who would have thought that the name of the Spanish knight who founded the Jesuits, Ignatius of Loyola, the successor to the character Amadis of Gaul and then Jesus, would come up while discussing Sir John Oldcastle's books on knighthood? Sir Oldcastle grasped the spirit of knighthood; Loyola understood only the deadly letters of the books. That old buffoon Alonso Quejana, alias Don Quixote, consulted his books on knighthood day and night until they destroyed his brain. His old nag became the steed Rocinante, comparable to Pegasus or Alexander's trustworthy horse, Bucephalos. But then Don Quixote was far wiser than any buffoon.

— *In the Pentland Sea* —

We have left the North Sea and have entered the North Atlantic. Little by little, the lighthouses along the Scottish coast and the high mountains of the Orkney Islands disappear. The sea rises and falls in long and large waves. A fishing boat with a brown sail seems stuck on the horizon. The first breaker slams over the deck. Although it is night, it is so light, like a cloudy day in winter back home. We are traveling toward the midnight sun. Leaning on the railing, I watch for a long while. Back in my cabin, I have started to read and take some notes.

In Spain, as I read in Cervantes's *Don Quixote,* a priest, a barber, a housekeeper, and the homeowner's niece gathered in the house of a man whose brain was so burned by books of chivalry that he had dedicated himself to errant adventure.

> He was still sleeping; so the curate asked the niece for the keys of the room where they could find the books, the authors of all the mischief, and right willingly she gave them. They all went in, the housekeeper with them, and found more than a hundred volumes of big books, very well bound, and some other small ones. The moment the housekeeper saw them, she turned around, ran out of the room, and came back immediately with a saucer of holy water and a sprinkler, saying, "Here, your worship, Señor licentiate, sprinkle this room; don't leave any magician of the many there are in these books to bewitch us in revenge for our plan to banish them from the world."
>
> The naivete of the housekeeper made the licentiate laugh, and he directed the barber to give him the books one by one to see what they were about, for there might be some among them that did not deserve the penalty of fire. "No," said the niece, "there is no reason for showing mercy to any of them. Every one of them has done mischief; better to fling them out of the window into the courtyard and set fire to them, or else carry them into the yard and make a bonfire there so that the smoke doesn't annoy anyone." The housekeeper said the same, so eager were both of them for the slaughter of those innocents, but the curate would not agree to this without first reading at least the titles.

The first that Master Nicholas put into his hand was *Amadis de Gaula.* "This seems mysterious," said the curate, "for I have heard that this was the first book of chivalry to be printed in Spain, and from this are derived all the others. It seems to me, then, that we ought to condemn it to the flames as the founder of so vile a sect."

"Nay, sir," said the barber, "I too, have heard that this is the best of all the books of this kind. Thus, being so singular, it ought to be pardoned."

"True," said the curate. "And for that reason, let its life be spared for the present. Let us see that book which is next to it."

"It is *Las sergas de Esplandian,* the lawful son of *Amadis de Gaula,*" said the barber.

"Then verily," said the curate, "the merit of the father must not be put down to the account of the son. Take it, mistress house-keeper, open the window, fling it into the courtyard, and with it lay the foundation of the pile for the bonfire we will set."

The housekeeper obeyed with great satisfaction, and the worthy *Las sergas de Esplandian* went flying into the courtyard to await patiently the fire that was in store.

"Proceed," said the curate.

"This that comes next," said the barber, "is *Amadis of Greece,* and indeed I believe that all those on this side are of the same *Amadis* lineage."

"Then to the yard with the lot of them," said the curate, "for I would burn my father if he were going about in the guise of an errant knight in order to burn as well Queen Pintiquiniestra and the shepherd Darinel and his eclogues and the bedeviled and involved discourses of his author."

"I am of the same mind," said the barber.

"And so am I," added the niece.

"In that case," said the housekeeper, "here, into the yard with them!" The books were handed to her, and because there were so many of them, she spared herself the staircase, and flung them out of the window.

Another book was opened, and they saw that it was entitled *The Knight of the Cross.* "For the sake of the holy name of this book," said the curate, "its ignorance might be excused; but then, they do say, 'behind the cross there's the devil.' To the fire with it."

Taking down another book, the barber said, "This is *The Mirror of Chivalry.*"

"I know, his worship," said the curate. "That is where Señor Reinaldos of Montalvan figures with his friends and comrades, greater thieves than Cacus and the twelve peers of France, along with the veracious historian Turpin. I am not for condemning them to more than perpetual banishment, however, because at least they have some share in influencing the famous Matteo Boiardo. From the same place as Boiardo, Christian poet Ludovico Ariosto wove his web—and if I find him here, and he is speaking any language other than his own, I shall show him no respect whatever. But if he speaks his own tongue, I will put him upon my head."

"Well, I have him in Italian," said the barber, "but I do not understand him."

"Nor would it be well that you should understand him," said the curate, "and on that score we might have excused the captain if he had not brought him into Spain and turned him into a Castilian. He robbed him of a great deal of his natural strength, and so do all those who try to turn books written in verse into another language; for, with all the pains they take and all the cleverness they show, they never can reach the level of the originals as they were first produced. In short, I say that this book and all that may be found treating of those French affairs should be thrown into some dry well, until, after more consideration, it is decided what is to be done with them—except *Bernardo del Carpio* and *Roncesvalles.* These, if they come into my hands, shall pass at once into those of the housekeeper, and from hers into the fire without any reprieve."

Not caring to tire himself with reading more books of chivalry, he told the housekeeper to take all the big ones and throw them into the courtyard. This charge was given not to one dull or deaf, but to one who enjoyed burning these texts more than weaving the broadest and finest web. Seizing about eight at a time, she flung them out the window.

"But what are we to do with these little books that are left?" asked the barber.

"These are not chivalry, but poetry," said the curate, and opening one he saw it was *Diana* of Jorge de Montemayor. Assuming all the others to be of the same sort, he said, "These do not deserve to be burned like the others, for they neither do nor can do the mischief the books of chivalry have done. They are books of entertainment that can hurt no one."

And the barber went on, "These that come next are *The Shepherd of Iberia, Nymphs of Henares,* and *The Enlightenment of Jealousy.*"

"Then all we have to do," said the curate, "is to hand them over to the secular arm of the housekeeper—and ask me not why, or we shall never be done."

That night, the housekeeper burned to ashes all the books that were in the courtyard and in the whole house; and some must have been consumed that deserved preservation in everlasting archives . . .

One of the remedies that the curate and the barber immediately applied to their friend's disorder was to wall up and plaster the room where the books were, so that when he got up he should not find them. (If the cause was removed, the effect might end.) They could say that a magician had carried them off, room and all, and this was done with great haste. Two days later, Don Quixote arose, and the first thing he did was to go and look at his books, but not finding the room where he had left them, he wandered about, looking for it. He came to the place where the door used to be and tried it with his hands. He turned and twisted his eyes in every direction without saying a word; but after a good while, he asked his housekeeper where the room was that held his books.

The housekeeper, who had already been well instructed as to what she was to answer, asked, "What room or what nothing is your worship looking for? There are neither room nor books in this house now, for the devil himself has carried all away."

"It was not the devil," said the niece, "but a magician who came on a cloud one night after the day your worship left, and dismounting from a serpent, which he rode, he entered the room. What he did there I know not, but after a little while, he made off, flying through the roof, and left the house full of smoke. When we went to see what he had done, we saw neither books nor room . . .

"But, uncle," asked the niece, "who mixes you up in these quarrels? Would it not be better to remain at peace in your own house instead of roaming the world looking for better bread than ever came of wheat, never reflecting that many seek wool and come back shorn?"

"Oh, niece of mine," replied Don Quixote, "how much astray art thou in thy reckoning. 'Ere they shear me I shall have plucked away and stripped off the beards of all who dare to touch only the tip of a hair of mine."

The two were unwilling to make any further answer, for they saw that his anger was kindling. In short, then, he remained quietly at home for fifteen days without showing any signs of a desire to take up with his former delusions. During this time, he held lively discussions with his two gossips, the curate and the barber, on the point he maintained: Knights-errant were what the world most needed, and he would revive knight-errantry. The curate sometimes contradicted him and sometimes agreed with him, for if he had not observed this precaution, he would have been unable to bring Don Quixote to reason.

I put down *Don Quixote* for a moment and reflected.

The curate who chose the books for the pyre and would not budge a bit represented the Catholic Church. The "secular arm" was the housekeeper. Who were the niece and the barber? I dare not say. The books that were burned were undoubtedly written by the members of Lucifer's heretical court.

I continue reading:

Thus setting out, our new-fledged adventurer traveled along, talking to himself and saying, "Who knows but that in time to come, when the veracious history of my famous deeds is made known, the sage who writes it, when he has to set forth my first sally in the early morning, will do it in this way?: 'Scarce had the rubicund Apollo spread o'er the face of the broad, spacious earth the golden threads of his bright hair; scarce had the little birds of painted plumage attuned their notes to hail with dulcet and mellifluous harmony the coming of the rosy dawn which, deserting the soft couch of her jealous spouse, was appearing to mortals at the gates and balconies of the Manchegan horizon, when the renowned knight Don Quixote of La Mancha, quitting the lazy down, mounted his celebrated steed Rocinante and began to traverse the ancient and famous Campo de Montiel.'" In fact, he was actually traversing this path. He continued, "Happy the age, happy the time in which shall be made known my deeds of fame, worthy to be molded in brass, carved in marble, limned in pictures for a timeless memorial. And thou, oh sage magician, whoever thou art, to whom it shall fall to be the chronicler of this wondrous history, I entreat thee to forget not my good Rocinante, the constant companion of my ways and wanderings."

So he went on, stringing together these and other absurdities, all in the style taught him by his books, imitating their language as well as he could. And all the while he rode so slowly and the sun climbed so rapidly and with such strength that it was enough to melt his brains if he had any.

Nearly all day he traveled without anything remarkable happening to him—which caused him despair, for he was anxious to encounter someone at once upon whom to try the might of his strong arm. There are writers who say the first adventure he met with was that of Puerto Lapice. Others say it was that of the windmills. What I have ascertained on this point, however, and what I have found written in the annals of La Mancha, is that he was on the road all day, and toward nightfall, he and his hack found themselves dead tired and hungry. He looked all around to see if he could discover any castle or shepherd's shanty where he might refresh himself and relieve his wants, and he perceived an inn not far from his path. It was as welcome as a star guiding him to the portals, if not the palaces, of his redemption. Quickening his pace, he reached it just as night was setting in.

At the door were standing two young women, girls of the district, as they call them . . . and so with prodigious satisfaction, he rode up to the inn and to the ladies who, upon seeing a man of this sort approaching in full armor and with lance and buckler, were turning in dismay into the inn. Yet Don Quixote, guessing their fear by their flight, raised his pasteboard visor; disclosed his dry, dusty visage; and addressed them with courteous bearing and gentle voice: "Your ladyships need not flee or fear any rudeness, for it belongs not to the order of knighthood which I profess to offer to anyone, including highborn maidens, as your appearance proclaims you to be."

Don Quixote asked the name of one of the women in order that he might forever know to whom he was beholden for the favor he had received, for he meant to confer upon her some portion of the honor he acquired by the might of his arm. With great humility, she answered that she was called La Tolosa. . . . Don Quixote said in reply that she would do him a favor if from that time forward she assumed the "don" and called herself Doña Tolosa. . . . He then asked the name of the other woman, and she said it was La Molinera, and offered that she was the daughter of a respectable miller of Antequera. Likewise, Don Quixote requested that she adopt the "don" and call herself Doña Molinera.

In this way, Don Quixote, that pure and wise comedian, returned the Tolosa and the Molinera to honor.[27] Tolosa is an Albigensian and Molinera or "miller" is a Waldensian. The Cathars were tisserands, or weavers, who were easily found in weavers' cellars. The Waldenses were also called millers. Milling grain was the same as sacred weaving. In the Tyrol, a knight in the service of Dietrich von Bern left the mill to enter the rose garden and eternity.

I continue:

Sancho Panza [who was also called *hombre de bien* by Cervantes, or *bonhomme*] saddled Rocinante, readied Dapple, and stocked his *alforjas* [the leather pack on a mule] along with which went those

---

[27][Tolosa is the Occitan name for the city of Toulouse. —*Trans.*]

of the cousin, likewise well filled. And so, commending themselves to God and bidding farewell to all, they set out, taking the road to the famous cave of Montesinos.

"Now tell me," said Sancho, "who was the first tumbler in the world?"

"Really, brother," answered the cousin, "I could not at this moment say positively without having investigated it. I will look it up when I return to my books, and I will satisfy you the next time we meet, for this will not be the last time."

Sancho continued, "Look here, señor, don't give yourself any trouble over it, for just this minute I have hit upon what I asked you. The first tumbler in the world, you must know, was Lucifer, when they cast or pitched him out of heaven, for he came tumbling into the bottomless pit."

"Sancho," said Don Quixote, "that question and answer are not thine own; thou hast heard them from someone else."

"Hold your peace, señor," said Sancho. "If I take to asking questions and answering them, I'll go on till tomorrow morning. Nay! To ask foolish things and answer nonsense, I needn't go looking for help from my neighbors."

"Thou hast said more than thou art aware of, Sancho," said Don Quixote, "for there are some who weary themselves in learning and proving things which, after they are known and proved, are not worth a farthing to either understanding or memory."

Like Hölderlin, Don Quixote, the knight of the rueful countenance, beat Apollo!

⁓ In the North Atlantic ⁓

High seas. Our ship, the *Gullfoss*, a twelve-hundred-ton Icelandic vessel, is struggling hard against the sea. Silvery North Sea dolphins accompanied us for a while, jumping out of the waves. It was marvelous to see their glittering bodies shoot up out of the water and dive back in again. As I watched them, I had to think of Orpheus, the divine singer. Apollo's favorite animal was the dolphin who carried him over the clouds. As an Argonaut, Orpheus traveled to the north and maybe even came from there. His mother was a mortal: Chione, "snowy." The singer charmed even the animals with his music. He descended to the deepest part of hell to rescue his love Eurydice and bring her back to the light of day.

Now the night is no more. Like mother-of-pearl, the sea shines in the twilight between sunset and sunrise. Our flag is a blue swastika on a white ground. When I asked him on the bridge, the captain told me that we will soon reach the 60th parallel.

In the ninth century and later around the year AD 1000, when King Haraldur Harfagri and then king and saint Olaf Haraldsson began the suppression of the free pagan farmers of Norway, the country's best immigrated to Iceland to recover their old freedoms and found a new homeland.

Olaf is one of the many saints of the Catholic Church who should no longer be praised. The celebrated skald Snorri Sturlusson (who was the author of the *Younger Edda*) reports in his *Heimskringla*: "Olaf severely punished everyone who did not abjure paganism; he drove some out of the land, others had their hands and feet crushed or their eyes poked out, and still others were hanged or slain in other ways."[28] So the flower of Norway's farmers fled over the North Sea to Iceland, among them those who inherited their fathers' beliefs in never being enslaved.

Thanks to the Icelandic *Landnamabök* (Book of Settlements), which was begun in the thirteenth century, just as Iceland was becoming Christian, we know how long the voyage took from Norway to Greenland and Iceland:

---

[28][Skald Snorri Sturlusson (1179–1241) was an Icelandic historian, poet, and politician. He is author of the *Younger Edda*. The *Heimskringla* is a compilation of Scandinavian history. —*Trans.*]

Experienced seamen say that it takes seven sailing days from
Stad (the west point of Norway) to Horn in eastern Iceland. Sailing straight across from Bergen to Hvarf in Greenland, a traveler
passes Iceland at the twelfth sea mile. One must sail so far north
past the Shetland Islands that these are visible only in calm seas,
and so far south of Iceland that birds and whales come from there.
From Rekyanes, in southern Iceland, it is three sailing days until
Jölduhlaup and a day trip from Kolbeinsey (a small island in the
north of Iceland) to reach the Einöd coast of Greenland.

Iceland's first settler was named Ingolfur. The *Landnamabök* informs us:

> Every summer, Ingolfur sailed out to Iceland, 6073 years after the
> the world began or 873 in the year of the Lord. When Ingolfur
> sighted Iceland, he threw overboard his carved wooden pillar. He
> would settle at the spot where the wooden beam washed ashore.
> Ingolfur landed at the place that is called Ingolfhoefdi. Vifil and
> Karli were Ingolfur's serfs. They were sent out by him to find the
> pillar, which they did by the third winter. In spring, Ingolfur reset-
> tled at Reykjavik. Ingolfur's son was Thorstein and his grandson
> was Thorkel Mond, who was a law-speaker. When Igolfur fell ill
> and lay dying, he had himself carried out into the sunshine and
> there commended himself to God, who made the sun. He led a life
> as pure as the most pious Christians could ever lead.

Another settler was named Thorolf. Because he sacrificed to Thor, he
fled to Iceland to escape the violence of King Haraldur. As he arrived at
Breidifjord, he threw overboard the beam with Thor's carved image. He
would settle where Thor landed. He fulfilled his promise and consecrated
the land in the name of his god and friend, Thor. Thorolf sailed into the
fjord, where he found Thor's image washed ashore. Farther on, he and
his shipmates landed in a bay. There he built a farm and a large temple,
which he consecrated to Thor. The fjord was hardly settled. Thorolf put
down roots there and called the entire area Thorsnes. He had such a
strong and profound belief in the mountain that dominated the penin-

sula that he called it Helgafell, or "holy mountain," and stipulated that nobody should look upon it who was unwashed. He made the mountain into a place for eternal peace; nothing should happen to anybody there, neither man nor beast. It was Thorolf's belief that they should all die on this mountain. Later, as the *Eyrbyggjasaga* describes, when his son Thorstein drowned in the sea, he too went to the mountain. Fire burned and horns blew. The son should rest upon a wooden pillar.

Two other men, both incredibly strong and familiar with magic, threw their wooden pillars overboard when they sighted Iceland. These men were Lodmund and Bjolf. Their home was Thulunes in the Norwegian countryside north of the Hardangerfjord.

It is ten o'clock, and an evening tea is being served. At home, it is midnight and the stars are sparkling. Maybe the moon is casting Germany in silver. Here it is day and will stay so for weeks.

There is a storm and it is pouring rain. The waves are slamming against the portholes of the dining room. From a total of around seventy passengers, only a dozen or so have made it to tea. The cups and saucers are placed within wooden frames that are screwed tightly to the table, and still things are broken. The stewards move like trapeze artists in a circus. The ship experiences heavy going. In my cabin, the bed heaves up and down under me, and sometimes I feel like I am floating in the air. The ship cracks and groans at every joint.

I am reading. According to the sagas, the first colonists of Iceland were the Westmen, the Irish. In his account of 825, an Irish monk named Dicuil wrote that he had spoken with fellows who had resided on the extreme northern island of Thule of Pytheas. "Thirty years ago, some priests told me that on such an island, from the first of February to the first of August, and not only by the summer solstice but in the days before and after, the sun hid itself just behind a small hill so that it was not dark, even for the shortest time."

So much for the account of Friar Dicuil. "It is fact that before the eighth century, Iceland was uninhabited. This speaks against those who seek Pytheas." Thule in Iceland. How could the earlier population have died off? Given that the island was hermetically sealed from contact with the outside world, we must rule out epidemics. Mutual destruction through war can be ruled out as well because hostile natives did not exist. Even if we refuse to accept this reasoning and hold as possible that outside interference caused the extinction of the inhabitants of Thule during the age of Pytheas, some archaeological remains of their settlements should have been located. Yet no trace can be found that would contradict the evidence that the handing down of the sagas began with the arrival of the first residents of Iceland in AD 795. In addition, the supposed inhabitants of the Thule islands spoke more often of volcanoes and hot springs than of a sea of ice in the far north.

Couldn't fire and lava have depopulated Iceland without a trace?

With more assurance, I read in another book, "According to Strabo (the celebrated Greek geographer of antiquity who lived in Rome at the beginning of the first century), Thule could be found six sailing days north from Britain. This can only mean Iceland."

Where was Thule?

I am shutting off the lights. My cabin is on the inside of the ship, so it is always dark. The ventilator blows rough and cold sea air into the room. The ship's sharp prow cuts into wave after wave, sure of its way despite the high seas. I can hear the noise of the water. I will put away my writing paper and books now and try to sleep. We have it easier than the Vikings.

Once there was a king of Thule who was faithful up to the time of his death. Where lies Thule, which has the sun to thank for its name? Was it in Iceland or in a Norwegian region called Thulunes at Hardangerfjord, where Lodmund and Bjolf brought their pillars to Iceland?

Thulunes means "island" or "peninsula." Thulu . . .

~ *REYKJAVIK* ~

After a rainy and ultimately quiet voyage, our brave ship entered the harbor of Iceland's capital at around four o'clock in the morning. Heavy rain clouds hung over the mountains; we can only guess their elevation. The sea was ashen and the ladies were made up garishly. Despite the time, pale sightseers walked through the streets, and there were still many cars on the roads. The city is "beautiful!" Concrete walls, corrugated iron roofs and high-rise, American-style buildings . . .

The interior of our hotel is bright and surprisingly comfortable. For the first time in weeks, I could empty my suitcase and hang up my clothes. How I missed the throbbing of the ship's engines, though, and the darkness of the night! Are there days when you can escape the light? I couldn't sleep. I was overtired, and a phrase from Goethe echoed in my brain: "Now, you are at wit's end." Why did you seek companionship with the devil if you are so afraid? Why did you want to fly and yet you are still frightened? Are we pushing you, or are you pushing us? This is more or less the manner in which Mephistopheles spoke to Faust. My thoughts rush through my head and I leave the room. Once out of the hotel, I start to amble down the street.

Now the ugly city is sleeping. The Icelandic sun shines through the clouds, but only for a moment. There seems to be some life in the harbor, but otherwise, all is quiet. No tree rustles in the wind, no bird sings on a branch. The concrete walls are soaked with humidity. I am going to the harbor.

Bedlam is loose aboard our *Gullfoss*. Cranes are lifting from its hold boxes, barrels, sacks, bales, barbed wire, and iron bars. A little farther on, a fishing boat is docking. I look on as they shovel its thrashing and silvery cargo into baskets. A bearded fisherman, dressed in a water-resistant coat covered in fish scales, holds a fish high and calls over to me. Thinking that he wants to show me his catch, with my hands and feet I try to make clear to him that I don't speak his language. He throws the fish in a basket and wipes his hands with a sack. Jumping over to the quay, he extends his hand and says: "Welcome to Iceland! I know that a guest from Germany arrived today. Welcome to our homeland!"

I was almost at my wit's end. And why? I dreamed of a fairy-tale land and suddenly found myself in a country that isn't at all like a fairy tale. I was impressed by the loneliness of this deserted island on the edge of the polar sea—an island where night's veil covers nothing, like eyelids that keep closed eyes from seeing what they do not wish to see. In a way, however, I was guilty: I wanted to "fly" like Lucifer, but I was dizzy. Yes, this was what made me so uncomfortable.

No matter where I went and stood and thought and saw, everything has drawn me here. Are Iceland's shores the key to understanding the Viking song of sailing? Is Iceland Pytheas's island of Thule—for which he risked his life? I dreamed of a fairy-tale land. Gruesome reality surrounds me. No trees, no forest, no flowers or field; just tasteless houses jumbled together between shop counters, clothes shops, newspaper offices, and movie houses. Everything gives the impression of being transitory, unripe—what must be but in reality is quite unwanted. Gold-rush towns must have looked like this place, the towns founded when men dug for Californian or Klondike gold and most of the time fell into the graves they had dug for themselves.

When I think about our Upper Hessian farmers—who, despite their difficulties in feeding themselves on twenty or thirty *mornings* (a common measure in Germany) of land (which is successful only if they choose their belongings as cautiously as possible), have never forgotten their dignity and love of beauty—and I contrast them with the capital city of the Vikings and skalds, a cheap imitation of the worst Europe has to offer, I am forced to look from the north to the south!

A pious Christian pilgrim to Palestine once told me that he had very contradictory feelings when he visited the church of the Holy Sepulchre in Jerusalem: Arguments and brawls were common, and you could count the days when murder was not reported. This journey to Iceland should be my pilgrimage. Yet disappointment speaks its language within me and I cannot silence it. Not that I am repulsed or disgusted—if I have communicated this, then I have exaggerated. No, simply put, I have nothing to do here. That's it. What Reykjavik has to offer I could have found more easily in Marseille.

Today we went to Thingvellir, or Parliament Field, the location of Iceland's world-famous Althingi, or Parliament. A great deal has been written about it, but I didn't feel a holy shiver. I was shown around and thought of Germany, and not only because praise was written in German for Germany's most illustrious communist leader in big red letters on the basalt walls. In the Walhall Inn, we had cake and coffee. Then we drove back to Reykjavik. The earth couldn't even offer a tree, shrub, or bush, and what I believed to be a mountain range when we arrived in Reykjavik was revealed to be a heap of volcanic ash. The only life we saw was a rider on a pony; three mother sheep with their offspring; and a few patches of dry, yellowish green grass as well as a bit of moss with a few flowers. In the end, we drove to our hotel down a straight, asphalt road between ugly houses.

My room is comfortable and friendly, with a bed, a desk, a steel chair, a built-in closet, and on the wall five paintings by four Icelandic artists. In their frames I find deeply knotted, wonderfully green trees with large crowns. Do Iceland's artists yearn for the south?

One of my traveling companions—twenty of us came to Iceland—told me that he is counting the days until he is back home. He promised to himself to hike through the Teutoburger Forest when he returns.

The Icelandic word for "commemoration" and "recollection" is *minni!*

Iceland's artists yearn for the south! Yet when they're south, they want to return home. Given the choice between the south or their barren and lonely island on the edge of the Arctic Circle, they would always choose their island. I posed the question and that was the answer I received from a painter. We had become friends. His wife is German. The painter, Mansi, and his only brother, Sveni, are the last surviving relations of the celebrated Icelandic poets Snorri Sturlusson and Egil Skallagrimson. Sveni is moving to Germany for an extended stay. He is twenty years old and still hasn't seen a tree! Although there are a few trees and even forests on Iceland, so he explained, until now he had never managed to visit them, wherever they are. By contrast, he knows all the glaciers and deserts. Mansi will also visit Germany this year for a few months. We have arranged a small alpine expedition to scale Rose Garden Peak in the Tyrol. He has already climbed the Dolomites four times and painted them. He showed me the four paintings, which are not for sale. He must really love Rose Garden Peak! Mansi said that it was time for him to leave Reykjavik. He could understand that I was homesick or disappointed, but only I am to blame. Iceland is not to blame—and Reykjavik is not Iceland. I had everything to seek and find in his island homeland, but I must not forget to look to the Icelandic heavens.

⁓ LAUGARVATN ⁓

Sunday: Jazz music penetrates through the thin walls of the hotel where we are resting for a few hours. Young people who made it here over the incomparably bad roads are dancing. The ladies are made up and are dressed in the fashion of a few years ago. The men are well dressed and sporty. The latest hits are played on a gramophone. Just played was a fox-trot that an organ grinder tortured passersby with every Wednesday morning—for months—in Berlin.

As I look out the window, the hot waves of Laugarvatn Lake slap against the shoreline as steam rises in the air. In the distance, the snow shimmers on the slopes of Iceland's most famous volcano, Hekla.

In 1300 CE, Hekla broke open and spat "earth fire." It was so dark that nobody knew if it was night or day. "At the same time, there was an eruption of lava on Sikiley that burned two dioceses." (Sikiley is Sicily.) Three hundred years later, when Charles V reigned as emperor over half of Europe, an imperial courtier named Walter van Meer visited Iceland and saw how "the souls of the condemned were brought to Hekla on a dark ship that was steered by a Moor." So, just like Sicily, Iceland had its own fire mountain—Bel! Both Hekla and Etna were supplied with the same firey brew—"earth fire"—from the forge of the divine blacksmith Hephaistos-Vulcanus, the spouse of Venus.

Dietrich von Bern, who was Thidrek in the Norwegian sagas, lived in Bel Mountain.

A few hours ago we visited the big geyser. We were forced to wait for hours until the waterspout shot up. In the end, to get the geyser to erupt, sacks of soap were unceremoniously dropped into it. Soon afterward, the earth began to shake and make noises until suddenly the enormous cooker expelled hissing steam and threw up its waterspout in strong puffs. The height of the cooking water was estimated to be about four meters at the highest.[29] Then, suddenly, the earthly cooker was silent and empty. Here and there a cloud of steam puffed. The bowels of the earth still rumbled. Steam clouded the whole valley and the air smelled of sulfur, which you felt in your chest.

---

[29][About thirteen feet. —Ed.]

A geyser was frothing on a winter or midwinter night. The snowy shroud lay endlessly and profoundly over the land. The polar star cried. The steam clouds hissed and the earth rumbled. There was no living creature to be seen. The reflection of volcanic fire reflected somewhere. The colors of the northern lights rolled across the heavens. In Iceland, the lights of the stars like to wander in wintertime. Now it is summer and day.

~ REYKHOLT ~

I am spending a very bright night in a house that is an ugly concrete box. During the winter, it serves as a school. It is ten o'clock in the bright night of the summer solstice. I am in my room, writing. My companions are frolicking downstairs in a large swimming pool, which is fed by hot water from thermal springs. I also enjoyed a dip after a long and uncomfortable trip and I rather unhappily left the warm water to write these lines. My swimsuit, which hangs over the radiator to dry, smells of sulfur.

The sun is high in the northwest. The sky shines in bright colors. A light and hardly noticeable mist hangs over the Reykjadalsa Valley. There is not a tree to be seen. The bleakness of the patchy green fields makes the place look much more dead than it is.

I don't think that I could live here willingly. If I were forced to do so, then every bone in my body would soon be yearning for the forests and pastures of my homeland.

Seven hundred years ago, the law-speaker and poet Snorri Sturlusson lived here in Reykholt. His warm bath encircled by a large wall is still here, just a few steps from the inn, past a row of miserable peat houses with smoke rising from their chimneys. Did Snorri, a contemporary of Wolfram von Eschenbach, Walther von der Vogelweide, Peire Vidal, and Peire Cardinal, write the *Younger Edda* and the history of the Norwegian kings, *Heimskringla,* in such a hut? On his farmstead, did homesickness and the forgotten memory of his forefathers' ways guide his quill during those long winter nights that were shrouded in icy cold and blackest dark and only now and then were brightened by the northern lights so far from this world?

We want to drive past the vicinity of Borg, where Snorri also lived. There he inhabited the same homestead where his ancestor Egil Skallagrimson lived two hundred years earlier, before some daring Viking seamen took him roving on the high seas to faraway lands.

Around the house, the storm is howling and bellowing. I am going down to my companions. It is summer solstice in the land of the *Edda.*

One hour later: The new day soon began as the sun moved closer and closer to the north. I had a look at the Steindorsstadaöxl [a place in Iceland]. The play of colors on the bleak stones was spectacular, and the endless expanse of the Langjökull Glacier just behind was both attractive and imposing. Wherever I looked, the hues wandered from a soft mauve to a glowing red, from the brightest white to the darkest black-gray. On the other side of the river, some dots moved in the yard of a farm that appeared on my map as Hoegindi. Through fieldstones, I could see Icelandic ponies moving slowly to the river. All was quiet at the farmhouse. I turned my telescope back toward the Steindorsstadaöxl. Its delicately rising slopes stopped midway where some rough basalt walls rose steeply. If my eyes didn't deceive me, those black spots were entrances to caves. As I concentrated, I heard the familiar voice of a traveling companion asking if I wanted to start poking around caves again. When I answered yes, he proposed walking over to the mountain when all were asleep, because tonight was the solstice. Although the bed of the Reykjadalsa was wide, he knew that there was a ford in the vicinity. Before dinner, he had taken a short walk down to the river and saw where a farm wagon had crossed. We could also wade to the other side and climb up to the caves, because, as he admitted, he too believed there were caves located there. I didn't hesitate, and we started off.

The storm was almost over. We went down to the river, took off our shoes and socks, rolled up our trousers, and started across in the water. It was so icy that I must have flown to the other side. A long hike to the Hoegindi farmstead made our blood rush. The mountain was less steep than it appeared. Finally, we reached our goal: the basalt wall—but we were mistaken. What we had taken for cave entrances were grottolike niches in the rock where brooks and rivulets ran in cascades down to the valley below. At the prettiest waterfall, we rested, facing the sun. Reykholt was below and looked like a toy. We marveled at the Eyjafjallajökull Glacier for a very long time. Who broke the silence first, I don't remember, although a few hours had certainly passed.

"There is an Indian word, *titthakara,*" I said. "It once meant 'he who finds a crossing': those men who found their way across a river at a shallow place where others had searched in vain. A titthakara understood that a ford represents a transcendental passage over the darkest abyss that separates man from the ultimate truth, which he can learn only after his death. It is a crossing that poses an eternal question: Can we acquire the knowledge of that dark abyss, of the hereafter, and cross in spirit to the other side of the river as a way to understand the meaning of our existence? There were people, spiritual pathfinders, who answered this question. *Titthakara* is a word in the ancient Pali language that could be easily translated as 'pure one' in Europe."

I remember my companion's words. I never interrupted him. As the sun rose gently between rose-colored clouds over the bleak heights and water ran down to the valley, at Reykholtsdalur, where the river widens out into a lake, swans flew into the sky singing. Or did the wind create a massive aeolic harp in the niches and clefts in the rock? There were songs in the night of the summer solstice. My companion, who was more Christian than I, said:

"Christianity is concerned above all with mankind. Either it condemns nature as nondivine or hands it over to nonspiritual 'natural sciences' or modern technology. By contrast, paganism was nature itself, with 'real gods.' All natural events were the result of the actions of genies or spirits. In that sense, paganism should be considered more pious, insightful, and Christian than the power-hungry and structurally rigid Roman Catholics or Protestants, who were more often than not inspired by Rome or Israel than by Christ himself.

"Ancient myths are inseparable from the power of gods. This spiritual association is part of a blood bond that gives a people their inner strength. For that reason, the *Edda* chants: 'In the old times, as the eagles sang, holy water ran from the sacred mountains of Paradise.' Yet every people—yes, every tribe—looked to its own, sharply different gods. They were inspired by the power inherent in them as a force for unity in the face of famine-induced migration and war, as well as in wisdom and law-speaking. In this way, the 'gods' were absolutely real, as language and people were.

"These popular and tribal gods were rooted in the countryside (the epicenter of popular belief), groves, and wells. Certain preferred places—such as caves and grottoes, for example—are indeed places that radiate subterranean activity, just as mountains and peaks are summits that reflect planetary and stellar activity. A mighty tree is a place where the water element and earth element rise up and meet the air and light elements that descend from above.

"In this period of prehistory, the divine did not reside in an unfathomable Paradise that was attainable only through faith. There was no mechanical legitimacy. Instead, nature was the all-powerful and ever-present countenance of divine reality. Above all other peoples, the Germanic tribes encountered their deepest spirituality in nature. Their gods were natural gods, their mysteries were the mysteries of nature. The Germanic soul was immersed in the sunny and innocent dream of the spiritual revelation of nature. That was the realm of Odin's son Baldr, the darling of the gods and mankind. This part of history cannot be understood until we see where crucial gods were scattered about the country and steered toward central strong points. Neither individuals nor even tribes nor entire peoples (which means groups of mortal men who fought with one another or allied themselves with one another) could sway the course of ancient history. The inhabitants of the large, holy sites had to manifest their presence with their divinities in the populated countryside. At decisive moments, Germanic tribes undertook pilgrimages to their holy sites. They went to Irminsul or Teutoburger Forest or to visit Veleda, the soothsayer, at Lippe Spring. They believed that destiny was spoken more easily and more forcefully at these places by gifted persons—particularly women.

"That is why the destruction of sacred sites played such an important role in the devastation and domination of peoples. Only in these places could an opponent strike at the pounding heart. Although some isolated clans and families soldiered on, once they were robbed of their divinities and their relationship to them, they posed no military threat and were reduced to meaningless, nomadic peoples. This is why the Romans tried to influence Veleda with threats or gifts to sway the Germanic chieftains and why the Frankish emperor Charlemagne, like Varus and Germanicus before him, sent his armies into Teutoburger Forest, for this area, where the territories of so many large tribes met, was the spiritual heart of Germany.

"This mythological prehistory becomes understandable only when we recognize that our modern concept of the individual was nonexistent. Ancestral order dwelled in the deep subconscious, not in individual thoughts and desires. Nature is not only populated with gods, it is filled with the souls of the departed. Surrounded by the ghosts of their ancestors, the Germans went into battle, protected by a strong belief in reincarnation that was consummated by the presence of the Valkyries. These pagan warriors recognized that immortality was part of a mighty, spiritual process of divine inspiration. They possessed the ability to admire fallen heroes as 'spirits of light.' Their lives were a spiritual drama in which the living and the departed were united. The mythical and mythological revealed a faraway past where mankind was devoted to the supremacy of a divine, natural order. Whether we like it or not, we are very far from all things mythical. The realm of modern man is natural science and technology, and any impartial, historical review of paganism's gods is automatically disqualified as superstition. In this light, Christianity was in no way less intellectual than modern science. The mythological is inseparable from the revelation of the gods, which is gone forever. Modern man no longer lives in a cosmically inspired world; he thinks and lives in a world of inanimate things and bureaucratic abstractions.

"Myths have nothing to do with *faith* and *creed*. Because most faiths became organized religions when the physical presence of gods became nebulous abstractions, people have yearned for that missing soul in new faiths. If we accept the mythological world of the old gods and its roots in the legendary world of popular myths, any other analysis is illogical. The mythical world of the old gods is not the product of poetry. Far more, mankind is the product of the gods. First, the image of the gods is revealed in man. Woe to man if he wishes to see himself as a god! Then the gods, offended, leave him. His image takes precedence over that of mankind. Man's desires and knowledge of what mankind can and should be, he learned from the gods. Gods are always at the forefront.

"If the mythological being was the product of fantasy, then he was the product of a divine fantasy that invaded the imaginations of mankind. He belonged to a fantasy world that operated its own cosmology and hymns within a strict structure of pictorial imagery just as it appears in nature, but accompanied by words: in plants and animals, the seasons, and the course of the planets. Thanks to the strength of his soul, he told the truth as the practical part of this divine concept. In this way, humanity remained open to the cosmos without reticence.

"The source of religion is celestial, not human. First, a god must enlighten the dreams of mankind. Ancient religions were a fusion between the godly and mankind; they were a way to organize physical and spiritual existence and join it with the divine. The 'legendary' man was nourished from the cosmos and, like an embryo, formed in the mother's womb. As in all religions, divine revelation is not madness but the most authentic of all realities. It forged a people from the horde.

"Early cultures did not live in an indifferent world of things. Rather, they were brimming with significance and communicative sanctity. Human life won priestly, consecrated importance. As every divine manifestation touched the human soul, extraordinary creativity was unleashed. This encouraged man to speak about the immensity that had possessed him, and the most noble of these languages was culture. Yet culture as a divine language has become almost extinct, because it has been reduced to the all-too-human considerations of profitable usefulness. We have corrupted the noblest manifestation of ancient times through our self-centric lifestyle. Instead of measuring ourselves against the greatness of the past, we measure the past against ourselves.

"Culture is a service to our world, and cultural activity in the ancient world could be likened to a pair of arms outstretched to the heavens. The individual carried in him like a seed what man can give and take from the world. He stood between heaven and earth, funneling what was underneath to the world above and what was above to the world underneath. Children frolicking around a tree in a meadow are already a cultural event. They do not try to understand the world with their intellect; instead, they feel it in their breast as they breathe and their heart throbs. On a bright spring day, children bring floating elements and elementary spirits in consonance with a round dance. Culture is neither abstract symbols nor organized commemorations. It is the overwhelming presence of the powers of the earth. The world and God are no longer theories. Instead, they are served with pure emotion. The highest and most secretive pinnacle of culture is, of course, sacrifice. Any selfish intentions should be seen as corruption. An authentic sacrifice consummates human activity, because the cosmic order of the world is reinforced in the act. The 'victim' is dominated not by selfish greed or the cowardly desire to obtain the favor of the powerful, but rather by an inner richness that he wishes to spend for others in a life—spending revelation.

"As it is, human life is intrinsically a huge sacrificial rite in which all the elements, animals, and gods take part. A person not only receives, but also gives. A good portion of health and spiritual order lies in his ritual activity. Yes, even the gods favored these people who were willing to become part of the creative force through their selfless actions. Also, the sun sacrifices its rays when they descend to the earth. Water evaporation, the life of the plants and their colors, fruits, and aromas are all the sacrificial answer of the earth to the sacrifice of the heavens.

"Ancient sacrifice had no purpose other than the act itself. Nothing should happen or should be desired or should be influenced by magic. Its reality was within the act itself. Through it, a person announced his fusion with the powers and creatures of the world. That creatures in nature nourish themselves with one another is an expression of this generosity and reception; there is nothing selfish in it—rather, it is an act that gives all and receives everything.

"The profound bond that united the ancient Germans and the powers of nature was formed by the diversity of their sacrifices and how these acts contributed to maintaining their society. In this way, lighting torches, singing hymns and sayings, and sacrificing plants and animals pleased the spirits of the springs and trees. Hanging flowers, colorful bands, and fruits from branches or singing and dancing around them were just some of the ways these people chose to honor the living energy of trees. In ancient times, even houses were built around the trunks of living trees in order that people might grow with these saplings and give strength to and take strength from them.

"Celestially inspired nature became a bond that held mankind in a society. According to Tacitus, the Germans refused to honor their gods with humanlike pictures or idols inside closed rooms because this was incompatible with the gods' greatness. With their prayers, they dedicated groves and forests to their deities and they piously invoked the gods' names at every mysterious event. To undermine the old spiritual system of living with nature, the first Christians destroyed these forests and built churches with the wood. They taught the pagans to recognize only dead wood in the trees and prepared the way for modern man's ruthlessness and hostility toward nature, so that man now sees in his surroundings only working material for his purposes and pleasure.

"Although mythology remains in a sort of gray prehistory, it does not belong to the past. It is the ongoing and hidden strength of history, which reflects in events what mythology has already symbolized. Although these mythical powers remain hidden in prehistory, they are ridiculed as such in the new order. Make no mistake, however: They inhabit the dark corners of the subconscious, where their effect can still be felt. It is exactly there that myths, slandered as unreal and unhistorical, retain their metaphysical reality.

"We must demand an effort from honest historians to help us surmount the ever-present scourge of materialism. As reality becomes more mythical, it remains more real in both space and time, yet eventually it overcomes space and time. The labor is over; it no longer possesses any ability to reproduce. Only the powers of mythology alone could do this. As Schiller once said, 'What was never and nowhere can never grow old.' As a historical personality becomes greater than our powers of expression, he becomes more mythical.

"The transition from the legendary to human historical reality created tradition and living heroes. These gods appear in human form or as simple people who provoked the disgust of the other gods. They appear as founders of cities or as law-speakers in the dawn of human history, and are identifiable with particular historical events that guided the high priests and kings of ancient history.

"In the realm of legends, the nonhistorical and suprahistorical invade the historical. Yet legends do not reveal what conventional historians are used to. From the historian's point of view, legends represent a fantastic distortion that demands reinterpretation. Such tales may be more true than modern historical works because the popular soul speaks out with special strength in the construction of a legend. These tales, which were never intended to recount actual events, told the story of human destinies. All historians should take very seriously the legends that surround Arminius, Theodoric, and Alexander.

"If we understand the sign of the times properly, we are no longer interested in the old gods and other heroes because certain documents have been discovered that declare as imaginary the events that refer to them. Yet if we want to explore the deeper meaning of our past, we are only beginning to understand the destructive power of the forces of modernity and that this knowledge is more precious than ever.

"The twilight of the gods was at the same time the dissolution of tribal loyalty to the gods, heroes, and the almighty forces of nature. Only cosmic considerations of ancestral blood can free mankind. The twilight of the blood is the same as the twilight of the gods. As blood loses its spiritual significance, it dries, and likewise the ancestors go silent. Then begins the struggle of everybody against everyone. In place of mythical divine wisdom, a ritual mechanical intellect has assumed its place in the 'me'-addicted world of things. Individual freedom is bought with death and burial. These human realities are reflected in the cosmos as the destruction of the gods of light by dark powers.

"In a moving passage, the *Edda* mirrors this: Fear of the world afflicts the gods as they feel themselves threatened by Baldr's death, because he more than any other being was the embodiment of nature.

"The mythical world of prehistory also saw its destruction in the final battle of the gods. Thor fought with Midgardschlange: He overcame and killed her but nine paces from there, and then he was killed by her poison. Odin was eaten by a wolf, a revenge as great as the distance between heaven and earth. We should remember that Rome's mother was a she-wolf.

"Alsbald managed the turnaround: Odin's son, the silent Widar, killed the wolf in yet another act of revenge. As it says in the Edda, Baldr returned and announced to mankind the divine mystery of earth and the cosmos: 'On Gimil's heights, I saw a room brighter than the sun and decked in gold. Worthy lords must live there and enjoy its pleasures without end. There rides the powerful in instance of the Gods, the strong from above who steer everything. He decides the field of battle, and speaks the eternal rules.'

"What is that strength from above that conquers the power of death and hatred? Who can reawaken a very lonely mankind after the twilight of the gods and his 'me'-addiction, so that we can rebuild society in selfless service, taking care not to destroy freedom, but to heal it?"

I gave my companion my hand, and I thought that every strength from above is brought by the sun whose children we all are. In the New Testament, he is called Apollyon, and he suffered injustice.

Singing traveled through the air of the summer solstice in Iceland.

Was it sacred music that announced Baldr's death and return? As this dead god was consumed by the flames of the firethorn, his father, Odin, whispered in his ear the greatest wisdom. This same word could have come from Lucifer or Lohengrin or Hellias. These swan knights had a special, happy message to bring to the Christian people.

As we returned to Reykholt, I picked up a stone. I will take it home to join the piece of Delphi temple frieze and that stone that I dug from the ruins of Montségur.

~ BACK HOME ~

Made up of travel journal entries, this book was completed in a small Hessian town in the midst of the land of my pagan ancestors and my heretical forefathers.

The manuscript of this book that I am now finishing lies on my desktop. I have placed a stone, a piece of the Delphi temple frieze, on top of my filled pages. The window of my room is open, so a second and third stone are necessary to keep the pages of my journal from blowing away. After an oppressively hot day, a thunderstorm has begun. It is pouring down on the trees and bushes. My little Empire clock, a present from a dear friend who is no longer alive, quietly marks the time with its *tick-tock*. This friend now knows eternity—far more than all of us. I am estimating how many diary pages are on my right and left sides. They are the same amount. The stack on the left makes up this book. I will put them away, along with the stone I found at the heretical castle of Montségur, but from time to time I reread them, because they contain drawings I made for myself that I do not want to forget. Tomorrow morning, I will remove from the pile of paper on my right the stone I brought from Iceland, and I will begin a new book as a sequel to this journal, which I have now finished. The cover page was written in the Icelandic Arctic Circle, the others mostly in the heart of Europe and in my German homeland. I found these two stones in the craters of two volcanoes, Vesuvius and Etna, which was called Mount Bel in the Middle Ages.

As of tomorrow, the left side of my desk will be free and the pages of my new book will be protected from disorder by a piece of amber. Again, a hefty storm has broken; the thunder won't cease. From the sky in which stars remain invisible behind fast-moving clouds, lightning bolt after bolt crashes to earth. Perhaps the Great Mother has suffered or a farmer stands before his tiny possessions that were destroyed by fire. When a blacksmith forges pain in the heart of mankind, woe to him if his heart is not hard like an anvil.

There is a humming in my ear. A bee is crawling on the windowsill because her wings are drenched with rainwater. When the sun comes out, they will dry off and she will be able to fly to the heavens. During the night, the water will collect in a flower cup as dew, and then will sparkle like a precious stone. The bee will drink the dew, and then the way will be open for the bee to penetrate deep into the flower, where it can find nutrition enough for the cold and flowerless winter: delicious, golden honey. Our ancestors brewed mead—*minne*—from honey. *Minne* is "remembrance" and "memory," which are called a Paradise from which no one can be expelled. The pagan Germans believed that bees were the remnants of a paradisal golden age. The lips of a newborn child were rubbed with sacred honey from the flowers of apples, pears, and roses. Next to all flowers and blossoms, bees love the ash tree. Sometimes they sit by the thousands and drink the nectar of the tree. According to the *Edda,* the dew from Yggdrasil, or the Tree of Life, is a honey drop. Yggdrasil, or Tree of the World, is the Milky Way in the night sky. The Anglo-Saxons called it the Arian Way. In Sweden it is called Eric's Way. Eric is the name of the devil.

The sun has finally peaked through the clouds, and its beams make everything sparkle and glimmer. The forest steams. My little Empire clock will soon toll seven times. Nightfall is after nine. Then I will leave the house. I know a way through the forest that is overshadowed by huge conifer trees. The path comes from a place called the Free Man and leads over the Dornberg to Ransberg and a valley—the rose garden. The path is called the Thief's Path.

I am carrying a Dietrich with me . . .

As I traverse the old Thief's Path, I will keep the Great Bear in my sight. In ancient times, this constellation in the northern sky was called Arktos, Arthur, Artus, Thor, or Old Grandfather. Thor the Bear, the old grandfather and source of divine strength in the *Edda,* like all bears, cared for the nectar collected during the spring and summer by the bees. To Thor and the Minne of the dead, our ancestors drank this honey as mead in the rose garden.

Despite its heavy wings, the bee circled my worktable and flew off into the night. Maybe it will spend the night in a rose hedge, and so begin a new day.

BIBLIOGRAPHY

Albert, G. "Der Jesuitenorden." *National Socialist Monthly* (1936).

Aroux, E. *Les mystères de la chevalerie et de l'amour platonique au moyen âge.* Paris: J. Renouard, 1858.

Bachofen, J. J. *Urreligion und antike Symbole.* Leipzig: Bernouilli, 1926.

Baetke, W. *Islands Besiedlung und älteste Geschichte.* Jena: E. Diederichs, 1928.

Baur, F. C. *Das manichäische Religionssystem nach den Quellen neu untersucht und entwikelt.* Neudruck: Vandenhoeck and Ruprecht, 1928.

Broeckx, E. *Le Catharisme.* Hoogstraten: J. Haseldonckx, 1916.

Classen, W. *Der Eintritt des Christentums in die Welt.* n.p., 1930.

Eggers, K. *Die Geburt des Jahrtausends.* Leipzig: Schwartzhäupter, 1936.

Evola, J. *Erhebung wider die moderne Welt.* Stuttgart: Deutsche Verlags-Anstalt, 1935.

Fülöp-Miller, R. *Macht und geheimnis der Jesuiten.* Leipzig: Grethlein, 1929.

Gibbon, E. *Die Germanen in römischen Weltreich.* n.p., 1935.

Grimm, J. *Deutsche Mythologie.* Berlin: M. Schröder, 1934.

Hartmann, O. J. "Volkstum und Götterwelt." *Die Tat* (1935).

Henke, E. L. T. *Konrad von Marburg.* Marburg: N. G. Elwert, 1861.

Hennig, R. *Von rätselhaften Ländern.* München: Delphin-Verlag, 1925.

Hertz, W. *Gesammelte Abhandlungen.* Stuttgart: Cotta, 1905.

Heusinger, C. F. *Geschichte des Hospitals sankt Elisabeth in Marburg.* Marburg: N. G. Elwert, 1868.

Höfler, O. *Kultische geheimbünde bei den Germanen.* Frankfurt am Main: M. Diesterweg, 1934.

Jiriczek, O. L. *Die deutsche Heldensage.* Leipzig: G. J. Göschen, 1902.

Kaufmann, A. *Cäsarius von Heisterbach.* Köln: Heberle, 1850.

Krebs, R. *Amorbach in Odenwald.* n.p., 1935.

Kunis, H. Wildenberg. *Die Gralsburg im Odenwald.* Leipzig: M. Schäfer, 1935.

Lea, H. C. *Geschichte der Inquisition im Mittelalter.* Bonn: Georgi, 1905.

Leschtsch, A. *Der Humor Falstaffs.* Berlin: Hermann Paetel, 1912.

Ninck, M. *Wodan und germanischer Schicksalsglaube.* Jena: E. Diederichs, 1935.

Raab, G. *Ewiges Germanien.* Leipzig: Hase and Koehler, 1935.

Rehorn, K. *Der Westerwald.* Frankfurt am Main: Knauer, 1912.

Ruland, W. *Die schönsten Sagen des Rheins.* n.p., 1934.

Schaeder, H. H. *Urformen und Fortbildung des Manichäischen systems.* Leipzig: n.p., 1927.

Schmidt, C. *Histoire et doctrine de la secte des Cathares ou Albigeois.* Paris: Genive, 1849.

Simrock, K. *Wartburgkrieg.* n.p., 1858.

Spiegel, F. *Die arische periode und ihre Zustände.* Leipzig: W. Friedrich, 1887.

Suhtscheck, F. V. "Wolfram von Eschenbach Reimarbeitung des Pârsiwalnâmä." *Klio* (1932).

von Wesendonck, G. *Die Lehre des Mani.* Leipzig: O. Harrassowitz, 1922.

Wechsler, E. *Das Kulturproblem des Minnesangs.* Halle an der Saale: M. Niemeyer, 1909.

Wesselsky, A. *Die germanische Kulturtragödie und Deutschlands Erwachen.* Wien: Selbstveri, 1933.

Wolff, E. *Die Heldensagen der Griechen.* Berlin: Verlag Die Runde, 1936.

Wolff, K. F. *König Laurin und sein Rosengarten.* Bolzano: Ferrari, 1932.

Zander, F. *Die Tannhäusersage und der minnesinger Tannhäuser.* n.p., 1858.

TRANSLATOR'S BIBLIOGRAPHY

For a complete bibliography on Catharism, the Minne, the legend of the Grail, the Albigensian crusade, and Provençal culture, please consult Otto Rahn's *Crusade Against the Grail* (Rochester, Vt.: Inner Traditions, 2006).

Aguirre Delclaux, Maria del Carmen. *Los Agotes, el Final de una Maldicion.* Madrid: Silex Ediciones, 2006.

Benoist, Alain de. *Jésus et ses frères.* Paris: AAAB, 2006.

———. *Tradizioni d'Europa.* Naples: Controcorrente, 2006.

Baroja, Julio Caro. *Las Brujas y su mundo.* Madrid: Alianza, 1997.

Bonomo, Giuseppe. *Caccia alle Streghe.* Palermo: Palumbo, 1985.

Cervantes y Saavedra, Miguel de. *El Ingenioso Hidalgo Don Quijote de la Mancha.* Madrid: Alfaguara, 2005.

Dumézil, Georges. *Les dieux des Germains.* Paris: Presses Universitaires de France, 1939.

Fülöp-Miller, René. *Macht und Geheimnis der Jesuiten.* Wiesbaden: Fourier-Verlag, 2000.

Greub, Werner. *Wolfram von Eschenbach und die Wirklichkeit des Grals.* Dornach, Switzerland: Verlag am Goetheanum, 1996.

Grimm, Jakob. *Deutsche Mythologie.* Vols. 1 and 2. Wiesbaden: Marixverlag, 2007.

Niel, Fernand. *Montségur: la montagne sacrée.* Paris: La Colombe, Editions du Vieux Colombier, 1954.

Pallis, Marco. *Peaks and Lamas.* Berkeley, Calif.: Shoemaker and Hoard, 2004.

Rachet, Guy. *La Bible, mythes et réalités, l'histoire de l'ancien Israël.* Paris: Le Rôcher, 2004.

Rahn, Otto. *Crusade Against the Grail.* Translated by Christopher Jones. Rochester, Vt.: Inner Traditions, 2006.

Schmidt, Charles. *Histoire et doctrine de la secte des Cathares.* Paris: Jean de Bonnot, 1996.

Simrock, Karl, ed. and trans. *Der Wartburgkrieg oder der Sängerkrieg auf der Wartburg.* Stuttgart: n.p., 1858.

———. *Handbuch der deutschen Mythologie mit Einschluss der nordischen.* n.p., 1855.

———. *Das Heldenbuch.* n.p., 1843–49.

Stein, Walther Johannes. *The Ninth Century and the Holy Grail.* London: Temple Lodge, 1991.

Sturlusson, Snorri. *Die Edda.* Edited and translated by Karl Simrock. n.p., 1851.

Tacitus, Publius Cornelius. *Germania, Zweisprächige Ausgabe lateinisch-deutsch.* Translated by Josef Lindauer. Munich: Deutsche Taschenbuch Verlag, 1991.

Teudt, Wilhelm. *Germanische Heiligtümer, Beiträge zur Aufdeckung der Vorgeschichte.* Bremen: Faksimile Verlag, 1982.

von Eschenbach, Wolfram. *Parzival.* Translated by A. T. Hatto. Harmondsworth, Middlesex, U.K.: Penguin, 1980.